ARE YOU SOMEBODY?

the life and TIMES *of*

NUALA O'FAOLAIN

N E W
ISLAND
BOOKS

Dublin

Are You Somebody?
was first published in October 1996
in Ireland by
New Island Books,
2 Brookside,
Dundrum Road,
Dublin 14,
Ireland.

Grateful acknowledgement is made to the following for permission to reproduce. Excerpt from *Philip Larkin: Collected Poems,* excerpt from *Ezra Pound: Selected Poems 1908-1959,* and excerpt from *The Collected Poems of Wallace Stevens* are all reproduced by permission of Faber & Faber, Ltd. 'Late Fragment' by Raymond Carver, from *A New Path to the Waterfall.* First published in Great Britain by Collins Harvill 1989. Copyright © Tess Gallagher, 1989. Reproduced by permission of The Harvill Press. Excerpt from *Happy Days: My Mother, My Father, My Sister & Me* by Shana Alexander reproduced by permission of Constable & Co, copyright © Shana Alexander, 1995. Excerpt from 'Meditation in Time of Civil War' from *Collected Poems of W. B. Yeats,* reproduced by permission of A. P. Watt on behalf of the W.B. Yeats estate. Excerpt from *Sean O'Faolain: A Life* by Maurice Harmon reproduced by permission of Constable & Co, copyright © Maurice Harmon, 1994. From *The Poetry of Robert Frost,* edited by Edward Connery Lathem. Copyright 1942 by Robert Frost. © 1970 by Leslie Ballatine Frost. © 1969 by Henry Holt & Co., Inc. Reprinted by permission of Henry Holt & Co., Inc. The author and publisher have taken all possible care to trace the copyright holders of the materials used in this book, and to make acknowledgement of their use.

ISBN 1 874597 46 4

Grant-aided by the
Arts Council

New Island Books receives financial assistance from
The Arts Council (An Chomhairle Ealaíon),
Dublin, Ireland.
Cover design by Jon Berkeley from
Angel With Arms Akimbo 1994 by Alice Maher,
courtesy of Green on Red Gallery.
Cover photo by Joe St Leger
Typeset by Graphic Resources
Printed in Ireland by Colour Books, Ltd.

5 7 9 10 8 6

CONTENTS

ISSUES

BELIEF

Are You Somebody?

INTRODUCTION

When I was asked by New Island Books to put together in book form some of the opinion columns I have been writing weekly in *The Irish Times*, I said I would. They're no good to anybody in a pile of back-numbers. A book, at least, goes places. It might be the only thing to read in a trekker's hut in Nepal. My grand-niece might pick it up. It would be in the catalogue of the National Library. And I said I'd write an introduction, to pull the columns together. Because nothing makes one piece of mine belong beside the next except my self, the person who wrote them. So the introduction became not an essay setting out my world-view — something I couldn't write, anyway — but an autobiographical memoir. Anything I write comes from me, and my life made me.

But who am I? I've been on television, so it sometimes happens that in a lounge-bar, say, women at another table, as the night goes on, start looking at me and pointing, or in a supermarket, someone who's just pushed their trolley past me pulls it back to peer into my face. They think they've seen me before but they're not quite sure ...

"Are you somebody?" they frankly ask.

To answer that question seriously, I look at where I am in life. But I'm very uneasy, trying to find a voice for the personal. I can only persist in trying because of the strength I get from having a public voice — from being an opinion columnist. I relish having my weekly say. Since the very beginning, I've been conscious of the ease of speaking in that particular place, at that particular distance from the reader and that particular distance from the subject. In public print, my voice is disciplined by conventions. I know where I am. But I feel that utterance, in my personal life, was nearly always not right. It was trying to please or it was too aggressive or it was miming someone who was not me or it was loudly over-confident. It makes sense to me to begin the reminiscence which introduces this selection of columns — things my public voice has said — at a moment in my personal life when I could not speak at all.

When I was in my early thirties, and entering a bad period of my life, I was living in London on my own, working as a television producer with the BBC. The man who had absorbed me for ten years, and who I had once been going to marry, had finally left. I came home one day to the flat in Islington and there was a note on the table saying 'Back Tuesday'. I knew he wouldn't come back, and he didn't. I didn't really want him to. We were exhausted. But still, I didn't know what to do. I used to sit in my chair every night and read and drink a lot of cheap white wine. I'd say "hello" to the fridge when its motor turned itself on. One New Year's Eve I wished the announcer on Radio Three "a Happy New Year to you, too". I was very depressed. I asked the doctor to send me to a psychiatrist.

The psychiatrist was in an office in a hospital. "Well, now, let's get your name right to begin with," he said cheerfully. "What is your name?" "My name is ... my name is ... " I could not say my name. I cried, as from an ocean of tears, for the rest of the hour. My self was too sorrowful to speak. And I was in the wrong place, in England. My name was a burden to me.

Not that the psychiatrist saw it like that. I only went to him once more, but I did manage to get out a bit about my background and about the way I was living. Eventually he said something that lifted a corner of the fog of unconsciousness. "You are going to great trouble," he said, "and flying in the face of the facts of your life, to recreate your mother's life." Once he said this, I could see it was true. Mammy sat in her chair in a flat in Dublin and read and drank. Before she sat in the chair she was in bed. She might venture shakily down to the pub. Then she would totter home, and sit in her chair. Then she went to bed. She had had to work the treadmill of feeding and clothing and cleaning child after child for decades. Now all but one of the nine had gone. My father had moved himself and her and that last one to a flat, and she sat there. She had the money he gave her (never enough to slake her anxieties). She had nothing to do, and there was nothing she wanted to do, except drink and read.

And there was I — half her age, not dependant on anyone, not tired or trapped, with an interesting, well-paid job, with freedom and health and occasional good looks. Yet I was loyally recreating her wasteland around myself.

One of the stories of my life has been the working out in it of her powerful and damaging example. In everything. Nothing matters except passion, she indicated. It was what had mattered to her, and she more or less sustained a myth of passionate happiness for the first ten years of her marriage. She didn't value any other kind of relationship. She wasn't interested in friendship. If she had thoughts or ideas, she never mentioned them. She was more like a shy animal on the outskirts of the human settlement than a person within it. She read all the time, not to feed reflection, but as part of her utter determination to avoid reflection.

What made her? Her father — my Grandad — wrote his memoirs, a few pages in pencil, in a lined copybook. He was one of fourteen children on a smallholding, and perhaps because, like his brothers and sisters, he had had to emigrate when he was a boy, and there was never a family again, he remembered his childhood home with an abundance of sentiment. "I will try and give you a typical family scene as I saw it in the beginning of the 1890s," he wrote:

Father would enter the kitchen after dark and would start making and mending — a chair, a basket, or some harness. He would always sing at his work, he having a great variety of songs in both English and Irish. The babies would be asleep and the next elders would have their feet washed in a wooden vessel, then follow. After the rosary was said the next elders would retire. Mother would be putting the last thread in her needle. An oil lamp hung before the window and a turf fire in the hearth would be supplemented by a piece of bog deal which cast a light on the dresser so that the jugs and other ware would gleam as if alight. Sometimes, when not engaged in work, Father would pull down the weekly paper and read aloud, mostly the political news — stopping now and then to put his own interpretation on it. Mother, near at hand, would be an eager listener ...

My mother, the grand-daughter of this ideal pair, was anything but an eager listener. I don't know what happened, down the generations. I don't suppose that history explains it — that the individual person comes out of a vessel into which two jugs called Heredity and Environment have been poured. But perhaps emigration did something to the relationship between women and children. Children were toughened early — sent out into the world with their cardboard suitcases, one minute warm in the tribe, the next minute walking down the steps of some distant railway station into a world they must handle on their own. Under the surface competence, they must have been infantile. Somewhere in the years that fed down into my mother there were too many children and too few resources. She was the most motherless of women, herself.

Her own mother, in the little account anyone ever gave of her, was angry and energetic, and running a tailoress operation in the front room of the red-brick terraced house in Clonliffe Road, sewing shrouds late at night for the dead of the parish. Tuberculosis makes you feverish, and she was slowly dying of TB. "She threw a red-hot iron at me," was all my mother ever said — sulkily — about her. "She said I always had my head stuck in a book." But then, one child had already died. One grown-up daughter was dying of TB along with the mother. There were seven more being reared for emigration. It was an ordinary, respectable, Dublin household of the time. The woman of the house never went out, never had money, never stopped having children. My own mother held herself at arms' length from this reality. She grew up with no skills. She didn't know how to make small-talk or cook a breakfast or tie up a parcel or name a tree or flower.

When I knew my grandfather he had long been a widower. He dreamt of champion greyhounds, and hobbled up Clonliffe Road to a public bench where he talked slowly with other patriarchs, other countrymen displaced. I didn't know why my mother feared him. He ate bullseyes and read *The Saint* thrillers. He would say to me from his frowsty bed, "Hand me over those trousers." He'd fumble in the pocket, and give me pennies. He sat on the upright chair to put on his long johns and his penis was like some purply barnacled mineral thing, found on a sea-bed. He expected his tea and bread-and-butter brought to his chair. He would certainly have denied that the fact that three of his children were ferocious alcoholics had anything to do with him. No one takes responsibility for the big Irish families that in generation after generation are ravaged by alcoholism.

My mother didn't want anything to do with child-rearing or housework. But she had to do it. Because she fell in love with my father, and they married, she was condemned to spend her life as a mother and a home-maker. She was in the wrong job. Sometimes I meet women who remind me of her when I stay in Bed & Breakfasts around the country. They throw sugar on the fire to get it to light, and wipe surfaces with an old rag that smells, and they are forever sending children to the shops. They question me,

14

half-censorious, half-wistful: "And did you never want to get married yourself?"

The one thing my mother knew definitely existed was her body. She was sent home from convent boarding-school because of dancing too close to the girl she adored. She was baffled by the punishment, never having heard of lesbianism. I remember a Henry Green novel which passed through the house when I was a child, whose cover had a sketch of girls in white dresses waltzing together in the half-dark. Mammy blossomed for a moment, seeing it. "That's exactly what it was like! In the big hall in school! The night I danced with her!" Decades later, not long before my mother died, a bright-eyed middle-aged lady came up to me at a reception. It was in the offices of the then Council for the Status of Women, as it happens. "How is your mother?" she asked. She, it turned out, was the other girl. The love-object. I didn't dare ask her what had really happened. Anyway, by then what mattered was the contrast between this spry woman, obviously someone who knew what status was. And the wreck of my poor innocent and ignorant mother, out in the little flat, making her way through days of shakiness and gagged-on gin, while her husband blandly went about his business, and the last of her children — a schoolgirl, then — brought herself up.

This was where grand passion had left her.

Her foremothers knew how the tribe expected women to behave, and how it would protect them in return. But when my grandfather came back from exile in London to work in the GPO in Dublin around 1910, and the link with Kerry was broken, no one belonged to a tribe. My mother was on her own, but without hope of independence. Nowadays she could have stayed in the civil service, even after she became pregnant. But 1940s Ireland was a living tomb for women. For men like my father, out and about in Dublin, the opposite was true. Broadcasting and journalism were beginning to open up. He had begun as a teacher, in the 1930s, and if he had stayed in teaching — coming home in the afternoons every day, and free in the summer — his children would have had a wonderful father. But he had many gifts and ambitions: he was a traveller in Europe in the summers, and a linguist and a sportsman and a happy, proud patriot. And handsome as anything. There are photos of himself and my mother on the beach at Ballybunion, all white teeth and strong limbs. She was blissfully happy with how he made her feel about herself. They were mad about each other from the start. They hiked over Howth Head and Bray Head and up the Dublin mountains and made love in the heather. He bought her a hot port one chilly evening. Her first drink ever. They married very early on a January morning because my sister Grainne was a little bump under Mammy's dress. The Second World War started. He joined the Irish Defence Forces in 1939 and loved army life. The next year my mother was pregnant again: he cycled up from the Curragh to the Rotunda to greet me. But I spent my infancy in Donegal, because the Army brought my father there. The first few pages of a letter from him to my mother arranging the move survive. She was pregnant again.

'A chroidhe dhil,' he begins. For years I could not read this letter. 'Beloved heart', when they ended so badly! He is writing from Fort Dunree, up on the Inishowen peninsula. He has found a little house for the family — he encloses a sketch and continues:

> For Grainne and Nuala there is quiet, air, sun and sea, chickens for Grainne not to mention an occasional *bó*. For you there are these things, plus me, plus an odd weekend trip to Derry and evenings in Buncrana. As regards books, Father Dolan has a pile of great stuff, which I know he will lend to you. There are other things — eggs, milk, potatoes straight from their cradles. And even though coal will play second-fiddle to turf, there will be no pennies in the gas. The reek is about twenty yards of a walk — no trouble to an enthusiastic husband ... Today is Wednesday —

and I find I will not be paid my 6/2d until tomorrow
— but I am borrowing money for a stamp. Almost
a week now since I saw you last and it feels like a
month. I am counting the days till we all get
together again in the lovely sunshine. Today the
sun shone for twelve hours, and all the day, from 9
a.m. till 6 p.m. I was on duty on a grass-topped cliff,
giving a hand to recruits who were engaged in rifle
practice...

His letter is overtaken by one from her.

...Your letters usually make me feel bloody awful,
but this one was not too bad! I notice that I have
influenced you to the extent that you say "a bit
difficult" when you mean "quite desperate". Good
girl ...

"Ah so!" I say. "She was already provoking him with her
despair." But then — three children in four years! The end
of the letter is missing, so the taboo on a parent's intimate
life was not breached, if there were intimacies there.

He treats my mother as a partner in this letter. He's doing
freelance journalism, and she's helping him. But when I knew
them, he went out: she stayed home. Nobody treated her as
a partner. When she died, a few years after him, this letter
was found in the old tin biscuit-box which was her only
possession, apart from clothes. She didn't own a single thing
in the little flat — not a book, not a record. In the biscuit tin
there were the scrawled pages of book reviews she had
written, in pencil and biro. They had moved house at least a
dozen times. She had gone to great trouble, then, to keep this
letter and the reviews. A few of her book-reviews were
published in the paper. That was the only money she ever
earned for herself, apart from the children's allowance. That
was what she talked about — the money. But it wasn't for
the money that she kept the crumpled drafts in the biscuit
tin, when she had nothing else. She could have been
respected, if things had been different. She could have done
something other than be the drudge she was.

It seems that very early in the marriage she was overwhelmed. She foundered, and either he didn't see it, or he saw it but couldn't help. It must have happened quickly. A woman who worked for my parents when they came back from Donegal told me Grainne and I were always identically dressed in pretty clothes. What I remember, from only three or four years later, is the teacher in Miss Ahern's school in Malahide calling me in to her office and fingering my dirty cardigan. "Couldn't your mother find anything better to send you to school in?"

She was to have thirteen pregnancies altogether. Nine living children. She never had enough money. She did her best for years. She made crab-apple jam. She gave us jam sandwiches and a Milk of Magnesia bottle full of milk for our picnic. She bought us wellington boots for the winter. She fine-combed our hair, us kneeling before her, bent into the newspaper on her lap. Think of all the clothes she must have bought, washed, dried, sorted out, put on our backs ... We lived in a rented bungalow meant for the farm-labourer, on an estate in north County Dublin. The bungalow was surrounded by fields with ditches and hawthorn hedges in what was an isolated landscape, then. The railway line from Dublin passed the other side of a turnip field. Sometimes Daddy jumped from the train and rolled down the embankment as a short-cut home. But he began not to come home. He was a clerk in the Irish Tourist Board after the Army, but then he began to get work in Radio Éireann, and to get jobs — like the 'Radio Train' to Killarney — that took him away. His life became more exciting all the time. He brought his *joie de vivre* home with him when he came striding across the field to where we were playing — making "houses" and "shops" from stones and mud — around the house. We would hear the bright whistle of 'Beidh aonach amárach', and we'd run to jump up on the fence to see him. "Daddy's home! He's home!"

Her life got harder. The Calor gas cylinder under the two rings she cooked on would run out, and she had no phone or transport. She washed clothes in the bath, with yellow soap and a washboard. We were no consolation. Once, when my father had gone down the country on a job, she broke the unwritten rules by daringly going into Dublin, and going to Kingsbridge station, and surprising him by being at the barrier, when he got off the train. He was with people. He leaned down to aim a kiss at her cheek before hurrying off with them. "He didn't even take the cigarette out of his mouth," she told me, not once, but over and over again, in years to come.

I imagine her making her lonely way back to us children. She was still in her twenties. She would have taken the bus out to the terminus, then walked out past the last street-lamp, then down the dark country road to the estate's gate-lodge, then ducked under a fence and followed the path we'd worn in the tussocky field across to the bungalow ... Nothing there but children. Another time — it was late at night, but I was awake in my bed because I was counting my Communion money for the twentieth time — I heard him come in and then I heard her shrieking: "That's not my lipstick!" That would have been near the end of the ten perfect years she always claimed they had. Around then, one of his women (she had a daughter by him that she called Nuala, oddly enough) came out to our place to bargain with my mother. This woman had money. She offered Mammy a large allowance to let him go with her to Australia. I remember this woman leaving hurriedly along the path through the field, and my father running after her, and my mother running after him, crying. Then Mammy fell in a heap in the grass. It was a summer's day, and the cattle were already sitting quietly around the field. She was a rounded shape in the grass, like a small cow.

Soon after, my mother had an affair with my father's friend, though she didn't like him at all. What other weapon did she have? To make my father take notice? But the men took no notice of her. They absorbed her protest: it didn't cause a ripple between them. So then she had nothing left to protest with.

Unhappiness settled on her gradually. She was gauche. She had a more charming sister who sometimes came home from abroad and brought fun into our house. This aunt used to seek our company. I learnt to believe that she enjoyed being with us. She was with us when we were packed into a bulging Ford Prefect with just clothes and dishes. We had been evicted from the bungalow, and ended up living in a small town, further away from Dublin.

It was in that grey little town that my mother began to drink by herself. She went out to the pub in the evening. She began to look around to see where there might be chemists' shops where she could get what she wanted to help her to diet. We were living then in a crumbling rectory with lovely drawing-rooms and an overgrown garden with a dog's graveyard behind the apple-trees, and stone-flagged sculleries full of spiders. The first year we were there, the suave American voice of Perry Como was everywhere, singing "Don't let the stars get in your eyes, don't let the moon make you cry ... " And Daddy was in America, too. At Christmas, he brought Mammy home a figure-hugging black dress. "I like you thin," he said. By now my father had turned into a journalist under the name "Terry O'Sullivan". He went away around the country five days a week, now, writing for the *Sunday Press*. Her sister, who was more fun than she was, sometimes went with him. There was no question of my mother going: she had seven children in the house.

"I like you thin." That edict of his echoed in my life, too, and in some of my brothers' and sisters' lives. I went around the chemist shops for my mother. I internalised her panic at not being able to sleep. I was addicted to sleeping-tablets for years. It is hard for children to withhold assent from their mother — to stand far enough apart to judge that what she is doing is not part of nature.

I once asked my friend, the broadcaster and writer Sean Mac Réamoinn, who knew my father and mother in the 1950s, what class we belonged to. We had very little money, and home was bleak, compared to the homes of our school friends. But my mother read all the time, and my father taught us the words of German songs, and we played extracts from *Swan Lake* on the gramophone and we put on plays, whereas the other families we knew did not do those things. "Were we working class?" I asked him. "Because we certainly weren't middle-class." "What you were was bohemian," he said. But bohemians care about music or literature or art. My parents had no real resource there. Any more than they had positive values — actually believed in the merit of individual freedom or anything else. The values of their own parents seemed to have no meaning for them. They didn't know their place. Mammy would send me up the field to the big Georgian house where the landlady lived, with the rent. She hated paying the rent. "Throw it at her!" she'd hiss at me. They were not practising Catholics either. We had to go to Mass, certainly. But they didn't. Whatever the people they came from had lived by just fell away in their generation. But they didn't have other values, to replace what they had lost. They were just careless.

It is only in looking back that I detach a narrative about my parents from all the rest. I didn't know much about them, though down on the floor of the ocean, where I lived in my child world, I could sense disturbances up above on the surface of the water. We used to rock for hours at night: two children to a bed, one at the bottom, one at the top, arms crossed, rocking and rocking. Nor was I living just in this world. I had another world. In school, I ruined the Christmas tableau on the nun. I was the Archangel Gabriel, and I had to stand behind Joseph and Mary and the Infant Jesus on a kitchen chair, and look down on them piously and hold my arms strapped to great feather contraptions — my wings — over them. But I saw someone I knew in the audience, and I waved my wing at her. The nun was so angry afterwards that she broke the chair to hit me with a leg of it. Yet I walked home leaving room between me and the verge of the road, as always, for my Guardian Angel.

Then we went for a while to a different National School. My mother sometimes didn't get up in the mornings and we had to go out empty-handed, though she would come down later on the bike she had learned to ride, and pass a pudding-bowl of potatoes in salad-cream through the bars of the playground. But when we had lunches we put them with everyone else's in a cupboard in the room. Sometimes we'd hear a chomping noise. "Miss! Miss! The rat is in the cupboard!" The teacher would swing the door open and hit the rat with the shovel she had for the stove. On the way home from that school, for a long time, I climbed down into a quarry where a pool of water had collected, and there was a rusted barrel on its side in the water. If I lay down and looked along the surface of the water in the barrel at eye-level, I would see lovely little fairies, with straight partings in their blonde hair, and pink ballet skirts. They were about the size of flies.

I knew other places besides home. They sent me to Kerry, to the relations. There were pig-hairs in the yellowy skin of the fatty, boiled bacon the lady draped across the cabbage I had to eat. But on Saturday nights a technicolour trifle was installed in the parlour, under a white cloth: we got that after Sunday Mass. The north Dublin fields where we lived were silent and bleak, so it was like going to New York to be sent to my great-aunt in Athlone. She was the mistress of a tiny, hardly-used pub, Egan's of Connaught

Street. Mr Egan kept a big hoinking pig in the slimy yard. Myself and Auntie Kit used to go around the public grass of the Battery on our hands and knees collecting a certain weed for the bristly old thing with its watery eyes. The shed the pig slept in was full of disintegrating sheet music from when Kit as a young woman had been a pianist accompanying the silent movies in Listowel. "Me and Jane in a plane/ Soaring up in the sky/ No traffic-cop/ Will ever stop/ Me and Jane in a plane." I loved the streets of Athlone — the lights, the chip-shop, Broderick's Bakery a few doors away where a machine sliced the pans. I was even a small celebrity among the street's boys and girls, being thought to be from Dublin city.

There was the big world too, presenting us isolated children with puzzles. I went into a sweet shop one day. The woman behind the counter was showing something — big photos — in a low-voiced, secret way to another woman, bent over the counter. I glimpsed the photos. They were of desperate bony fingers reaching out from under the wooden walls of huts. Fingers like sticks. These were photos from the Holocaust. I saw gas ovens. Piles of bones. That night our friends came across the field, for us to go down the railway line and rob Williams's orchard, as usual. But as we were going along I told them about the evil in the world, and we all decided to repent. We went home and upended the kitchen chairs to kneel at, and said a very long Rosary. A year later — we were now living in a temporary cottage — the maid, who was never paid, and never went out, fell to the floor and gave birth to a baby. It transpired that the butcher, when he called with the meat, had been having sex with her. The baby went to the maid's mother. My mother happened to call to that house a few weeks later. The baby was emaciated, immobile, sinking into death. "Sure, who wants it?" the grandmother said. It did die, as far as I know. It was 1953. Then we were again in a new school. We were assembled in the concert hall to listen to the Coronation of Queen Elizabeth in

Westminster Abbey on the convent radio. "Always remember, girls," the nun said, "that 'God Save the Queen' is the most noble tune ever penned in eight bars."

I started looking at things. We used to come in from the country to visit my Nana, my father's mother. I don't know how it was allowed, but when we got to her house, a bit down Clonliffe Road from my mother's family house, I would go out again and start walking. I could not get enough of looking at Dublin, which was Joyce's Dublin still, then, brown and dusty and dense with street life. Later in life, my father told me things about the city. He told me that the sea used to come in at the North Strand which is why it is called a strand and that they reclaimed Fairview Park with the rubble from the ruins of O'Connell Street after the Rising. They laid a rail, and a bogey-car to transport the rubble out, and the bright young people after a night out would jump on the bogey-car in their gowns and tails and push it off and come whizzing out from town. But when I walked around Dublin as a child I knew nothing, except what I noted with my own eyes, like a spy behind enemy lines. I would walk along Summerhill, which was a canyon of Georgian tenements then, with women sitting on the worn and beautiful front steps all the day long. I'd read the writing on statues. I liked 'ne plus ultra' on the Parnell one though I did not know what it meant. I would go into the Protestant cathedrals and go down the quays, and around behind the distillery in Smithfield, and stop to look at anything — a horse and cart backing into a yard, a woman calling down from a window, a butcher emptying a basin of pink water into the gutter. No one sees a child watching. I was never afraid till I went to *The Messiah* in the Theatre Royal when I was eleven, and a man put his hand up under my skirt and hurt me with his fingers.

Perhaps that habit of observation helped me to get my job with *The Irish Times*. I was offered a try at writing a column, as far as I know, because of a conversation I had, in the late 1980s, about the physical beauty of the seaside places north of Dublin when I was a child. I had this conversation, on radio, with Gay Byrne. I was a television producer with RTÉ then, and I'd read somewhere that if you watched a year's television only three per cent of the human faces you would see would be those of women over, say, fifty or fifty-five — older women only figure on television in ads and soap opera. So I had made a series of short programmes in which elderly Irish women just looked into the camera and told the story of their lives. The women's personalities, and the twists and turns of their lives, and the compelling effect of a face looking out at the viewer without any intervening interviewer, had added up to something strong. The series won a Jacob's Award which had been presented the night before and Gay was interviewing me on his radio programme as a result.

Gay Byrne reminds me of my father — whom he knew, of course. My father and Eamonn Andrews were doing a kind of 'In Town Tonight' programme on Radio Éireann when Gay was starting out in broadcasting too. The careers of the three men could have gone any way: that they ended where each of them did was due as much to chance as to their talents. The three of them shared a kind of impersonal charm — an ability to stand in a room and be the one others wanted to please, rather than the one to work at pleasing. They each found ways of keeping their dignity against the flattery of a small town.

Gay evokes for me — not that he means to — my father's mild and decorous childhood home in Clonliffe Road, where no one ever used the front door dressed in its striped canvas blind, and down in the basement my grandmother swept the bobbled chenille tablecloth with its own little brush and pan after the meals — rabbit stews, rice puddings — she served to my Granda and my Auntie when they came home from their respectable jobs at dinner-hour. Gay's people and my father's people would have been alike, I think. Mass for the women every morning, and First Fridays, Novenas, the seven churches on Holy Thursday, Tenebrae on Good Friday, Exposition of the Sacred Sacrament and so on. At Christmas, card games and the odd bottle of stout and the married sons and the handful of old friends calling. No new kind of people ever coming into the house. No new opinions or ways of behaving penetrating it. The only fiction, the didactic fable at the back of each copy of the *Messenger of the Sacred Heart.* Even history was somewhat frowned upon for showing off. I pressed my grandmother about The Rising. "Oh, yes, there was terrible trouble in town that year," she said, her face wrinkling up with disapproval. "We could hear it all from here ... " Then she brightened. "But we got vegetables in 1916 that we never got before or since! The carts from Rush couldn't get into the city with all the trouble. They could only get as far as Drumcondra — here, at the top of Clonliffe Road — and we'd go up and get the best of vegetables for half-nothing!"

Gay and my father both transcended the cautiousness of their backgrounds. Though Gay was more committed than my father to the values of that background. If the two of them walked towards me now, I'd see two dapper, smallish men with attractive voices and quick minds, both using a natural charm and courtesy to keep other people at a distance from them. Behind Gay I'd see an orderly and consistent life. Behind my father, chaos accumulated.

But around 1950, in the place Gay and I were talking about that day on the radio — in the pristine countryside to the north of Dublin with its string of seaside villages — my father and my family were still well. He responded to even that quiet countryside with brisk enjoyment. He took us on walks through the woods and told us what "Indian file" meant. He planted potatoes, and named the ridges after the stations on the Dublin-Belfast railway line.

Where we lived was beautiful, then. Not the big flat fields around the bungalow — though even there, on a winter afternoon, I saw my first heron rise into the sky from a pond, grey on grey. But the beaches and the cornfields and the old woods. And the winding country roads, so little used then — at Malahide and Rob's Walls and the front at Portmarnock — that sand drifted across them and collected on them. In winter great wild waves crashed up the sand at Portmarnock, and broke over the road, and across from the dunes there was a little wooden pub and some holiday shacks, and then fields. The road around the estuary to Baldoyle flooded quickly and silently in winter, and we ran along the grassy bank to school between silver sheets of floodwater. There were no new houses. The parkland and fine houses of the landlords stretched back almost to the edge of the city. Near us, there was a deserted big house, shuttered and silent in the middle of woods. The peacocks had been left behind there, and gone wild, and they called to each other all the night. We walked a mile to where the bus from Dublin turned around. It was a country bus, going through countryside on its way into town, stopping at the pubs that marked each little hamlet. Everything was clean and bright. At the shabby end of the main street of Malahide, where the air was scented by a little sweet factory, you turned down past a decrepit, elegant, terrace, and at the bottom, at the water's edge, a man with a row-boat would take you across to the sand and marram grass of Malahide Island where seabirds' eggs lay lavishly on the ground, as at the Creation. You rang a big bell on a pole, at the end of the day, and the boatman came back across the water, shining and still in the evening, to collect you. Or you stayed on Malahide beach with your jam sandwiches and bottle of milk, and the people in the houses would boil your kettle for the tea for a penny.

That sparkling world was what I was talking to Gay Byrne about, on the radio that day. He has an intimate appreciation of how idyllic north Dublin once was, and what we have lost. But I remember trying to convince him that Ireland is a much, much better place now than it used to be, even though so much beauty has disappeared with development. When the interview was over, I went back to the day's ordinary work. But Conor Brady, then deputy editor of *The Irish Times,* rang me. I'd never met him, but I knew who he was. He'd heard me on the car radio. Would I like to try my hand at a few opinion columns? This was the circumstance that led to this last, deeply satisfying, decade of my life, and to this book, of course. Conspiracy theorists, who think that columnists are carefully chosen for their "liberal" views, had better apply to Conor Brady to identify the conspiracy. He never said what he heard in me that made him ring me. I wasn't talking about my views. I was talking, to someone who reminded me of my dead father, about a long-ago childhood.

2

The most useful thing I brought out of my childhood was confidence in reading. Not long ago, I went on a weekend self-exploratory workshop, in the hope of getting a clue about how to live. One of the exercises we were given was to make a list of the ten most important events of our lives — the key moments that brought us from birth to wherever we are now. Number one was: "I was born", and you could put whatever you liked after that. Without even thinking about it my hand wrote, at number two: "I learnt to read." "I was born and I learnt to read" wouldn't be a sequence that occurs to many people, I imagine. But I knew what I meant to say. Being born was something done to me, but my own life began — I began for myself — when I first made out the meaning of a sentence.

I remember everything about it. The page was a double-column, small-type account of someone's verbatim evidence in a Scottish murder trial. I don't know how it made its way to north County Dublin. But I was puzzling at a line when all of a sudden the meaning of one word I understood hopped across — like the ping-pong ball hopping along the line in a sing-along — to join the meaning of the next word I understood, until there were enough words that meant something to make sense of the sentence. I was overcome with delight. I was still small — not yet four. But I ran across the field and up the road, speeding along through the summer dust — I see it as if it were yesterday — to the shop, a long distance away. "I can read! I can read!" I shouted up at the woman who ran the shop. She bent down. "Well, aren't you the great little girl ... "

I must have picked it up already from my mother — that reading is a defence. That "they" can't get at you, when you have a book. Of course — my mother was the "they" in this case. Any demand she made — get sticks to start the fire, take the baby for a walk in the pram — interfered with my reading. I found ease and comfort in books. The little Carnegie Library in the village, complete with display cases of dusty exhibits like an ivory back-scratcher from an Egyptian tomb, was a cornucopia, even though the pitch-pine bookshelves were half-empty. I don't remember a children's section. I read all the volumes of James Agate's diaries, though I hardly knew what a London theatre critic was. I read all the volumes of *Stories From the Opera*. The library didn't get new books very often. A teacher lent me *Anne of Green Gables* and *The Road to Avonlea*: I nearly died of pleasure. In Newcomen Mall library I got *Heidi*. I read the easy bits of *Ulysses*. I made no distinction between children's literature and other literature. For a while the Americans had a library in Dublin — it was part of the United States Information Service. My mother borrowed books there, and I read them after her. Dos Passos. Dreiser. And there were a few books at home. Francois Mauriac's life of Shelley. A thriller by Francis Stuart with the pages of the dénouement missing. *Bright Day* by J. B. Priestley. Its epigraph was the first line from Shakespeare I ever encountered.

I liked the words as much as the plots. In a scandalous book called *The Kansas City Milkman* — Mammy vaguely said I shouldn't read it — one character said about a woman, "What she needs is a roll in the hay." I didn't know what this meant — I saw a barn, in my head — but I loved it being a metaphor. A local boy was known as Buggy. "Don't call me that," he said. "I've a handle to me mug the same as you have." I murmured it over to myself. "A handle to me mug ... " Halfway up the hill in Malahide there was a bench, with a little plaque on it that said '*pro bono publico*'. And on the side of the Chef sauce bottle — often on the table — there was a vertical column of words. Piquant was one of them. "Piquant," I would say to myself as I dodged along beside the gurgling ditches on my way to school. "Piquant. Appetising." Best of all was the beginning of the Last Gospel — in those days, it was said at the end of every Mass. "In the beginning was the word and the word was with God and the word was God ... " I loved the sonority of it, and that I didn't know what it meant. No one was ashamed of words, at home. The teacher took us into a room in one school to listen to Daddy doing a commentary in Irish as well as English from an army Tattoo on the wireless.

But really respectable people were cautious in speech. The girls at school would say to me sourly, if I used an unusual word, "Did you swallow a dictionary, or what?" They had more sense than to risk exposing their selves in essays that might be read out. My essays were always being read out. There I'd be, a confused and emotional exhibitionist, and there they'd be, silent and politic. Being known to be imaginative made you marginal because it was close to "making a show" of yourself, drawing attention to yourself, showing off, exaggerating, telling lies. I was more an entertainer than a serious student because it was a useless thing like English I was good at. Girls were good at English, not boys. Because of all this, the women who taught English had an intense secret life. They slipped books to fellow-enthusiasts, like Russians passing *samizdat* literature along the underground. I went to seven schools. I was no good at anything else, but I was good at English. I needed the love I got from English teachers, and I returned it, and return it.

"I don't know whether she's intelligent, Sister," my father said when he delivered me to the Mother Superior of my last school. "But she and her mother can take a book apart ... " I see him saying this, sitting in the shiny brown parlour, automatically trying to charm the nun as quickly as possible. He was paying me a compliment, certainly. But one he could place at a genially baffled distance from his own powers. Since I knew, too, that Mammy was his dependant, not he hers, it wasn't such a great thing to be lumped in with her ...

It was at secondary school that reading books took on depth, and became the study of English. From then on — all my life, and still today — reading for pleasure and reading for study or work were never very different from each other. After school — to digress — I did formally study English at UCD, and after UCD I worked on medieval English prose romances at the University of Hull, and eventually, back in Dublin, I prepared for an examination on the whole course of English literature for a big scholarship, and when I got that I did a B.Phil. in English at Oxford. And I suppose I've read a book every few days or so throughout my life. Apart from a few writers who don't make up in anything else for their lack of inner life — Chaucer, a lot of Balzac, Scott, the jollier Dickens, Salman Rushdie — and apart from a few writers I'm completely cut off from — Lamartine, Hawthorne, Richardson — I have enjoyed everything of any importance I've ever read. In any case, I would prefer to read something I don't enjoy than do almost anything else. I like the act of reading in itself. Following the line of something — not just the story but the rhythm, the tone, the feel of what has accumulated from before and what is beginning to impend — becoming sure-footed on the high-wire of the author's intention. I liked everything to do with English as a school subject. Textbooks. Vocabularies: the set anthologies of my day began with examples of metrical schemes and figures of speech — words to marvel at, like rhodomontade, anapaest, or onomatopoeia. I liked English exams — I remember drawing a diagram of the shape Shelley's 'Ode to the West Wind' made inside my head as a treat for the examiner, on the blotting paper sheet, at the Inter Cert exam.

Reading certain books was a complex and complete experience. I had a room in a squalid mews in Dublin for a while when I was a student — the landlord had whips hanging from his bedstead. I remember it only because one summer morning I settled in the weedy yard when I had done the housework, and began reading *Madame Bovary*. Hours later, the sun had moved to the other wall, and my heart was beating heavily as Flaubert led me, under his perfect control, into the last chapter. I remember gasping — involuntary, light, gasps — as James added another circle to the rings of consequence that expanded from the actions of the principals in *The Wings of the Dove*, until the void settles around Densher and Kate. I lived in a hotel in Teheran for a few months in the 1970s. The revolution was near. Men with machine-guns patrolled the lobby in front of the lifts. Places you could buy alcohol — dim shops like cupboards in the alley-ways around the Russian embassy — were closing down. I didn't care. Every evening I'd hurry back to my room to pour out a glass of mild Iranian vodka and settle with perfect happiness into wherever I'd got to in *Remembrance of Things Past*. It took me eleven weeks to read Proust, that first time. His world was my real world: I just bore with the days, exotic as they were, until I could get back to it.

And Yeats. At various times in my life, themes or tones of Yeats have been the only right ones. These days, the grave and majestic turn at the end of 'Meditation in Time of Civil War', where he pays his respects to Wordsworth, and to reality, and acknowledges his own incompleteness, is especially meaningful to me:

> *But O! ambitious heart, had such a proof drawn*
>   *forth*
> *A company of friends, a conscience set at ease,*
> *It had but made us pine the more. The abstract joy,*
> *The half-read wisdom of daemonic images,*
> *Suffice the ageing man as once the growing boy.*

The simplicity of the last line — arrived at, after all the complexities of the poem — moves me almost to tears. This passage, and all the other bits and pieces which are in my memory, are always available. There is grandeur in there, no matter what appears to be happening — waiting at traffic-lights, peeling potatoes. I learnt T. S. Eliot's 'Portrait of a Lady' when I was fourteen or fifteen and an enthusiast of world-weariness. My head would be full of the smell of hyacinths across a garden, conjuring up things that other people — Eliot and myself being too fastidious — had desired. To look at, I was just a spotty girl.

If there were nothing else, reading would — obviously — be worth living for. Saul Bellow. Alice Munro. Chekhov. Keats. Eoin MacNamee, Montherlant. James. James Joyce. Tolstoy. Mailer. Dacia Maraini. Dermot Healy. Douglas Dunn. Trollope. Richard Ford. *Caoineadh Airt Uí Laoghaire*. Donne. Colette. Robert Lowell. *Jane Eyre*. Naipaul. Kafka's 'Up in the Gallery'. Roddy Doyle. John McGahern. Racine. Kawabata. I don't have to observe any hierarchy. But I recognise that there is a hierarchy. There is great and less great and so on, down to trash. When I was a teacher I had to avoid quoting some things because they moved me so deeply that I was afraid I'd cry in front of the students. The big speeches in *King Lear* did that, and the end of *The Tempest*. And 'Death be not Proud ... ' and 'So we'll go no more a-roving ... ' And what Ralph says to Isabel Archer just before he dies, in *Portrait of a Lady*. And Keats' wonderful letters. I presented writing like this to my students with confidence, just as it had been confidently presented to me. I think classic literature is deservedly so-called. I might never have read *Phèdre* or 'Dejection: An Ode' or 'Samson Agonistes' or *Les Liaisons Dangereuses* or Pope or Hopkins or Ben Jonson but that they were prescribed "texts". I don't have any objection to the art made by dead white males. Far from it — the thought that I might have missed this literature — that I might have been born later, when it was decided it was too difficult for young people — fills me with horror. I never think of gender when I'm reading. If questions about it force themselves on me, I have to come out of reading, into this world.

And I like what derives from literature — fine commentary, like Cynthia Ozick's, or Seamus Heaney's, or Henry James' prefaces. Biography. Autobiography. The only thing I don't read much of now, when time is so precious, are middle-range authors — Kundera, say, or Paul Auster. Writers who play middle-level games. When I want pleasure I want perfect trivia — romances by Judith Krantz, thrillers by Scott Turow, moral tales by Maeve Binchy. Or else I want the real, the great thing.

The worst deprivation of boarding-school was that we weren't allowed to have fiction in our possession. I longed for it as someone thirsty longs for water, because the language of the school was Irish and I couldn't read Irish, and could barely speak it. I was half-gagged, all the time. On a few very special feast-days the "library" — a glass-fronted bookcase — was opened. You had an afternoon to devour as much as you could of, say, Annie P. Smithson. But every year some young Frenchwoman would come to the convent, to help with teaching French, and though she slept in a cubicle in the dormitory like us, the usual rules did not apply to her, and she often had novels in her locker. I needed them so badly that I made the stories out through the barrier of French. *Les Clés du Royaume*, and all the rest of A. J. Cronin. *La Chatelaine du Liban*. Novels were about what I cared about. They asked the questions I wanted answered. How do lives get lived? How is love found?

3

I was sent to boarding-school— where I arrived on my fourteenth birthday — because puberty got me into so much trouble. Not that I knew what it was called or what was happening — all I knew was that something had run over me like a train, and simplified everything. I was stunned by the demands of the body I had barely noticed. I didn't care for anybody or anything in the small town we lived in except going to dances and being left home and walking around the dark and windy lanes that led down to the harbour in the town, talking to my friend about boys. My father came upon us mooching furtively along. "Button your coat!" he snapped at me. "You look like a mill-girl." It wasn't just my sexuality he was recoiling from: I was becoming *déclassée*. In that town, then, the convent girls didn't go the Town Hall to jostle at the mirror in the Jeyes Fluid-smelling Ladies and then sit on the bench at the edge of the dance-floor, burningly aware of the males around, waiting to be asked up to dance, till four in the morning. Only working people, or people who went to the Tech, danced. By the time the band had got to "Goodnight sweetheart / See you in the morning", the Hall was a sweaty, shuffling mass of solid eroticism. After the National Anthem, and finding my coat, I'd go out into the dark night. Whoever was "leaving me home" would be waiting in the shadows past the street-lamp, speechless. Often, we didn't know each other's name. But for the sake of those bouts of devouring each other — in doorways, against trees, under the wall of our house — I would do anything. For instance, I stole. My mother was poorer than ever. She made me do a humiliating thing every so often — call to the gasworks, down behind the harbour, and walk

36

past the men to the office, and ask for a man to call to the house to free our jammed gas meter. Everyone knew the meter wasn't jammed but that when he counted the money there might be a few shillings surplus, and that she was desperate for them. Still, I took her money to pay into the dances.

The nuns knew everything about the town. When they heard I was being left home by a married man — I didn't know that, or anything about him except that I was wild about him — they called in my father to tell him to take me away from the school. I was thirteen. I was supposed to be bad.

I was the second eldest. My parents still had the energy to do something about my crisis. My mother, on the telephone from the Red Bank bar, got me into St Louis' Convent, far away in Monaghan. My father sold his car. I was bought a trousseau in Gorevan's: napkin rings, three pairs of shoes, a dressing-gown, a hairbrush — things no one in the family had ever had before. Then he borrowed another car — putting himself out for me to an extent that I still feel guilty about, compared to the care my brothers and sisters got — and drove me to Monaghan himself. There was snow on the roads, and he couldn't manage the strange gears and it took us two days to get there. But in the end, on an Ash Wednesday, in mid-term, we went to Mass together, and then he brought me up to the grey granite building and left me with the Mother Superior. There were shards of ice on the lake in front of the school and motionless swans on the black water. Not much more than a week before I had been slow-waltzing half the night, pressed into men's bodies by their big heavy hands on my back. By comparison, I had now landed on a planet that could not support life.

I had to forget, when I was away at school, what I knew
about bodies. Yet when I was at home in the holidays, I was
in the company of girls whose destiny was marriage, not
further education. Their lives depended on the quality of
the man they got, and the only way to get a man was to go
courting. So the important things in life — the career tools
— were manner, figure, clothes, carefully-judged liberties
allowed to this boy friend or that. By the mid-1950s my
family had moved to a house in Dublin, in Clontarf. My
sister and her friends were soon working in offices and
shops and could buy some clothes and make-up for
themselves. When I came home, I didn't belong. I'd go to
hops and not get asked up at all. I was dowdy. I didn't know
the argot. *Rock Around the Clock* came to Dublin and
cinema seats were ripped up. The idea that young people
are different from older people in every way was starting,
with Elvis, and James Dean. But up on the border in our
Irish-speaking convent we were simply imperfect adults,
and living somewhere between twenty and two hundred
years in the past. I was sent back there after every holidays
— pale from smoking, hollow-eyed from silent explorations
with boys in bus-shelters — no matter how hard I argued
that I would be better off getting a job in Clery's. "I could
hand up money," I'd say. No one listened. When I got to
school there was no one I could talk to about what I'd done
in the holidays. Any more than when I went home, there
was anyone interested in what happened at school.

But school had its own tangy, dense, atmosphere. It was
a complicated, cerebral, place. We might as well have been
disembodied spirits for all the attention that was paid to
our bodies. Getting out of bed in the dark mornings was
hard, and we got chilblains, and pimples, and we weren't
allowed wash our hair often enough, or take enough baths.
If there were others like myself who already knew
something about sensuality, I presume they suppressed

the knowledge, as I did. (It was to be another twenty years before, idle on a bed in Paris on a hot afternoon, masturbation re-emerged from where it had hidden since kindergarten). Our underwear was inspected. Stockings fell in wrinkles from grey elastic garters. Girls outside wore high conical bras those days, but our young breasts were flattened by our gymslips, and you could see nipples through the fabric. There was a lay-woman who came in to school to teach. She had what might have been two puppies wriggling in her jumper just above her waistband. We never mentioned such things.

Any luxury was most intensely felt. The classes who didn't have a state exam did an operetta at Christmas. To the exam-doers, coming from an evening of silent study, scurrying past the *halla cheoil* to late prayers in the dim, cold chapel, the sound of the soaring orchestra and chorus as they reached the finale inside — "We do not heed their di-isma-al sound," the year they did *The Mikado* — was beautiful. It coloured the wintry night. On the morning of St Patrick's Day, too, girls from the orchestra sat out on chairs with their fiddles and played a jaunty jig as we hurried past to a special Mass. There were daffodils in a vase in the refectory, and a fat little sausage each, to mark the feast-day. Anything special — a lie-in, a parcel from home, a puff of another girl's talcum-powder, the little altars we made to Our Lady in our cubicles in the month of May, a fresh loaf when we expected stale, two pats of butter instead of one — was deeply pleasurable.

School was full of tingling excitement, too. When I mentioned this recently, to the only nun I still know, she said angrily, "Oh, no, Nuala! For heavens' sake don't be coming out with all that!" But there is nothing to be ashamed of in how we made a romantic system to contain our rampant emotions. There were boarding-schools all over Ireland then, and all of them must have had girls who had crushes on other girls and on nuns. And each place must have had a special vocabulary peculiar to that sub-world: all those words and concepts which will be lost for ever when women my age die, because no one values them enough to record them. In Monaghan, the girl with the crush was called a "daftie": a popular senior girl might have eight or ten dafties. The dafties competed to get the loved one to accept presents. The point of the present was to be thanked for it. You hung around, perhaps for weeks, always knowing exactly where in any crowd the loved one was located, and whether she was moving towards you or away from you, for the saliva-drying excitement of the moment when she might mutter a few words of thanks. Being thanked was called a "soirée" — pronounced swarry by us. (Perhaps the term survived from the nineteenth century, when the St Louis sisters came from France to Ireland.) After a soirée, your friends would have to help you walk, your legs would be so wobbly. The few nuns who played this delicious game had great scope for effect: they might thank you among the dim rose bushes in the nuns' graveyard.

The emotions we felt as schoolgirls were volatile and exaggerated and they have always been despised by the world. But they were not trivial. They were a grounding in the affective dimension that was to matter most to us all our lives. They were not a mere substitute for what we would have been doing with boys if we weren't in boarding-school, which is what the patriarchy has always arrogantly presumed. Emotion was an element in the process of our putting ourselves together — learning appropriateness, learning control, learning to differentiate our selves from the other selves around. The satisfaction of feelings was the engine that drove us on, rather than competitiveness, or ambition. There was a nun who was tempestuous and brilliant, who strode everywhere, a high colour on her handsome face. Engagement with her on the level of feelings was serious. And fine — finer by far than any relationship I had known before. She bent our incoherent feelings to the purposes of learning and talking and thinking — to goals beyond personal gratification. At the time I was ashamed of my own emotionalism. I admired the girls and nuns who held themselves apart. Not long ago, I stopped the car in a remote part of Ireland where I was lost, to ask a woman walking along ahead of me the way. She turned out to have been at Monaghan at the same time as me. She remembered me, but I, to my embarrassment, did not remember her. "Oh, I wouldn't expect you to," she said. "I wasn't the kind of girl Sister was interested in. You were." That's a remark that cuts both ways.

Not everyone can have forgotten all this. A girl I was the daftie of back then contacted me not long ago to see whether I could help her residents' association to save their local church from demolition. I could hardly say to this respectable matron, "Do you remember the afternoon I lay on the outside of the counterpane when you were ill in bed, and I told you the fine hairs at your hairline, behind your fringe, were the most beautiful things I'd ever seen?" And near me there's a pub where a group of rather smart work-mates — perhaps they're estate agents — sometimes have a drink after work. One of them waves to me. I remember the pretty necklace she gave me when she was my daftie. It says something about the way the sexuality of girls, and even their innocent sublimation of sexuality, is stigmatised, that if I were to indicate to her that I remember, she would faint with shame.

I'm not ashamed of our fervours. But I am ashamed that twice, I stole the gifts I gave to my heroine. I took Tweed talc or round soaps in tissue paper from other girls' cubicles. I had to. I had no money. I didn't take them for myself — just to give to her. And I think that she may have known. And that the nuns knew, and never came out with it. They knew I told lies. They knew I read under the blanket. They knew (this was nearly the end of me) that I smoked, perched in the window embrasure of a lavatory high up in the attics, listening at the cold glass to the noises of the town, like the great roars from the rallies for the IRA men — one of them was a local — who were killed on the Border in 1956. They knew that it got harder and harder to get my fees from my parents (though as it was I was costing the family a fortune, with my uniform and my books.) My mother sometimes got a crony from the pub she drank in to drive her up to Monaghan, but she was afraid of the nuns, so she would stay in the bar of the hotel in town, and send the crony to get me out of the convent. The nuns probably knew about my thefts. I think they were probably enormously kind. But they weren't straight with me. I didn't trust them, any more than they trusted me.

I have no doubt that being sent to this school was the biggest single stroke of luck in my life. When I have criticised it in the past, the nun I'm friendly with has gently suggested that I brought a troubled self to the school — that I projected my own unhappinesses onto it. It does frighten me that I remember the bad times rather than the good ones. "But don't you remember when you led the strike?" she says. "Don't you remember the special Virgil grinds and how exciting they were? Don't you remember the fun we had rehearsing *Blossom Time*? Your essay that we published in *The Oriflamme*? The time I lent you 'J. Alfred Prufrock'?" I'm middle-aged now. I don't want to be engrossed in old hurts. But they are there. The time the nuns ostracised me because I didn't go straight to the chapel to thank God for coming first in Ireland in French. ("No, Nuala, it was certainly not a punishment. It was just that we're very, very disappointed in you.") The time they wouldn't let me be a Child of Mary. The time my friend Breda and I had to apologise on our knees in front of the whole school for taking bread from the refectory, because we were hungry.

We were expected to be the best in Ireland at school subjects. But also to be more than exam-passers — to appreciate art, for instance, though, music apart, "art" might be an illuminated scroll recording the prayers that had gone into a Spiritual Bouquet, or a recitation, with gestures, of 'Glory to God but there it is/ The dawn on the hills of Ireland' for a visiting American Bishop. We did debates. There were engravings after Claude and Poussin on the walls. But intelligence or artistry were nothing much in themselves. They were to be put at the service of God. The nuns were the most powerful women in Ireland. But they didn't have any ideals for the secular world. The thing that would bring a girl most praise was a desire to enter the convent — to be a Bride of Christ. When I left school, the head nun — who could have run General Motors, she was so competent — advised me, earnestly, that in whatever situation I might find myself I should think what the Virgin Mary would have done, and do the same.

I left school, full of furtive resentments against it, and didn't go back for thirty years. But there's a small museum open to the public in a yard of the buildings now. One day not long ago, driving through Monaghan, I thought I might sneak in and maybe get a look at the hidden courtyard and the glassed-in corridor — scenes of such epic events in my adolescence — without meeting anyone. But as I hurried into the museum, a nun came flying down a fire-escape. "Nuala! Nuala!" she cried, with unmistakable delight in her voice. I couldn't believe it — someone in the world remembered me by name after so long! This particular nun I recalled with untroubled affection. She had taught languages with clear-minded vigour. But when she linked my arm and took me — protesting — to meet the terrible ogre who had been the head nun in my time, I was even more amazed. "We're so proud of all you've done, Nuala, and it's wonderful to see you looking so well — you'd be — let's see — you'll be forty-seven soon now, won't you ... " This person, in all the world, remembered my birthday! They wove a little feeling of family around the tea they gave me in the nun's parlour. Afterwards, I helped Mother Dorothea — tiny and frail — to shuffle into the chapel, where she said a prayer and I stood transfixed. Then she kissed me, and I ran out and got into the car, and bent over the steering-wheel, crying too hard to drive.

When I got going, a mile or so down the road, I saw a phone-box. I rang my friend Marian who'd been at the same school ten years after me, and who knew the dread Mother Dorothea had evoked in generations of girls. "We were wrong, Marian, " I sobbed down the phone at her. "They really liked us. They understood the girls: they just didn't let it show!"

"Our first revisionist," Marian said.

4

I left school after the Leaving Cert, when I was seventeen. I hoped to go to college, but it would be a while before I could do the entrance scholarship exam, and another while until I would know whether I'd won a scholarship. I also hoped I wouldn't get into college so I could get a job as an assistant in Clery's, like my friend. At that time, young men as well as young women worked behind the counters in the old wooden-floored Clery's, where the cash zinged around the shop on pulleys and burst up from vacuum pipes. The shop-workers seemed to me to have the best of fun. I had a job, but I had no company in it, working as a clerk in the hire-purchase office of a furniture shop in Grafton Street. Hire-purchase was for the very poor, then. The customers walked down a long room to the hatch where I sat. I saw from the way they walked towards me how bitter it was for them to be still paying out for things they'd got long ago. Money was dominating me, too. I was living at home but I was giving money up. From leaving school on, how to earn enough money to keep myself was my biggest single problem for years and years.

In that interval between school and college, I was as devout as I was ever going to be. I joined the Legion of Mary in Dublin — we had a barrow displaying pious literature near O'Connell Street, and we had a special mission to street-walkers. I said prayers every day, and I went to Mass. I did read during the tedious bits of Mass — a ploy discovered in Monaghan where we were sometimes marched through the town — longingly past the sweetshops and the chipper — and up the hill to the Cathedral, across from its twin hill where hunched figures prowled the paths of the lunatic asylum. I read, concealed in my Missal, anything that was a bit religious — the poems and sermons of John Donne, for instance. I was a member of the Pioneer Total Abstinence Association: when I did take my first drink I went back to it, and then again, and again .... I went to Confession a lot, to help me with boys.

One of the reasons I was doing my best to be a normal girl and a good Catholic was the terrible shock of losing my virginity. A while earlier, home on holidays from school, I'd been messing with a boy friend on a sofa in his house. His mother was upstairs. Lionel Hampton was on the record-player, plinking out 'So High the Moon'. My panties were off. The boy suddenly, terrifyingly, pushed into me, all the way. I ran along the suburban streets to home, panting, crying, praying out loud not to get pregnant. I locked myself in the bathroom to wash off the blood and kneel, in privacy, to beg Our Lady to save me. Some of the girls I hung around with had come up the stairs to the bathroom door and were taunting me through it — I must have said something, when I ran the gauntlet of them, sitting on the wall outside. "What happened to your knickers?" they shouted, like the Furies. "What happened to your knickers?" The fear and revulsion drove me almost into believing that I had a vocation to be a nun. But the more lasting effect was that I was enthusiastic with boys from about the waist up, but the rest of me was so self-conscious that I wouldn't even say that I wanted to go to the Ladies.

When I knew that I'd got the scholarship to UCD I went on holidays to my aunt, who had been such fun when I was a child. She was living in someone else's house in a dreary east-coast seaside resort where the sea went out so far at low tide that you couldn't see it. We sat at night under the seawall in our coats, and she drank whiskey from the naggin bottle of whiskey she always had, by now, in her handbag. She was like a loving child, herself. But she had become baffled. She knew she loved her own children, and us, her sister's children. But she didn't know why she was married at all or why to the particular man who was her husband or why she was afraid of Grandad or why anything. She was always called "wild". Her husband worked abroad. She was summoned off to live with him from time to time. More than once, she drank the ticket money, so as to get out of going. But then her husband and her father would arrange her deportation over her head.

My family's house in Clontarf was packed and clamorous. My father was "Terry O'Sullivan" through and through now — the idealistic schoolteacher and lieutenant in the Army, Tomás O'Faolain, who had written to his *"chroidhe dhil"* with such affection and energy about the arrangements for the moving of their little family to Donegal, had been overtaken by another identity. Partly it was the size the family grew to, along with my mother's refusal to be satisfied with serving it, that killed his enthusiasm. But mostly, he was alienated from a domestic role by the opportunity which Lemass' Ireland happened to present to him. He was not a journalist in the ordinary meaning of the word. He was a small god in the world, which was then very new and innocent, of people who wanted publicity. His successor on 'Dubliner's Diary', the distinguished journalist Michael O'Toole, talks in a reminiscence he published about the way my father made semi-majestic entrances into this or that event around town. Holding himself aloof, he would wait, with melancholy calm, for the customary adulation. He would have risen in our house out on the seafront in Clontarf around two in the afternoon, and freshly washed and shaved, and often wearing evening clothes, he would have stepped into the car from the *Press* when the driver brought it to the gate to read his invitations under the special reading-light that had been installed over the back seat. He would make a round of social events until settling down to write, around midnight, a 'Dubliner's Diary' for the next day's *Evening Press*. Restaurateurs would send exotic meals under silver cloches, and wines, and brandy, in to the office. He banged out the Diary on his old typewriter, come what may, with the discipline that was his second nature.

He wouldn't have spent more than a couple of hours, awake, in his home. When he was a young father, an old woman who worked for my parents told me recently, he always spoke Irish to Grainne and me, the two eldest. Now, he had no time to speak much to his children in any language. When he was a young husband — this woman told me, unwittingly — he and my mother were very close. "I think they must have fought a lot," this woman said to me. "When he came home from work he used to tell me to take you children out for a walk and not come back for an hour." Nobody knows the interior of other people's marriages, and the one and only thing my mother was confident about all her life was the perfection of their physical relationship. But he avoided home. Even on Christmas Day, when we had charming rituals to do with the tree and presents and champagne — things we'd always done, like a family in a book — he eventually went out. He often took a child or children or his wife to a function, or arranged a treat for them from some grateful hotelier or the like. But he never spent a full day at home. And my mother wasn't at home much, either. She went up to the pub two times in the day. One was in the evening, till closing time. The other was at lunchtime, when she went up to get the messages. And to steady herself, to face him.

Who knows where he got to? He had lots of things going on. All of us were dependant on him. Grainne — "Grainne's the pretty one," my mother would always say — was exceptionally smart and attractive and had jobs as personal assistant to various managing directors: this was as high as a young woman could expect to go in the world of work at the time. I — "Nuala's the brainy one," my mother would say — had temporary jobs and my scholarship was coming up. My next sister down, Deirdre — "Deirdre's the nice one," my mother would say, thus finishing off any general confidence the three of us might have had — was engaged to be married, and had an office job. But emotionally, we were in thrall to him. Then there were the brothers, always in difficulty or in trouble, then my little sisters and then my youngest brother. None of them got much attention. But they were members not just of a family but of quite a self-consciously distinct — even a superior — family, all the same. I have a brother who used to be in the British army. He sits in a room in London now, and drinks and reads. "I loved my mother and revered my father when I was a boy," he has written to me, in a letter that captures all our confusion. "They were Mother and Father, and does a child know any different? Sure it made me bed-wet when he came home pissed and pummelled my mother. Her cries for help were heartrending, and made me try to sleep in a chest of drawers. You didn't get to see father much, but I loved him from afar."

The stranger would see my father's suave manners, his detachment, his humour, and think he was a modern type, and that things must be lovely for us at home. And so they often were. He was usually delightful. And he was the head of the family, even if the family was going to ruin. His iron will created a version of a home life for himself. When he came in at night he would go out the back to the roses he grew and inspect them in the dark. He took his own clothes to the cleaners and polished his own shoes. He was invariably dapper and almost always cheerful. He whistled beautifully while he shaved. Nothing would have stopped him from surviving. He drove my mother into a frenzy: "I've asked your mother to come to the Wexford Festival with me," he'd say airily — or a garden party, or a reception. "But she informs me she has nothing to wear. Isn't that so, Katherine? I gave you *carte blanche* to go into Brown Thomas — tell them to send the bill to me — and get something nice, but still, apparently, you claim you have nothing to wear ... " She choked with frustration, unable to find the words to say that she wasn't able to do things like that, and he knew it: that she had no good underwear or shoes even if she had a dress, that she was too shy of shops to tell them to send bills, that one of the children was mitching again, that he hadn't said how long they'd be going for and who was supposed to be minding the house and whether he'd give her money for herself when they were there or she'd be waiting for him to buy drinks all the time — she was unable to say what she felt: that he was mocking her in her cage. She would be dying for him to get the hell out to work, so she could go up to the pub and get a quick double gin down her to stop the shaking.

But even his cruelty to her was not simple. A couple of times, when I went up to his bed to give him a message, I saw Rosary beads under his pillow. He must have prayed by himself. He must have felt helpless, sometimes, under his apparent insouciance. During the next few years, when I was gradually getting away, the house — four bedrooms, ten of us — vibrated with all the different individuals who lived there, each fighting to have some, at least, of their needs met. The hot press in the kitchen was a hopeless chaos of jumpers and socks, and sugar crunched underfoot in the kitchen. I brought home an English actor I had a crush on. No one had cleaned up the pools of tea on the table — crusts in them had gone soggy and looked like snails. "Good God!" he said. "It's like a set for an O'Casey tenement!"

At night, the house was completely undefended. Gangs of boys used to come at least as far as the stairs. The local gurriers knew they could take liberties. There was no one there to care for my little sisters and brothers. My little sisters made a regular life for themselves. They put themselves to bed at nine. They tried to fix the clock to go off to get them to school on time. I remember the beds. My aunt's children often slept in Clontarf, too. There were so many of us that there were beds on the landing and in a windowless box-room. The bedclothes were supplemented by coats. There were only torn pieces of sheet — enough to put under your chin, to soften the rough coats. I do remember my mother pausing to fix a strip of cotton under some sleeping child's cheek. I never remember my father doing anything like that.

We all hated asking for money. I often stood on the landing outside my parents' bedroom trying to work up the courage to knock on the door and wake them to ask for it. Even when I was doing the entrance scholarship for UCD at Earlsfort Terrace, I had to get off the bus at the North Strand and walk the rest of the way because I hadn't the full fare. Yet we were not poor by the standards of the time. Many years later, I was interviewed on television, by Anthony Clare, in a series about Irish people. I said I was poor when I was a student and, so as not to seem to be making exceptional claims for myself, I said that lots of people in UCD then were poor. Eamon Dunphy reviewed the series, and I've just tracked down his piece. 'Watching Nuala O'Faolain depict herself as poor,' he said, 'I longed to kick the television set.' He said, 'Nuala's Daddy was one of Ireland's most celebrated journalists, Terry O'Sullivan. Was she "poor", was "everyone in UCD", poor? As anyone who was actually poor in the 1950s knows, the answer is no. No, no, no. In fact, nobody who went to UCD in those bleak years was poor. They were only playing at poverty ...' This is true, in a way. In the late 1950s, there were big marches of unemployed men in Dublin. They looked and they were desperate. They had no alternative to emigration.

But I was hurt, all the same. My father himself often didn't have a penny. And though the driver and the Austin Princess might occasionally be waiting for my little sisters at the gates of the National School when they came out, they might not have socks. They might not have copy-books. One of my little sisters had TB and lay around all the time. No one noticed, or if they did, they did nothing. An older man friend of mine, a doctor, happened to call for me and he saw her languor. She spent a year in a sanatorium. Otherwise, I suppose, she would have died. My brothers, at that time, were the worst victims of the neglect that has left me with such an impression of poverty. They needed to be helped to get through school. But they never got through school. They were to stumble from one dead-end job to another. My friend, the doctor, and a Jesuit from Gardiner Street tried very hard to keep my eldest brother going towards Matric, and the possibility of college. But they were defeated by my mother wanting him to earn money, and my father washing his hands, and pretending there was no problem. We were not poor. We had aspirations the really poor did not have: it wasn't strictly speaking because of money that we didn't attain them. I once heard about a Dublin journalist my own age who at that time was very poor. His mother was a maid in a hotel. The children would wait in an alley-way out the back of the hotel at night till she found out what bedroom was empty and smuggled them in. I envied him. I envy him that his mother took such care of them.

At the Fianna Fáil Christmas party for the press, the year Eamon Dunphy wrote that piece, I turned away from him. Charlie Haughey laughed at the two of us and made us shake hands. Back then, when we were poor inside our house but not outside, I used to drink with my parents in Groome's Hotel. I remember Charlie Haughey giving me a lift home from there once and settling down when he pulled up at the gate, and my mother coming out and rapping on the steamed-up glass of the car. Charlie Haughey and my father were very alike in a certain ironic grandeur of manner. They both came from modest backgrounds, and "Joey's" in Marino, where they both went to school, was no academy for the élite. Yet — what a great time they were having, in their prime! But my father was skating on thin ice. The bailiff often waited outside the house, propping himself on the wall of the shelter across the road. We survived from day to day. My brother's brilliant potential was ignored, and he went away on a merchant ship.

It wasn't possible to go to college from the house in Clontarf. It was too crisis-ridden. There was too much pain

52

in it. But I didn't know that. I was proud of my family. You wouldn't often meet a man and woman as charming as my father and mother at even their half-best. I was charmed by them. My mother made me her confidante. I listened to the details of my father's betrayals and her riposte — she was having a gauche little affair with a man in the pub. I didn't see this role as destructive. I thought I was living my own life. But when I got my scholarship I actually lost the money — lost the actual bank-notes. This was exactly the kind of catastrophe I was used to. On top of that, I didn't even go in to my first-year exam. I had become a supporter of Noel Browne's socialist group, and because I thought canvassing for it in a bye-election was more important than my own life, I hadn't done any study. I remember my friend Nessa Boland begging me, at the main door of Earlsfort Terrace, to at least go in to the hall, but I turned on my heel and walked out. I was drinking not just like, but often with, my "wild" aunt. I would never have got through the next years but for the older man, the doctor I had met at a Noel Browne meeting, who tried to keep an eye on me and all the family, and who saved me as certainly as he saved my sister with TB.

Because I was so involved with them, and because none of us had the slightest bit of insight into what we were doing, I almost sank with the sinking ship of the family. But luckily, I was pulled towards safety by the strong forces of love and sex. I was in town every night. I wanted my own place. I always worked part-time, and for a while I had a full-time job as a shopgirl in Boyer's, and only went up to college to socialise. But my father didn't let me go without a struggle. There were repeated, bitter, rows. He'd slap my face one day and take me on a luxurious skite down the country to a race-meeting or something the next. But I rented a bed-sitter, high up under the eaves, in Nassau Street. He called on me once, unexpectedly. When I opened the door he walked past without a word, and went across to the sink and kicked the little tin I was using for rubbish out from under it, so that the tea-leaves and peels went all over the floor. Then he ran down the stairs.

5

The outer boundaries of my experience, when I was a student, were in one direction, the literature and the people who were opening my mind, at college; and in the other direction, the business of love. Those were what mattered. I had confidence about the learning. One day I was idly listening to someone talk about Milton's sonnet 'On His Blindness' and I suddenly understood the interrelation, and the third thing made by the interrelation, of form and content. This was a revelation almost as important as learning to read. The English Department in UCD was just coming into the modern world then, at the end of the 1950s. Denis Donoghue introduced us to American poetry. To this day, the poems he showed us have a dimension of magic for me. He showed us Pound — 'When, when, and whenever death closes our eyelids,/ Moving naked over Acheron/ Upon the one raft, victor and conquered together,/ Marius and Jugurtha together, one tangle of shadows...' He showed us Wallace Stevens. He began with the beautiful conclusion to 'Sunday Morning': 'Deer walk upon our mountains, and the quail/ Whistle about us their spontaneous cries ... ' He showed us Robert Frost — 'She is as in a field a silken tent/ At midday when a sunny summer breeze/ Has dried the dew and all its ropes relent ... ' I remember those three poems, in particular, because they fixed me in a preference for a magisterial tone in poetry. I find anything more friendly in lyric poetry not sufficiently grand.

Yet I had no confidence at all at the other boundary — at the business of love. Over the next few years, the few times I more or less went "all the way", it wasn't because I wanted to, but because I was too shy about intimate things to talk about it. I didn't have the self-confidence to indicate "no". Or — when it came up, wordlessly, the first time, I didn't have the words to say that I didn't want to. Then, by doing it, I gained the confidence to say we should stop. This was the worst possible way of being with young men who were at least as confused as I was.

The boys and girls at Earlsfort Terrace, as far as I know, were prudish, and they often lived at home or in hostels run by priests and nuns, and they were prone — I was, anyway — to ambush by Catholic scruples. Honest randiness was not admitted, even by Trinity students, except by some wistful rugby types from Northern Ireland I somehow knew, who persisted in believing that Catholic girls were "easy". But even the older men at Trinity — men from Britain who had done National Service, or former servicemen from America — had to bow to the customs of quiet, contraceptive-free, Dublin. Drinking and talking and incessant going to the pictures were, among other things, sublimation.

There were different styles in lots of things between Earlsfort Terrace and College Green. But a certain kind of person from either place — someone involved in theatre and drinking and literature — met on the shared ground of Grafton Street. "Oh them — they're students," the middle-aged would say, because middle-aged men — the ones with money in Jammet's and the Russell and the Shelbourne, the ones with artistic reputations in McDaid's and the Bailey and O'Neill's — were the kings of the little city. I remember Dublin as dark and dramatic then, at the end of the 1950s, the streets drifting with smoke and rain. I see it in my mind's eye in black and white. Pubs and cafés were thrilling, because light and warmth spilled from them. The students moved like guerrillas around the centre of the city, hardly visible. They walked everywhere. They borrowed each other's coats. They lent each other books, and ate egg-and-onion sandwiches and chips with mince sauce and if they had money, at three o-clock potato cakes came on the menu in Bewley's. You ate them slowly, a whole pat of butter on each one, sometimes accompanied by the snuffles of Myles na Gopaleen, toying with a white pudding on toast at the next table.

Middle-aged or young, city people lived alone in cold bed-sitters that smelt of gas, with stained curtains, and dripping bathrooms down lino-covered halls. There were hundreds of these lairs, and young men and women walking and getting busses from one to another. Even Trinity students, supposedly patrolled by proctors, could disappear into a network of rooms in Kenilworth Square and Waterloo Road and under pavement level in Leeson Street and up in the attics of Nassau Street and over the shops in Baggot Street. Couples went into the musty beds in the afternoons, by silent agreement — she in her jumper and skirt and suspender belt, he pushing down his trousers under the blankets. The fumbles led to this and — ugh! ouch! — that. Buddy Holly serenading Peggy Sue on the Dansette so that the fellows playing cards next door wouldn't hear.

Everything I was learning was new to me. Caring about issues — de Valera's attempt to remove proportional representation, for example — was new. Politics was new. Nationalism was new. I had a boy friend, that is to say, from a Tipperary Republican family who used to walk me up and down Molesworth Street while he plotted to blow up the Grand Lodge of the Freemasons: that was nationalism. Standing on O'Connell Bridge watching the unemployed men march, and wondering whether anything could be done — that was politics. There was no party politics. It wasn't even that Fianna Fáil ran the country: de Valera, personally, ran the country.

Having friends was new. Learning from the enthusiasms of other people my own age was new. Knowing boys and men as companions was new. Not many people got to college thirty-odd years ago, and my fellow-students, though often poor, were usually carefully raised. Most people left school at eleven, or fourteen, or after the Inter. They didn't get much of a chance to make friends of the opposite sex. They were meant to sense each other out at dances. That I did know about — the intensities in the laneways behind dance-halls, and coming out of the cinema with sore lips and swollen breasts. I did not know in any stable way how to behave. There was a cheap 'invalid' wine, then, called Vintara. I used to drink a lot of it. Onlookers, particularly if they had led sheltered lives, were appalled by how uninhibited it allowed a person to be.

It seemed to me that I was finished, when I dropped out of UCD. Months of despair in London followed. I didn't even have the money to go to London, but that I took a job as a domestic in a hospital there. An agency in O'Connell Street paid your boat-fare to that kind of job, the lowest of the low: then they took the money back out of your wages, so that it was nearly impossible to save the fare home. I lived in a hostel near the hospital. I worked by myself in a basement room. There was a big tin machine that took dirty dishes in at one end and produced them at the other, a bit less dirty. I was in charge of that. I had been having a wonderful time at college. I'd had friends. Now, I was so lonely, in the evenings, lying on the bed, looking up at the window high in the wall, that my skin hurt. I tried not to think about Dublin, because all that was over, and as far as I knew, for the rest of my life, I'd be some kind of an Irish worker in England. This experience of complete hopelessness went very deep. There were hardly any black people in England then, and no Asians. The Irish and — more recently — Cypriots, were the servant class. Down at my level you just lived to work to earn enough to live another week of work. I didn't see any way out.

An accident got me the fare back to Ireland. Lives were ruined at that time, thousands and thousand of them, quite casually, by the rules the patriarchy made for young women. They were hotly-pursued, and half-longed to yield, but they were not able to defend themselves against pregnancy, and they were destroyed if they got pregnant. I got the fare back to Ireland through one of those tragic pregnancies.

An Irish woman I knew — a successful, well-dressed executive assistant who normally wouldn't have mixed with me — thought she might be pregnant. She came to me and we went to a doctor. She took off her jumper and bra and he just peered at her and said yes, she was pregnant. He said it coldly. She paid him. Outside, it was a winter night. She held on to the wall, dry-eyed, trying to grasp the ruin that faced her. Almost the worst thing was — how would she tell her parents? In the end, I was given the fare to go back to Ireland to tell them, while she waited in London to hear how they took it.

That was how I got back to Dublin.

This young woman had barely begun her life, when pregnancy struck her. But that is her story, for her to tell. All I know is that she hid out in Belfast, and that I was there with her for the last few days before the baby was born. We walked around all the time, aimlessly, because we had no money to go in anywhere. I saw her a few hours after the birth, weeping in her bed, her milk seeping through the bandages she was tightly bound with. Her father came up from Dublin and he and I were the only people in a side-chapel when a priest baptised the baby. Then I took the baby to the train for Dublin. In Dublin I got a bus to Blackrock. I handed the baby in to the nun in a home there, to be kept until it was adopted. All that way, the baby never cried. I didn't know until many years later that the mother used to go out to Blackrock to that home, and look through the hedge at the children's playtime, in the hope of seeing a child who looked like herself.

And still, I was having unprotected sex myself. I didn't know how to get out of having sex. I never thought of the man as having a responsibility to me. Though now I don't forgive the older man, for instance, who took me on a holiday to the west of Ireland, which I'd never seen before, when I was nineteen. This man was Irish, but he had been travelling abroad. He was the first travelled man I ever knew, and I revered him for his knowledge. I felt I had to sleep with him to keep him interested in me. But I only knew how to court. I remember him bending over my naked body — I hated it being out in the open — in the bed in the damp cottage we'd had to pretend to be married to get (I wore the twist of gold paper from a cigarette packet as a ring when I met the landlady). He was pulling at the hair under my arm, as a sort of playful, initiatory move. "Relax," he ordered. "Come on, come on!" he urged me. "Be a bit more relaxed, can't you?" But I was coldly embarrassed by him. We sat on cliff-tops in the windy sunshine and he told me about his sex-life. I was supposed to be inducted into adult sensuality by his confidences. I sat in the glass porch of the little hotel near the cottage and read my way through back copies of *The New Yorker*, grimly putting in the time till I could get away from the holiday and from him.

This man later wrote me a letter about what "a man" wants from "a woman". I enter it here as a document from patriarchal times:

Dear Little Sister,

You can give him (by "him" I mean the man you will want to give to) first of all companionship. You can be the sieve for his ideas and his enthusiasms, the moderator of his superfluous angers, the soft bosom of his hard days, his scourge to action — or his dangler of promised sweetmeats — when he slackens. You will give him the freedom of loving you exclusively. You will tie him to this stern, sweet discipline, let him feel the demands of your love.

> For he lives only as a shadow-man if his heart can know no outpouring, his selfishness no merciless self-destruction, if his countless good impulses and scattered loves have no single gathering-point and centre where they realise themselves and have meaning. You will give him this — you will give him the manly task of earning your love again daily. You will give him the delight of his eyes when he looks at you bright and neat and clean, when he notices yet once again that your eyes heed him. You will give all these things to him no matter how strong or wise or world-famous he may be. And when you make the gift of yourself, please let it be with humble awareness of all these things which you are giving — that's what will make your gift very rich and meaningful. You are right to prize highly "interesting people," brain knowledge and the world of books and to seek after them. But I have told you the things your man will want from you. Believe me.

This ineffable letter — particularly the veiled threat at the end about a man (him) not wanting a woman (me) to go seeking after knowledge and books and so on — ranks in its small way with Mr Collins' proposal in *Pride and Prejudice* as a piece of perfectly unqualified egotism.

In those years, sex only made sense to me once. I was friendly with an American man who was doing a post-graduate degree in Dublin. He was much older than the rest of us — he'd been in the CIA, even, according to himself. He had the records of *West Side Story* and J. D. Salinger's stories. He shared a basement in Waterloo Road with a lot of other men. One afternoon when I went round there, he was the only person in. We flirted around on the bed in his room, not very seriously. Then the doorbell rang and he went off down the passage to answer it. He came back in and with his face all screwed up, and feeling his way, blindly, and without a word, he pushed and pulled my clothes apart and forced himself into me. After a few awful minutes of red-hot pain he collapsed onto my shocked body, sobbing dreadfully. He sat on the edge of the bed after a while and put his head in his hands. "That was a telegram," he said. "My mother is dead."

I did, after a year of near-desperation, get back into college. The writer Mary Lavin — whose fondness for me was one of my strokes of luck — gave me an allowance for six weeks, to study to re-do the exams. I had exactly enough for a room in Pembroke Street and a chip supper — which I thought about all day — in Cafolla's of Baggot Street Bridge. Then when I got back in, I had no scholarship so I couldn't pay the fees. But a Jesuit in Gardiner Street who was told about me by my doctor friend, gave me the fees — a sum I could never have hoped to get for myself. Eventually I won a minor prize and along with having jobs all the time, I got through to my degree. Not without constant trouble with the college authorities — I was reported to them, for example, for "unbecoming behaviour" at a party. Vintara-induced behaviour. But I was also kindly helped by UCD, especially the women who ran the front office. I loved the place. I love the memory of Earlsfort Terrace.

I was twenty when I met Michael. My mother said, "Are you sure you love him?" "Oh Mammy," I said. I was at the end of her bed, and she had put down her book and pushed her specs down her nose because this interested her, "Oh Mammy, I'll die if I can't see him. I'll die!" I had bumped into him a few weeks earlier on the steps of the National Library. I saw him lifting his face to the sun there — the curve of his cheekbones, the shadows of his eyelashes. I knew him slightly — I'd borrowed his cottage on a hill near Dublin once. Now, the cottage gave us something to talk about while we stood — in the middle of a crowd in a *bona fide* pub outside Dublin — like poles connected by a high-tension cable. Going back into town in someone's packed car I sat on his lap. We hardly breathed. "I'll ring you" was as much as he could say when they dropped me, and I just swallowed, and walked away.

He rang. "Come down to the cottage on Saturday" — as-it-were lightly. "You know the way. We can go for a walk, have a bit of supper ... " But it was the winter. Snow started falling. Then a blizzard set in. By Saturday morning there were drifts, even in Dublin. All the main roads were closed. There was no chance of the bus going. He had no phone at the cottage. And even if he had — I didn't want a new arrangement! I had to have this one! I had been living for this one! I was asking my mother to give me the train fare to the nearest station. "But how far is the station from the cottage?" "I don't know, Mammy, but if I can just get there I'll get to the cottage somehow." Mammy got out of bed and looked in her coat pockets and her bag and gave me all the money she had.

Down the country the snow had stopped falling. It was a still, glassily cold winter afternoon. The sky was palest yellow. A few cars had been along the road from the station earlier, and made deep ruts in the snow. Now the ruts hurt my feet as I crunched along, because the rough edges of snow had frozen again. I had ordinary shoes on — I wouldn't let him see me in rubber boots. The road went into woods, and snow sifted down from the branches and trickled down the inside of my polo-neck and spread across my back. A man in a car going not much faster than I was gave me a lift. I was so numb that I could not pull the door of the car towards me. He was worried about me, when I said to drop me where a lane went up to the cottage. It was getting dark. "I'm fine," I said, "and my friend is just up the road!" I didn't want to be delivered to the cottage with a fuss. I had to seem casual.

But when I crunched through the snow and up to the door of the cottage, red-faced with exertion and shyness and anticipation, Michael wasn't there. The fire was still warm. But he had gone — inching his way, no doubt, to Dublin.

I cried. Then I took the lamp I had lit, balancing its glass chimney carefully before me as I climbed the steep wooden stairs. I took off my skirt and stockings and got in to what must be his bed. I had a last miserable cigarette, and the blankets gradually warmed up and I went asleep. Some time later I woke at the sound of the bedroom door opening. He stood there. The lamp was still lighting. He was quite unable to say anything, or smile, and neither was I. Then he came into bed and his warm arms rolled me on top of him, so that my mouth was exactly positioned where we could be at ease. And sometime that night, not moving much, he melted into me and moved me with all my assent, up and down, in and out. And in the end, I lay in the crook of his shoulder, new-minted. So that was it! That was what it had all been about! I got to know every detail of that bedroom. That night, the frost would have filmed the diamond panes of the little window beside the bed, but where one pane was cracked the glass was always clear. I would have seen the stars through it.

───────────

From then on, Michael was my man, though the "my" sounds more assured than it ever was. But I was still a student and a Dubliner, whereas he lived in the country, mostly, reading and playing the piano. He took no interest in the society we were part of. Not many people did. Noel Browne's socialist party had ended in an impassioned meeting in Moran's Hotel where the various personalities split. I remember David Thornley stumbling down from the stage, crying. The big, bitter marches of the late 1950s against emigration and poverty and hunger had long since stopped — the Archbishop got the leaders good jobs, was what was said. The Republic had settled into being a one-party state. In the early 1960s I knew more about Welsh politics than Irish ones. I had long had a crush on a Welsh nationalist, and when I'd gone to see him in Wales I had stood transfixed in Woolworth's in Bangor, because the shopgirls spoke Welsh. I'd been to Mass with him in an upstairs room: it was more like glamorous, embattled, early Christianity than the huge, ordinary churches of Dublin. I stayed for a while on a Welsh nationalist farm. I read the texts of Welsh cultural nationalism like Saunders Lewis' *Why We Burnt the Bombing School* and I had a Welsh phrase-book I studied. When I went with the Welshman to the currach races in Galway I dimly noticed Irish-speaking Ireland. But I had no interest in Irish. Of course — this says little or nothing about the Ireland of the time. No doubt if I had had a crush on a Connemara man, I'd be a fluent speaker now.

Nevertheless, it was a feature of the intellectual life — if that is not too grand a word for it — of the Dublin I knew then that it wasn't interested in the condition of Ireland. Nothing was happening. Northern Ireland was a far-off place. When Edna O'Brien's first books came out they were a catalyst for women to exchange confidences, and I learnt that quite a few people went to Belfast to get condoms. Condoms, hats, cheap butter: that was the extent of it. *The Bell* magazine had no successor of the same importance. Things were happening in England. Artists seemed to have more money in England — they could hardly have had less than the Dublin ones. I often stayed in the basement in Leeson Street (now, surreally, a nightclub) where the poet Leland Bardwell and her children lived, which was also an after-closing-time salon and a doss-house for people with no beds to go to. It was a centre for English and Scottish poets and painters who drifted across from Soho to see Leland, or Anthony Cronin. Maybe at the level of Anthony Cronin, contemporary Ireland was under discussion. But I was just a student, and perhaps the only student of my generation who never wrote a poem or a story.

Otherwise, there were poets, everywhere. And essayists. Erudite young men like Owen Dudley Edwards wrote essays for small magazines, or to deliver to student societies. Everyone tried to convert other people to admiration for this or that writer or historical figure. This was at a time when feature journalism was completely undeveloped. Ideas and information were on their first time around. So when Owen talked about Swift, say, or Parnell and Kitty O'Shea, or Housman's life and poetry, or Sherlock Holmes, it was all new. I began to write small items for Radio Éireann — Sean Mac Réamoinn got me the work. I'd bring my scripts in to him in the studio in Henry Street, tripping down the long passage with its coconut-matting runner and in one of the glass doors whose function was lettered in gold in an Irish replete with *fadas* and *seimhiús*. He'd run his pencil through the first paragraph; then, when we started broadcasting, I'd hear my first paragraph recycled as his introduction. Then he might take me across to the Tower Bar. He was a well-spring of enthusiasms — for Christianity, for crosswords, chess, women, Celtic literature, food, jaunts down the country in someone's rare car. Rural Ireland was far away in every way, then. The *Fleadh Cheoil* were just beginning to make an impact, and the music of the film *Mise Eire* left audiences rapt. But before I met Sean I had never known anyone to have a recording of Irish music. *My Fair Lady* I remember being passed around, but never Irish music.

Ideas were transmitted by talking. Student magazines mattered, and student societies, and what was said at them. There was a very severe eye kept, in UCD, on guest speakers. But soon after I went to college a paper somehow slipped the net, on religions of the Mediterranean basin. I got such a shock listening to it that I remember now the big oval mahogany table we were all sitting at, in a room just off the main hall in Earlsfort Terrace. I had hardly heard the word religion used in the plural before. No one had ever told me that trinities and virgin mothers and deaths and resurrections were known in places other than Christianity. I was still a practising Catholic then and I was very seriously shaken. I had taken it for granted that the alternatives were to be a good Catholic or a bad Catholic. My education had not prepared me for not believing at all. When I had my own first piece published, it was about the visual references to the Via Dolorosa in Bergman's *Wild Strawberries*. This was a real period topic — the few foreign films that came to Dublin were scrutinised up and down. And the Irish Catholic version of Christianity was more or less the only world system we knew anything about ourselves. We had been trained to read events — Hungary, the Bay of Pigs — in the light of their anti- or pro-Catholicism. The first stirrings of intellectual life, after school, were likely to involve trying to assimilate the new thing, whatever it might be, to the familiar religion.

There was an unselfconscious interest in ideas. A friend might send you a note to say that you absolutely must meet in Hartigan's: they'd had an idea for a short story. John Jay was trying to take plays from Player's in Trinity to Edinburgh, and in both UCD and Trinity French drama was having a passing currency. Claudel and Camus were grist to the mill of Irish youth. We student theatre types would try anything: Beckett's *All that Fall* was a perfect success, but a Strindberg one-acter was abandoned when the audience burst into hysterical laughter at the line, "I saw your feet in the bathhouse and ever since I have loved you ... " I put on a dire production of *The Lower Depths*, not least because Moscow subsidised publications like Gorki's *Plays*, and you could get copies in the Communist bookshop in Dublin very cheaply. If you had an enthusiasm you shared it. Paddy Connolly, later to be Attorney General, knew all about Wagner. My friend Eithne O'Neill wrote to me (in Irish and French — she was practising her languages) about the stories of Doris Lessing. Nabokov was passed from reader to reader. Paddy MacEntee and Henry Comerford had a plan to put on *Volpone* under the portico of the GPO as some kind of statement about neo-classicism. When you discovered something it was like winning a prize, and you went out to share it. John Montague's poem 'All Legendary Obstacles', I remember, was like that. Reading it for the first time was an event in one's life.

Leland read everything, and passed everything on. Her musty basement in Leeson Street was a most various place. It could be frightening. All the usual inhabitants decamped from McDaid's pub one night and went to see Jimmy O'Dea in *Mother Goose*. My friend Laila, an elegant Egyptian, baby-sat Leland's baby. He was no trouble — he drank his milk from a Gordon's Gin bottle with a teat and went asleep. But Laila was reading Poe and the shadows seemed to gather around her. She grabbed the baby and spent the hours out on the step. Then again, the basement was sometimes a bridge school. Leland comes of Protestant stock and she has her accomplishments. She was a bridge player and horse-rider. She did keep a horse, when the Corporation re-housed her in Tallaght: her neighbours thought she was a traveller. Leland was as poor as my mother had ever been, and she was perfectly capable of having as many babies. Yet she survived, and helped other people to survive. She was the support-system for a generation of writers, down in her basement, stirring a stew with one hand and comparing translations of Baudelaire, as it might be, with the other. Her head was stocked. In a note to me in London from Dermot Healy in Cavan, maybe ten years later, he remarks: 'Leland was just unbelievably good on the radio these past few Saturdays. A mixture of French singing, Mozart, Paul Durcan and her father. "Isn't that lady's voice beautiful," the girl said in the pub where I was listening. And when I returned this

Saturday she switched over immediately to Radio Éireann. The gypsies who occupy the pub nodded approval. They congratulated me when my own name was mentioned: "Very nice, mister, very nice indeed ... '"

Bohemia was where women and men were closest, in those days when the sexes were such strangers. But there was no equality. I once ventured to ask Leland why she was with a particular man, who was unpleasant to her. "Who else would I get?" she said. "At my age?"

———————————————

You could not, then, thirty-odd years ago in Dublin, just go and live openly with your lover. Formally, Michael and I did not live together. Even my mother only accepted the situation because we were going to get married as soon as we could. (He had been married, in England, but he and his wife had not been living together for some time. Divorces took a few years, then.) I spent a night with him once in a notoriously free-thinking boarding-house in Rathgar. When I came out in the morning, a car-load of men who had been waiting, crawled along beside me as I walked away. Leaning out, they half-threatened me and half-pleaded with me to go home like a good girl, and go to Confession. My patron — the doctor who had helped me and the family over and over again — went to my Professor of Old English, a priest, to ask him to use his influence to stop me seeing Michael. (No one expected anything of my parents.) The house Michael lived in was full of secret liaisons like ours, because the houses where unmarried couples were known to be tolerated weren't very many. The girl in the front room was visited every evening by a young man who lived with his mother in Fitzwilliam Square. They were actually married, but no one knew.

I was never part of my original family again. But their address was my permanent address: unmarried daughters lived at home, in principle, if they lived in the same town. Bed-sitter Dublin had different rules from today's apartment-block Dublin. The only definite break came if you married and had children yourself. Girls and boys married each other then who would have a passing relationship now: Michael and I would have married within the first few months if he hadn't been married already. I thought he was wonderful. He was very good-looking. And he knew about music. I listened to music in his room all one summer. He had a big pile of records — Clara Haskil playing Mozart, Bartok, Chopin, Walton, Telemann, Bach. He read in French and Italian. He looked after himself. He loved the outdoors, whereas I had hardly ever even been for a walk. He drank very little, disliked smoking, and he prepared fresh, vegetarian, food. This was the last straw for my mother. "Don't you think he's a bit dull, dear?" she'd say, when I went out to the pub she drank in to see her.

He was in every way a good influence on me. (What if I had discovered orgasm with a person as reckless as myself?) He took me abroad for a holiday at a time when there wasn't even a concept of "holidays". Most young people always needed work: I was a lunchtime waitress and had to keep the job. There was no television, and no travel material in newspapers. In the circumstances, even the bland British travelogues which came on before the main picture in cinemas — sunny Bournemouth, a flower festival on Jersey — were exotic. By the time I was twenty-one, I had only been to three or four places in Ireland, and nowhere else except the hell-hole of London, and to Paris, when I was at school and won a French government essay competition. I had never eaten in an outdoor restaurant. I had hardly ever seen a black person and never spoken to one. So when Michael took me to join his friends on a boat on the Mediterranean, I was aching with readiness to travel. The overnight train went down through France. As dawn came up, I saw from the rattling, hot, cindery-smelling compartment for the first time, vineyards, sunflowers, quilts hung out windows. That first night we stayed in a high room in a once-ornate pension somewhere in the dense alleyways between the station and the port in Genoa. We went out into the crowd and the noise. The air was pungent. Bright prostitutes sat on kitchen chairs at the corners of the streets. There was a smell of smoke, a vision of great church doors, children chasing each other, people haggling and shouting and laughing, and a big smooth rat who made his way along the side of a wall. We went down a step into an earth-floored café, and saw a pizza-oven, for the first time, and as I was to do for a long time, I ate just vegetable soup, because at least it had potatoes in it.

And another time, we went on a motor-bike through France. Every mile of the journey — before we puttered down the other side of the Alps, amazed at the soldiers holding hands in the dark park in Aosta — is still vivid. Like the bookish provincials we were, we went to Rouen to the Flaubert museum in a pavilion in his garden. There was a little greyish cloth under a glass dome. This was the handkerchief, the card said, with which Flaubert '*a essuyé son front, quelques instants avant sa mort.*' We went to Nevers, because in the movie *Hiroshima Mon Amour* — which had reduced myself and Laila to abject, quivering rapture — the Marguerite Duras character keeps saying, "*Je rappelle Nevers.*" We went to Autun, and looked at the Ghislebertus tympanum — Iris Murdoch had used the serpent in that carving as a symbol of evil in her latest book.

But in real life, after I got my degree, I was stuck again. Then a professor from UCD — Robin Dudley Edwards — came all the way out to my parents' house in Clontarf, where I was living, with a message from my own Old English professor. There was a scholarship in Medieval English being offered by the University of Hull. It was only a small scholarship, but there was nothing coming up in

Ireland for another two years. My patron, the doctor, bought me a suit and a ticket to Hull for an interview, and I got that scholarship.

In Hull, that winter of 1961, the skies were grey streaked with black. The wind sliced in from the North Sea. In a launderette once, a Ghanaian man urgently showed me photos of his wife and children in Africa. He wept. No one could do anything about the loneliness of postgraduate students. They'd come from warm, peopled, lives to a place with no reward except scholarship. I was no scholar. I began to wither. I went to tea — scones, marble cake — every Sunday on a rota of Christian families organised by the Anglican padre. I went to a double-bill of *The Rake's Progress* and *Don Pasquale*. I went to an Irish event: 'The dancing will consist of Ceilidhe Dancing and Old Time Waltzes. There will also be songs and request items. We look forward to your continued interest in this very necessary effort. St Enda's club has the formal approval and blessing of His Lordship, the Bishop of Middlesbrough ...' Michael had got work as an extra in a film some time previously, and when the film — *The World of Suzie Wong* — came to Hull, I sat all day in a freezing cinema waiting for the moment when you could see his head to come around again.

I had wanted to try to be independent. But I couldn't stand the loneliness. Michael came over, and we pretended to be married, and got a flat on a grey suburban street. We lay in front of the gas fire reading Flaubert's letters. We went south, across the flat plains of eastern England, and I thought his eyes were exactly the same colour as the roof of Lincoln Cathedral after rain. That was the sort of thing I thought, even if I didn't say, when I was twenty-one.

And at the end of one year at Hull I took the risk of coming back to Dublin, to work towards getting the big Irish scholarship which paid for you to study anywhere in the world you chose. Not that it was all that urgent that I go on studying. Michael and I would be getting married, wouldn't we? Just as soon as he got his divorce.

6

Years after I was in Hull, Philip Larkin apologised. "I was asked to look out for you," he said. "But I'm afraid I couldn't be bothered ... " It is a pity he didn't bother. We could have discussed, if all else failed, his state-of-the-art library at the university, which I sincerely admired. I would have been happy, tucked into the stacks, reading the publications of the Early English Texts Society, if I hadn't missed Michael so much. "I did see you coming in and out of the library," Larkin said to me. "But you seemed all right... " This was at lunch in a hotel in Cheltenham, ten years later. I was working for the BBC making Open University programmes and I was making one about poetry and television, and the problems associated with supplying images for a poem. I wanted to record him reading his own poem, 'Here', for the soundtrack. Normally, he didn't do that kind of thing. But because he remembered my name with a little guilt, he asked me to join himself and his mother in Cheltenham, where he would read the poem into my tape-recorder. Thus, I had one of the more disconcerting meals of my life. Both the Larkins seemed to be somewhat deaf. And the hotel-lounge we had pre-lunch drinks in, and then the dining-room itself, had a tin roof. It was raining very hard, so it was difficult to hear in any event. Philip would say something like "Another gin and tonic, mother?" and Mrs Larkin would reply with something like "I must say I agree with you about the fish" and I'd say something like "What amazingly heavy rain," and Philip would say "Certainly, I'll just catch the waiter's eye ... " We got through an extremely boozy lunch at these gentle cross-purposes. Then he and I went out the back, the two of us and the tape-recorder squashed under his big black umbrella. There was a stone-built shed there, where the staff kept their bicycles. We were away from traffic and people. We sat on a low wall, companionably, and he started off:

> *Swerving east, from rich industrial shadows*
> *And traffic all night north; swerving through fields*
> *Too thin and thistled to be called meadows,*
> *And now and then a harsh-named halt, that shields*
> *Workmen at dawn ...*

He was a wonderful reader, and a most attractive man, sending out both a non-threatening message and a message about being more threatening than his non-threatening image made him appear.

I've known a lot of writers on that kind of anecdotal level. I digress, and mention some of them, though I was never reverent about writing, myself. My father, after all, wrote, in his way, as the daily, bread-winning task. People I lived with wrote, banging away oblivious to me, often when I wanted them to do other things. I never even read what they produced — I was exceptionally uninterested in anything by anyone I knew myself. It wasn't until recently, when I presented the 'Booklines' programme on RTÉ, that I ever asked any writer about writing. This wasn't always easy. The living short-story writer I most admire, Alice Munro, told me that as a young woman in remote Ontario she'd read and been inspired by Mary Lavin, which was very pleasing. But when it came to her own writing and I started interviewing her in studio, she leaned away from me, her fine eyes looking at me warily, as if I'd gone slightly mad — as if she couldn't think why I was asking her all these crazy questions. Some kinds of writing, I thought afterwards, don't want to know their own methods. But some kinds of writing are almost as interesting to talk about as to read. I directed an interview with Norman Mailer about *An Executioner's Song* and I interviewed him myself about *Harlot's Ghost*: both interviews, it seemed to me, were legitimate, if tiny, offspring of the books. I interviewed Kingsley Amis in a very small hotel room in Kensington and afterwards we knocked back duty-free whisky and Amis was like a big, pink, particularly likeable baby. I directed an interview with John Betjeman and he gave us all champagne and pined for Anglo-Irish demesnes we Irish television people had never heard of. Seamus Heaney was always a selfless promoter of poets and poetry, which was one of the reasons the Nobel prize was so rightly given to him. If he agreed to talk about poetry on television, he prepared for the task. And he always found a way to be meaningfully generous. I remember, particularly, the way he talked about Derek Mahon's poetry (Derek Mahon himself could not be lured by any bribe whatsoever to appear in front of a camera). In Princeton, Joyce Carol Oates turned out to be an enthusiast for Roddy Doyle. In London, we had supper with Eileen O'Casey in an Italian restaurant and although she was in her eighties, she enslaved the waiters with her charm. In interviews you do get a glimpse of personality. But mostly it is rote work for the writers. Though few of them re-cycle themselves with quite the same economy as J. B. Priestley, whom I met once at a dinner party in London — delighted to meet him, because I'd read his *Bright Day* over and over when I was a child. Priestley amused the dinner-table with an improvisation about being on holiday in Ireland recently, and noticing that Irish girls have lovely hair but terrible legs. Flying to Dublin a few days later I picked up the in-flight magazine. It hadn't been an improvisation. There was an article by J. B. Priestley: 'Irish girls have lovely hair but terrible legs,' it began.

I have a friend who is a very successful writer — David Lodge. He's thought of, now, as a comic writer. But I loved about him, from the moment I met him, a sombre scrupulousness — of which his English Catholicism is part — which may be the ground of the comic necessity in him, but which makes the person (as often happens with writers) the very opposite of the author. The only writer who looked and behaved like 'a writer' all the time (and who I ever felt I worked with in a collaborative sense) was John Berger. This was when I was making television programmes for the arts faculty of the Open University. Zola's *Germinal* was one of the texts on the course on the nineteenth-century novel, and to do something about that novel, for the television component of the course, the Professor of English wanted his old socialist comrade. John Berger was an art critic and novelist, who had just had a great success on television with a series about the social role of paintings, called 'Ways of Seeing'. It was going to be difficult to get him to agree to do an Open University programme, and the professor and I flew to Geneva to try to talk him into it. It took a whole evening. John's wife mostly moved around the room preparing a meal, and doing things quietly with the children.

Things went stiffly at first. But a photograph of Zola's overstuffed sitting-room, in his villa near Paris, led to inspiration. It suggested to John something about the limits of the material. There is a gap between what you can feel and see, and what you can imagine. Zola, as bourgeois as his furniture on one level, could articulate what to the bourgeoisie is a nightmare vision of coal-miners, because they cannot see them. They imagine them, deep under the ground, menacing, formlessly, as the rise of the proletariat menaces the bourgeoisie. The argument wasn't linear — I only ever grasped its possible shape when John would turn his beautiful face to mine and earnestly go over it. But the programme wasn't just an illustration of an argument — that was what was creative about it. We went to Derbyshire and filmed, with immense difficulty, down a coal-mine. We filmed life above-ground and life underground and John talked about the gap between, and I freeze-framed images of people in the village and unfroze them and used a brass band playing Gounod's *'Mors et Vita'* on the soundtrack. We made a film about the life in

75

darkness. In general we thought we had been richly suggestive, rather than prescriptive. And perhaps we had been.

It was a wonderful experience, working with him. And knowing him, at that particular time. His novel *G* had just won the Booker Prize, and he was in the process of giving half his prize money to the Black Panthers, and was always taking taxis to Caribbean clubs in the Finsbury Park direction. And he was writing poems: he gave me some. He took me around a bit. I adored him. And he thought I was very gifted. When we were filming at the coal mine he used to hold me at night because it was very difficult work and I couldn't sleep from anxiety. "Think about Donegal," he used to say. "Think of the waves on the shore in Donegal." I didn't like to admit that he'd got it generously wrong. I wasn't from glamorous Donegal: I was only from County Dublin.

I mention this as an epitaph, almost, on unconsciousness. I was lost in hero-worship. I never gave a thought to his then wife — a very brilliant woman — or the children, back in Geneva. He was above all that, I would have said. No one is above anything, she implied, in a piece she published in the feminist magazine *Spare Rib* not long after. It was an account — a deadpan, detailed, account — of cleaning the inside and the outside of a lavatory.

Philip Larkin had been asked to mind me in Hull, when I went there in 1961, by Patricia Avis, who lived with Professor Desmond Williams of UCD, who later had a small dalliance with me. (We'd meet in London at the Ritz, or with his *Daily Telegraph* friends in 'The King and Keys' in Fleet Street. He was said to be on MI5 work, but mysteries were his stock-in-trade.) Patricia Avis had written two books. Charles Monteith of Faber wouldn't publish the first because, according to Richard Murphy, who was her husband, "it slandered his friends." I wish I'd known that when I was seated beside a gushing Charles Monteith at a dinner in All Souls, four or five years after Hull. I wish I could have told him what I think of such lethal arrogance.

She died — alcohol and pills — with no hope of either of them being published. Yet by all accounts, she was as clever as the clever men — Kingsley Amis, Conor Cruise O'Brien, Larkin — she knew. I see articles about her that imply that she was a doomed soul. That's an argument often used to cover up indefensible circumstances. She was nearly in time for the break-out — for getting support from other women, getting published by women's presses and so forth. But when she was in her prime, writing and publishing was a man's world.

Though — exceptional women could survive. One I knew personally was Mary Lavin, who so kindly helped me try to get back into college. Mary did not frequent pubs. But she was not a housewife, either. She had a town house and a country house and used hotels. She had the status of the respectable widow she was. She also had a great love. But the loved one, handily, did not impinge on her daily life, since he was a Jesuit, and usually in Australia. She had money and health and three daughters who interested her enormously. She could run things her way. Above all, she had been an only child, adored and affirmed by her father. When I knew her, she treated her widowed mother with harassed affection, as if her mother was her least favourite child.

But I did not know, when I was a young woman, a functioning wife or mistress who wrote. Most of them were too poor to be able to spare the time. Patricia Avis was wealthy, but though that might have helped her write her novels, it didn't (in her lifetime) get them published. It wasn't in the mind of girls to write. The young writers at

Mary Lavin's house were all men: the women were all women who were going out with the men. If you were a young female, no one asked you what you did, around the pubs of Dublin, or what you wanted to do. They assessed you in terms of themselves. You were welcome if you fitted in. The "literary Dublin" I saw lied to women as a matter of course, and conspired against the demands of wives and mistresses. Outside the home, in the circles where academia and journalism and literature met, women either had to be make no demands, and be liked, or be much larger than life, and feared. It wasn't at all easy to be formidable and also desirable. Patricia Avis was like a zombie with misery. I saw Maire Mac an tSaoi in the corner of an obscure pub once, in urgent talk with a man. She would have been the exception, but she wrote in Irish.

For a while when I was a student I lived on Leland's sofa, under a pile of coats, in one corner of the big front room, and Patrick Kavanagh had a bed on the other side. He was a terrible flat-mate. He coughed and hawked, and tramped, muttering, out into the area under the steps and pissed copiously and often, groaning and talking to himself while he did. His heartburn was not helped by his starting to drink again each morning, as soon as an inventory of his pocket and mine, and of the number of bottles that could be returned and their deposits retrieved, had established the day's opening budget.

He was too wrapped up in the struggle to keep himself going to take any notice of extraneous people. That's how it was possible to share a room with him. But though he was usually curmudgeonly, he took the trouble to amuse when he was feeling well and had a few bob. And his health did get better — or, didn't get worse at the speed you would have expected — over the years. The worst kind of end, which seemed to be lying in wait for him, was fended off, because his woman friend, Katherine Moloney, began to look after him. I used to meet him, a few years after sharing the basement in Leeson Street, in London, in a pub opposite the British Museum. He wasn't just better physically: he was in better humour than he had been in Dublin. Katherine lived in London, and she minded him. (Misogyny is so ingrained in some quarters that this important fact is overlooked.) I remember him positively entertaining the company once with tales of the millionairess' castle in Italy he'd just been staying in. "My hostess invented the brassiere," he rasped, startling the strangers around in the Museum Tavern. "That's what made Caresse Crosby rich. The brassiere did." He'd obviously been patronising Italian shops — he was eating straight *Bicarbonato di Soda* from a big packet. He went off with Katherine that night as spry as anything. And he wasn't impossible the day he and Katherine were married in Dublin. Eoin and Joan Ryan — I was always told that Joan was the woman the poet is grieving in 'Raglan Road' — gave the wedding meal in their house in Leeson Park. There was a big table covered in dishes, and lots of drink. Patrick looked a bit remote. But then, many of the guests were out of their element. There were people there who had never seen each other except in pubs, and flats that were extensions of pubs.

Paddy's presence was always the weightiest in any company he was in. But that was because of his self — the difficulty, if not impossibility, of engaging his attention, much less of charming him, unless he chose. If he did choose, the attention he directed at a person could be surprisingly warm and simple, behind his awkwardness. His personality would have compelled attention, even if he had been less of a writer.

Writing in itself was not revered in literary Dublin. A lot of people wrote, and no bones were made about it. It was not thought of as a raid on the inarticulate or anything like that, so much as a craft that you might keep yourself by practising. It was something anyone might be engaged in. When I was around Dublin in the early 1960s I might call in to the National Library to see Mary Lavin. She wrote there, and in the foyer of Buswell's and on a bread-board sitting up in her bed in Bective in the early morning, before she got her daughters up for school. Round in McDaid's, John Broderick might be getting ready to go home to Athlone, where his business was writing. Down in the Stag's Head Tom McIntyre might be talking about writing with Tom Kilroy, who was writing. Myles na Gopaleen might be in Neary's, not talking to anyone (I spent an evening there once with Louis MacNeice and the two men didn't address each other.) Ben Kiely might be in the White Horse on Burgh Quay, hypnotising some young woman with his talk. My friend Sean Mac Réamoinn might be in the Tower Bar with a visiting writer, like Anthony Burgess. Liam O'Flaherty might be walking home along the canal.

I knew John McGahern for a few years. We shared a Northside home-ground — me in Clontarf, he in his digs on the Howth Road. We met in high dim pubs at the bottom of the Malahide Road or further down Fairview. "I work much," he wrote to me — we wrote and sent telegrams across Dublin in those days, because there were no private phones at bed-sit level. "So much I hate the sight of a white page. I'll send you my work sometime. I think about you in some of it ... " He had already written *The Barracks* when I met him. We used to go to the pictures a lot — the five o'clock show, because he was well out of Belgrove School, where he taught, by five — followed by a snack in an O'Connell Street ice-cream parlour. We were in an ice-cream parlour when he showed me the telegram from Faber and Faber which accepted *The Barracks* for publication, with the greatest enthusiasm.

John was recovering from pain connected with the beautiful sister of a garda, as I recall. There was a cinema ad for Mystic stockings, where a kind of green witch writhed over a pair of stockings she was passing through her hands. The ad evoked this woman, and hurt John. But perhaps he was familiar with being hurt: perhaps he felt at home, hurt. The few letters of his that chance has preserved suggest that hurt was an element in our acquaintanceship. 'I waited and waited on Tuesday evening and that was all. Then I thought she might be ill, or some accident, but the obvious one is almost always right, the hardest one to admit. But it doesn't matter now ...' A postcard from Sligo: 'Thank you so much for the letter. It's far better to be honest. And of course it doesn't profoundly matter, anyhow ...' A terse letter saying: 'What you did that last evening the more I think wasn't very far short of criminal.' (What? What did I do?) A letter — 'The only world is the world of love, and if we're true we must be consumed in whatever reality there is. All the rest is silly business ... ' A telegram saying he waited till eight. A telegram to the Pike Theatre wishing me luck — I was an actress at the time, and opening that night in a Behan one-acter. A brush-off letter: 'I think it's better for us not to meet, there's too much brokenness in our last evening and yesterday, a kind of inconsequence without joy, almost mere pauses or waiting, both of us coming out of our different lives. So let us wait apart for a while ... ' Then he elaborately wishes me happiness. This letter is blotched: it was either rained on, or I cried when I read it.

Yet what I remember from the year or two we sometimes went out together are simple things. John knew the manager of the Capitol Cinema, for instance — they were from the same part of the country. And one day this manager stood us a meal in the restaurant, at a cosy table-for-two at the side, up against the flock wallpaper, with our own little lamp on the table. I can taste at this moment the rasher in that mixed grill. It was the luxury, the lavishness of it that made it so memorable. Because we were poor. Not intellectually — he gave me Rilke's *Notebooks of Malte Laurids Brigge*; I introduced him to Webster, and so on. But we walked everywhere. We had very little money. Once we went on the bus to Skerries, and relished the blowy air, out on a headland. I remember that day because we were lighthearted and friendly, and not at our usual edgy distance from each other. And I've seen that exact landscape, completely transformed, in one of his marvellous stories. That's one of the pleasures of having known a writer.

I think now that Mary Lavin, who spun many a plot in her mews in Lad Lane, promoted us to each other. There was a great deal of headlong drama connected with knowing her. She'd send me notes saying things like — of a man we were both interested in — 'he has done some bad things of which I'd like to tell you. He certainly came between us by a deviousness and secretiveness in his nature that is *not* in mine. Ah well ... ' and she would speed on to an instant portrait of the next person to cross her mind. She would bring her face close into my face and fix me with her gooseberry-colour eyes and enrol me in whatever the scenario of the moment was. She may have had plans for John or for me, separately or together. Underneath even her own consciousness she was frighteningly sure of what she wanted. She tunnelled towards her goals at a depth I, for one, have never been at. I hadn't read anything she wrote, at the time, so I didn't realise.

Certainly, John and I were misled by something. He was working himself out, at that time. He didn't look impressive — a slight young teacher from the country, with a slow way of speaking. But his pale glance was formidable. I wrote about him to Michael, when I was telling him everything in the first flush of love. I spelt McGahern wrong. 'He's the chap who is a good writer,' I wrote. 'This is how I classify him so you'll remember who he is — to me he's a million little things all complexed ... ' Then I give a pen-picture of him, in which I say that he is 'both lonely and contemptuous'. I think now that young writers toy with narratives. Maybe John toyed with certain possibilities as a way of settling himself. Certainly, we tried hard to know each other, if willing it could do it. I remember a miserable night — the last, I think — when we wandered the wintry streets for hours and still could not find any ease with each other. These things matter when you're young and have high standards. Nowadays, I bump into him once a year or so, and we just exchange friendly greetings. But I hardly know him less, in reality, than I did when we were meeting all the time.

Biographers of Irish writers will be scraping the barrel very deep if they ever come to me. But I'm representative of a certain milieu. For every real writer around, there were ten merely literary-minded people like me. Perhaps "literary Dublin" needed both kinds. It was a real place, even in the 1960s. Without question, writing mattered more than money or possessions or status in any other field. But the culture was terribly dependant on drink. There was too much public, anecdotal life, and not enough personal, lyric life. There was too much drinking. Drinking means bad breath and crusted shirt-fronts and shaking hands and bottles of milk wolfed down as a meal and waking in the morning on a pile of coats with no clean knickers and being thin, being cold, being sick. And drinking is, after all, about getting drunk. Fine people all but prostituted themselves to get the money to get stupidly drunk every single night. I saw Myles na Gopaleen urinate against the counter in Neary's one night. That's what being a drunk means — waking to the evidence of repeated lonely humiliations, that drive you further and further away from anything but drink. And whatever that kind of drinking did to men, it ruined women. I can think of only a few of the women (and I'm not one of them) who hung around McDaid's who were not, sometimes, squalid. You would think that way of life had been designed to test people to their limits. Certainly it could not be survived: only abandoned.

7

When I was first in Hull and separated from Michael, I wrote to him often. Sometime later — maybe during a row — he sent me back a packet of those letters. So I have a unique insight into a person called Nuala O'Faolain when she was twenty-one. She seems full of life, that young woman, and curious about everything around her and though obviously madly in love, not at all abject. The only thing is — she keeps asking this man to marry her. I am astonished now to see how persistently I asked Michael to hurry up his divorce so as to marry me. 'I always hope that one day you will see what I mean by marriage ... ' I write. 'I would like to get married soon, otherwise I can't really go to live at the cottage ... ' 'Marrying you wouldn't be my ideal, but the ideal might well grow up between us so I wish you'd marry me, quick ...'

It never crossed my mind to consider marriage as an institution you could look at, walk around, detach, as a social arrangement, from particular people. I saw no connection at all between what I was planning — a husband, children — and what my mother, the woman I knew best, actually had — a husband, children. Yet her letters told a clear story. 'I'm all fussed and financially desperate. Lost half-stone weight, though, and people — including Da — remark on it without being told ... ' I complain about my loneliness in Hull. She replies, 'I'm fat, tired, ugly, and old, and I have spent all my money and I'm not able to look after my home and my family. Contrast these truths with your easily-remedied ills and brighten up ...' She was still struggling with domesticity. 'The rooms are a mess. I'll pay you to help me one whole day when you come home — I can't find *anything* and dirt and destruction are overwhelming me. Daddy is fine — madly cheerful, ordinary and prosperous. Marvellous at the ostrichism, about me and everything.' She has a baby. 'I don't feel either well or happy — except with the baby. Money is the worst trouble — Dad never seems to get around to paying anything — ESB cut us off this morning and I have to wash filthy clothes. I wish there was some way to make him pay. The continual worry is bad for my ulcers ... ' She counts her blessings, unconvincingly: 'Still — I have good friends, a char, the weather is fine, I have plenty of books and every so often the companionship of the older children ... '

I knew marriage was perilous. I had met two women who in their different ways I admired, and wanted to copy. One of them was Harry Bewick — Pauline Bewick's mother. The other was the mother of Pauline's friend, Barry: Maura Laverty, at that time one of Ireland's best-known women writers. Neither of them had husbands.

Harry was English. She had been a married woman with two little girls, somewhere in the north of England, when she was young. Her husband was an alcoholic. One day, she told me, she finished reading a book by D. H. Lawrence. "That's it," she thought to herself, and put the children in their pram and walked out the door, never to go back. She'd worked — for example as a vegetarian cook — in progressive schools, all around England, and come to Ireland and lived in a cottage in Kerry, needing very little money because she lived very simply. Then she'd had a house in Dublin which was spoken of with awe because the lodgers — often grown-up men — were not stopped by Harry from sleeping with their lovers. She would have thought it was mad to do such a thing. When I met her, she lived in an ordinary, small, garden glasshouse in a field in Wicklow. She ate frugally, and boiled water on a little Aladdin stove, and slept when it was dark and rose when it was light. If a mouse, say, tried to get at her muesli, she would catch the mouse and carry it up the field and release it. If a slightly backward local youth spied on her sunbathing, she just moved. She liked company but she was just as contented if no one came. She read the same few books — the writings of the Indian sage, Krishnamurti — over and over again, peering at the pages through a magnifying glass. Other than that, I thought her way of life perfect. Yet it was the very opposite of marriage.

Maura Laverty's daughter Barry was as enviably exotic as Pauline in the Dublin of the time. They were art students. They had wonderful clothes — blouses copied from *Carmen Jones*, Capri pants, ballet-slippers. They had English men interested in them, not Irish boys. Maura had written novels and did a lot of journalism, and was an expert cook and author of cookery books. And she was the sole scriptwriter of the early television serial based on her play 'Tolka Row'. Maura was in the world of Ireland and Dublin as Harry was not. She knew how to earn good money. She got me my first ever professional job — passing on a commission to research authentic recipes for the new Bunratty Castle banquet. (They were only too authentic: Bunratty started off with braume brose and sew lumbarde and pety-toes in gelyce, and understandably, soon abandoned authenticity.) Maura lived in an elegant flat with great long windows hung with sweeps of soft muslin. But when we girls came in she would be in her bedroom. She would come out and greet us gently, and then go back into her room. She never had anything to eat with us. She never spoke about herself, much less uttered any complaint, but I used to feel loneliness coming from her. Three children were growing up on the proceeds of her hard work. Where was her husband? A husband was never mentioned. When that lovely woman died in her bed, her body was not found for days.

Yet love was supposed to work out differently for me than it had for any woman I actually knew. I went on believing that as soon as the man I loved (so far, the best candidate was Michael, because surely having orgasms meant you were in love? But there were always other candidates) loved me equally — as soon as some magic balance had been found — history would end. We would be married and an 'ideal would grow between us', to quote myself.

We would have been married if I'd become pregnant. Any decent man promptly married his girl friend in those circumstances. (Then you had to think of some way to explain things, when the baby arrived, seven months into the marriage. Couples suddenly emigrated to England and Australia. Women moved across the country and gave birth and hid the babies and put pillows under their skirts, when their mothers came to see them. Hundreds of babies were firmly said to be "premature".) No matter how progressive the circle you moved in, you lost almost everything if you became pregnant outside marriage. One girl in UCD did get pregnant — the others, through a combination of the most severe sanctions, and idealism about marriage, kept their sexuality and their boy friends', as far as anyone knows, in check. This girl was a distinguished person in every way. But I remember her hunched in her bed-sitter in Fitzwilliam Street — a pariah: I never pass that house without thinking of her with regret. Even to say the words "expecting a baby" wasn't easy. A man I knew had to tell his mother his girl friend was pregnant. His mother, who had been buying fruit, ran and got a big kitchen knife and plunged it into the melon in her basket. "That's what you've done to the Virgin Mary!" she cried. "That!" plunging the knife in again. "That!"

I gathered that the men I knew from down the country had lost their virginities, when they had, in the grounds of County Hospitals. Nurses were often singled out as "going all the way". But it was always someone else who was having sex — nurses, actresses, Protestants in Trinity, or from the Trinity point of view, Catholics, up in UCD. Sex was in everyone's mind, often obsessively. But no one believed it was a healthy thing, and good for you. Or that people who did it were altogether acceptable. In practice, in a place without contraception, the only women quite free to have sex were married women. There were so many children that it was easy to include one or two who might, or might not, be by the husband. Though — male lovers were dangerous. They'd get maudlin, and tell a whole pub about the son or daughter they had by so-and-so. At the other extreme, they forgot. I was with a friend of my father's once and he was saying to a girl in the company — this was in the early 1970s — "I don't know what you women's lib people think you're up to. Can't any woman who's worth her salt get what she wants from a man if she treats him nicely in bed?" He'd forgotten the young woman he was talking was his own daughter from a long-ago liaison.

An old Ireland was ending, in the 1960s. There were new possibilities. But what arrangement you came to with what kind of man was still the most important question by far for a woman. And it wasn't even seen as a question. I was asking Michael to marry me as if the act of getting married made no difference to one's independence. Yet the lives around me were full of hints that there were difficulties intrinsic to being a woman — married or not. Margaret got into trouble in her Catholic home for having an ashtray with a drawing by Matisse — just one sinuous line — of a woman with a baby at the breast. Dirty, they thought it. Laila, wealthy and elegant, played French ballads on her little white portable in her room in a hotel in Harcourt Street, sprinkling Mitsouko on her cashmere jumpers, not able to sleep for fear her father in Egypt, thousands of miles away, found out that she had a boy friend, and killed her. The women in my friend Geraldine's home town in Leicestershire, worked in the stocking-factories. On the way to work, they left their bowls in at the fish-and-chip shop, and they collected them, full of chips and peas and faggots, at dinner-time. There was great competition among them, someone remarked to me, about the bowls. The bowls were status-symbols —

bowls and prams. Whoever had the biggest, most decorated bowl and pram was the most respected. You would think I would have noticed that being a wife and a mother wouldn't necessarily suit me.

Yet there I was, in Hull, writing to Michael about going to a family-planning clinic to get fitted with a contraceptive device. 'The bloody thing is like a medium-sized rubber pudding-bowl,' I say. Then — this appals me, today — I say: 'We could see what using it is like, and if you don't like it then we'll stop. I'm longing for us to have a baby and I could do it too, without inconveniencing you in any way or stopping you being free ... '

My mother was as unaware as I was. 'I don't really care if you get a degree or not,' she wrote to me. 'I'd far rather see you with a husband and a few kids.' This — when her burning resentment showed that she felt as trapped as a slave, kept out in a suburb with children! But she blamed the person, my father, for that. Women did blame their husbands. The idea that it was desirable for all women to go off for their lifetime with one man and have his children as their life's task was completely uncriticised. I would have blamed Michael if I had spent an unhappy life with him. But perhaps my unconscious was more alert than I was. In the same letter where I claim I can have a baby without "inconveniencing" him I recall, for no particular reason, the baby the girl I knew had had in Belfast. 'I've been thinking,' I write, 'about the motionless sadness of bringing it down from Belfast in the train. And its grandfather, playing with its fingers in the big empty church ... '

As for the complex of man, baby, job — it was hard to get that right, either. In my own world, men had money and interesting lives and could show you things and bring you around. Whereas the radio personality, Frankie Byrne, I well remember, was the only woman I personally had ever met who had bought her own house with her own earnings. There were very few women teachers in UCD. Mrs Wall made things in history much clearer to me than Professor Dudley Edwards did, or Professor Williams. But she was a nobody in the politics of the college, compared to them. In English, Lorna Reynolds was a most generous patron — getting me proof-reading work, and taking me to tea (Earl Grey, and lemon cake) in her lovely house. I knew she was a friend of formidable women — Kate O' Brien, for instance, and — in Italy — Darina Silone. But I also knew that in UCD she had to fight the unequal treatment accorded to single women like herself, compared to the married men who were considered the norm. "I am not responsible for your nine children, Mr Tierney!" was the punch-line of an account of one of her many brave confrontations with the then President of UCD. She was constantly embattled. And she never won.

With marriage so unconsidered a condition, no wonder there were so many bitter wives around. I remember Anthony Cronin saying once, about the 1950s: "That was the era of the spectacularly difficult wife." He was thinking of Caitlin Thomas and Hetta Empson. They had the problem of their husbands, too, of course, as has any difficult wife I can think of. It was to be another twenty years, at least, before a wife might be perceived as herself as well as an appendage of her husband's. To be a wife, and hope for a career taken with the seriousness of your husband's career, was hardly possible. You would have had to go to the lengths of drawing him into a defensive *folie à deux*, like Queenie Leavis. You could best have a career — that is, express your gifts, and earn your own money — by either not having sex at all, or having it but somehow not getting pregnant. It happened that although I never used the device I got in the clinic, and never took the pill, I didn't get pregnant.

I count that, along with being sent to boarding-school, as the crucial accident that allowed me to survive. There were other great strokes of luck, like knowing Sean Mac Réamoinn, and knowing the older man — the doctor — who

kept an eye on me through college. But though I might
have managed something without them, I would not have
survived having a child. This has nothing to do with
children as such. I love them, now. I have very deep feelings
about being childless. But then, I was so unskilled, and so
confused, that I couldn't have raised a child well.
Childbearing, along with bad education, relationships that
managed to be simultaneously all-absorbing and
unrewarding, and financial dependance, were the enemies
of promise. But that's not why I'm glad: I didn't think of
myself as having promise. I'm glad because under the old
system it was so easy to rear children badly. The child
wouldn't have properly survived.

I didn't see that then, partly because I had no one to see
it with. When the women's movement came along, it was
collective — its insights were shared. But before it, when
"love" was all that mattered, solidarity between women
was correspondingly unvalued. I certainly thought of
married women as a different species from me — as women
who had retired.

There was a kind of fun that unmarried girls could have,
that married women were death to. I remember a glorious,
glamorous, night, just at the end of this period in my life.
I'd got my big scholarship and I was about to go up to
Oxford. I was twenty-three, and in Rome for the first time
and burning with excitement at being there. I was with
Michael and a group of theatrical people from Trinity who
were putting on an evening of the actor Pat Fay in Yeats
and Beckett monologues, in a crumbling old theatre near
the Piazza Navona. It was a privileged way to be in the city
for the first time — to belong to it by being sent out to buy
needles, or to stick posters to walls. Across in Vatican City,
Sean Mac Réamoinn, who was at the heady opening of the
second Vatican Council, might be in the bar for religious
correspondents, underneath the Via della Conciliazione.
Or he might be around a happy table in the garden of the
trattoria in Trastevere where Irish people met. And the

American I'd known in Dublin — who I had never blamed
for his use of me, the night his mother died — was living
in Rome. He flirted with me when no one was looking, and
arranged to meet me late one night in the dark hallway of
the pension where Michael and I were staying. This man
put me into his little car and we swooped around the
wonderful city, jumping out to go into a bar, to climb up the
steps of the Colosseum and sit and kiss, to walk in the still
countryside, out at the Via Appia Antica, stopping to kiss,
to look down on the rooftops from the Janiculum Hill,
kissing, and ending in the beautiful dawn in the
Campidoglio, where, beside the Renaissance square, there
was a plot of grass and shrubs, and a cage with two little
wolf cubs stretching and playing in it. I had seen Audrey
Hepburn in *Roman Holiday*. This was that, with me as the
star.

This man had a wife. It meant nothing to me that he had
a wife. Then, and for a long time afterwards, I was unable
to bring a moral sense or even common-sense to my
dealings with the opposite sex — and my own sex. I think
unconsciousness was the condition that allowed the
culture I grew up in to exist. When change did come, about
a decade later, the fog I had been wandering in was so
dense that it took me ages to make my way half-out of it.
Which is where I am now.

8

Being with Michael was wonderfully firm ground, compared to anything else I'd known. But it was an inconclusive relationship. I discovered, after we came back from Hull and were living in Dublin while I worked for the big scholarship, that he could have started his divorce. He could have moved to marry me. But he didn't. And I had reservations, too. I still prayed and went to Mass and had crises of conscience about sleeping with him. A deeper difficulty, welling up from some bedevilling idealism, was the incoherent feeling that there was something more difficult, and therefore more right, I could do, than just live pleasantly with a decent man. I was also imbued with the idea of "looking up" to a man. Michael was far too sceptical to accept the authority I tried to confer on him. But I hero-worshipped an intensely serious Catholic, a Welsh man I had met when he visited Dublin. The possibility of marrying this Welshman and being "good" for the rest of my life was a secret ideal — and although I knew no more about being a good Catholic bourgeois wife than the man in the moon, I was perfectly sincere. I knew him for years: we wrote scores of letters to each other; and he did in the end — out of niceness, when I was upset about something else — propose to me. When I said "yes", he immediately disappeared. It turned out that he'd gone to see his mother. Then he came back to me, and asked to call our arrangement off. He smelled the dance-halls off me, whether he knew it or not. I never saw him again, but I heard that he entered the priesthood, and eventually left it, and married and had a large family.

He did change my life, however, by asking me, when he was an undergraduate, to visit him at Oxford. I saw the little city for the first time, silent, after heavy snow, in the depth of winter. It was magical. Yet it wasn't magic: a person could go there. When I won the big scholarship a few years later, that was where I chose to go.

Yet even before I was there with the Welshman, I'd had a dream of Oxford. I had read a book about it one day, on my father's boat. This was a temporary folly of his. He kept it at the slipway at Clontarf Yacht Club, where his own grandfather and grandmother had been steward and housekeeper to the toffs. We puttered across to the mouth of the Liffey, once or twice, and left my father off at the water-steps at Butt Bridge, beside the *Evening Press.* Going to work by boat made us one with all the dead people who had used Dublin Bay. Sometimes we went the other way — the boat plunging and bucking — around past the Baily lighthouse to Howth. It was on one of those journeys, with the spray breaking over me, that I finished reading *Dusty Answer*, by Rosamund Lehmann. If the boat had sunk I would have gone on reading till I was under the waves. It had college friends in England in it, and it was the novel that formed my idea of college undergraduate life. I thrilled to all the great romantic books: my friend's mother threw a teapot at me during *A Farewell to Arms* and I didn't miss a sentence. Scott Fitzgerald made me tremble with empathy. My mother quoted bits of *Ballad of a Sad Café* to me. But it was English people in books — even as far back as *The Chalet School* stories and Angela Brazil — who summed up glamour. *The Constant Nymph* fed this fantasy, and *The Green Hat* and a Daphne Du Maurier novelette on a faintly incestuous theme which had a refrain — 'We were very young, We were very merry, We went back and forth, All night upon the ferry.' I yearned after the troubled, rich, English, upper-class people in books like that.

In real life, glamour consisted of my friend and I getting done up in high heels and tight black skirts. Tucked in to the skirts, and belted with waspies, we wore men's white

94

nylon shirts with the sleeves rolled up. We had big, pointy, breasts (old nylons stuffed in our bras), a thick layer of yellowy Pan-Stik on our faces, black lines going up from the corners of our eyes, vaseline on our shocking-pink lips. In the Crystal Ballroom we two beauties eyed guys with duck's-arse haircuts and crepe-soled shoes, while we condescended to dance with awe-struck Malaysian students.

I was wrong about *Dusty Answer*. The story turns out to involve Cambridge, not Oxford. And in the mid-1960s, when I went there, the generality of Oxford students were not glamorous. The *Brideshead Revisited* style was in temporary retreat. The Beatles had just burst upon England and were about to change it and the world. But I couldn't have been happier when I scuffed through the leaves to the college that had accepted me, one day in the autumn of 1963. I always knew underneath how near I had been to a lifetime of some clock-watching, achingly pointless, job. When I was seventeen, I'd worked in the canteen of a water-softener factory near Heathrow airport. That kind of job. Now here I was, in one of the first mini-dresses, with nothing to do but study, and a partner on the side. Michael was going to teach in Italy while I was doing this degree, but we would meet in the vacations. My friend Harden Rodgers started at Cambridge the same year. When the girl beside her at dinner the first night asked her where she was from, and Harden said "Ireland," the girl said, "Oh — you'll be wanting the praties, then." I never thought of being from Ireland. I belonged. I had read so many novels about this. That was where I came from — from inside the books I'd read.

Oxford was an unpretentious place, then. It was a provincial English town, which happened to have the beautiful buildings of an old university tucked away in it. The centre was decayed and ordinary. There were enclaves of small houses where working people lived and had prams and net curtains, behind and between the buildings of the colleges. There were brown, varnished pubs where locals with Oxfordshire accents played bar-billiards. There were corner shops, not wine-bars and boutiques. There was an old-fashioned department store, with a tea-room where you could get anchovy toast. It is a discount place now, featuring Evans Outsizes. There were ancient, crooked coaching-inns: only their names — the Mitre, the Golden Cross — live on in the shopping arcades full of souvenir shops that stand where they stood. There were proper cafés. I saw Auden trying to eat a poached egg in the Cadena, after a night presumably — by the shake in his hands — as miserable as his little basalt eyes. Nowadays, Oxford is full of tourists all the time. Then, it was sometimes so empty that its wonderful weathers filled it. In the sluggish summers, the foaming green countryside around seemed to press on it. Then cold seeped up from the flooded river, and fog rolled along the pitted golden walls of the colleges, and rainwater rustled down the gullies beside the footpaths. I once passed Elizabeth Taylor — in Oxford to stand there as Helen of Troy in Richard Burton's production of *Doctor Faustus* — hurrying along a back lane, just as the winter night fell. Her violet eyes when she glanced up were so intense, so exotic, that they seemed to fix like a flashbulb a permanent impression of the flint and wet cobble and black stone of winter Oxford.

I borrowed — this is an important period detail — a leather jacket, and auditioned before the board of the Oxford University Dramatic Society to direct their annual play in the Playhouse Theatre. This was a very prestigious thing to do, and that I was chosen to do it is a sign of how much change there was in the 1960s. No woman had directed the OUDS play for forty years. Not that I rose to the call of social change very well: my production of *The Importance of Being Earnest* was mediocre, except for Maria Aitken, and the set was terrible. The London newspapers traditionally reviewed the OUDS play, so this did not go unnoticed. One of them said it looked as if it were happening in a bed-sitter in Golders Green.

But leather jackets and young Irishwomen directors were all part of the new style. When I met people who had been up at Oxford only ten years earlier they remembered greyness and conservatism. But the 1960s were bright. There was a feeling of youthful licence. I remember a particularly abandoned party in Christ Church where the boys from the group The Animals were actually among the revellers. Most of the time, it was just young Oxford men trying to look as if they were The Animals. I was living my usual divided life. For the first year or so, I was a practising Catholic: in the ugly church in St Giles, one Good Friday, the liturgy was in English for the first time in my life. We, the congregation, had to say, "Crucify Him! Crucify Him!" I was very shaken by this. I went to the decorous events of the Newman Society, where young Catholics were meant to meet Catholics of the opposite sex. But I dropped that as my social life got busier and busier. I see now that being Irish was quite fashionable in that brief period between the 1960s' discovery of the working class, and the Northern Ireland troubles starting. I see that those years were a little space in history when young women were free and freely available, but hadn't yet woken to the implications of freedom. To think — I debated something about women, with the scholar Dame Helen Gardner, for the amusement of the hearties of a private dining-club called the Bullingdon. The fellows actually lolled around in evening dress and swigged champagne by the neck as we women sparred to amuse them! And we didn't see it! Class lines in England were not really under attack in the 1960s. You only had to look at these men to see they could never consider themselves anything but lords of the universe. And gender issues were deeply buried. I went to see Tintern Abbey, down on the Welsh border, with an American suitor of mine. I had a room of my own in the hotel, but I knew it was understood that a bed might be shared. But when he came to my room he found the door locked. This — with no explanation — offended him dreadfully, and we went back to Oxford in silence. But I couldn't say — I literally could not find any way of saying — that my period had unexpectedly started. I could have slept with him, but I couldn't say those words. I imagine that countless such misunderstandings happened, before the women's revolution took some of the power out of that kind of taboo. When I hear the Beatles 'I Wanna hold Your Hand', its slight plangency, more than anything, brings back the feel of those years. We were only young. There was something pitiable about our playing with freedom.

The poet W. R. Rodgers came to Oxford for a day. Bertie was my friend Harden's father and at her request, he took me around with him. He was a wild drinker. We racketed up and down Oxford in taxis — we even went to part of a lecture by Isaiah Berlin, on Herder. Bertie fell off the bench in the lecture hall in St Catherine's. Enid Starkie gave us drinks. She wrote me a note afterward that catches the flavour of the day:

> Dear Miss O'Faolain,
>
> I hope your uncle got back safely. I hope that you did not think me too unhospitable. If you are out of pocket for the taxi, will you allow me to pay for it? 1) I would have taken your uncle home if I had not been busy and 2) I have much more money than you have! Your uncle mentioned something about a cheque he had hoped the Davins would cash for him...

Acquaintances mistaken for uncles. Questionable cheques. It was that kind of day. But Bertie did me a very great favour when he introduced me to what, by the end of the evening, were his somewhat tight-lipped hosts, Dan and Winnie Davin. Their house was to be a second home — a first home, in many ways — to me. They were New Zealanders, and Dan had been a Rhodes Scholar and then a distinguished wartime officer and historian, and a novelist, and was now a fellow of Balliol and ran the Oxford University Press. I soon had a little attic room in their hospitable, book-stuffed house. In a recent biography of Dan, he and I are supposed to have been in love, but really we were that much more comfortable thing — a mutual admiration society.

I learnt, just from knowing Dan and Winnie and the people they knew. That's one of the great things about university towns. Picking up an education was a dimension of social life. The Davins had a corner they drank in in their local pub, and anyone might come along. Godfrey Lienhardt was an anthropologist, specialising in the Dinka of the southern Sudan, but a great generalist too, and a most cultivated man. He was there most nights. People talked about books, and when this or that book passed my way, I read it. Kierkegaard. Fontane. Benjamin Constant. Christina Stead. I met people. Iris Murdoch made it quite clear that just because she was born in Blessington Street didn't mean she was Irish. An American translator of the *Iliad* talked about Scott-Moncrieff, and how he'd picked the wrong line from Shakespeare to represent 'A *La Recherche du Temps Perdu*' in the title of his translation of Proust. "Remembrance of things past" was too soft, this man said. It didn't catch the hard stroke of '*recherche*'. The imperative tone of 'Tell me where all past things are' would be more faithful to Proust's rhythm. John Wain talked about Doctor Johnson and taught me to play shove ha'penny. Richard Ellman came in. The great biographer of George Eliot, Gordon Haight, came in. He was typical of the grandees of the American Wasp academic establishment, who would arrive in Oxford in the course of research visits they conducted like royal progresses.

They stayed at rich, discreet hotels and took people to dinner at their London clubs. If they were the definitive scholars in their field they were usually published by the OUP, so they came to see the Davins.

My thesis on 'The Reception of George Moore's *Esther Waters'* was about a kind of crossroads in late-nineteenth-century history of ideas, and it was full of interest. And once I did any work at all on it, by definition, I knew more about the subject than anyone else. But there were also set papers in the B.Phil. exam. And I knew hardly anything about that subject-matter. I cycled off from time to time to read a perfunctory essay to this old man in a study here, or this old lady in a set of rooms there — obscure dons who had somehow ended up with responsibility for Matthew Arnold or Kipling or Gissing or whoever. The university didn't teach at this level: if you didn't seek out learning for yourself, it would not be put your way. I wasn't learning.

I was saved, however, by the labour historian, Raphael Samuel. As if he were the angel of his name, he came to me, even though I hardly knew him, and presented me with a cake in a tin that his mother had sent him, and told me firmly that he would help me to work. He gave me essays to do every week — 'the growth of a reading public', 'Chartist oratory', 'the novels of "Mark Rutherford"'. He took me to a study-group in Nuffield where people talked about Paley and Defoe and Spengler and the Bryant and May strike and Dostoevsky and Henry Mayhew and Trotsky and Peterloo. Raphael was a pioneer of the inter-disciplinary approach. He believed that anyone who had done a specialist degree had been trained in incuriosity about everything else. He believed in starting again, from ignorance. I was rich in ignorance. I count it as one of the great lucky things in my life — besides going to boarding-school and not getting pregnant, and then, Michael being married and having Sean Mac Réamoinn as a friend, that Raphael took me in hand.

It was far more important than it seemed even at the time, to be introduced to labour history. It fed into the social revolutions that were just about to come. And one side effect was that the physical world of England began to be meaningful to me. I would know enough to understand why a canal had been cut in a certain place, or what the name of a pub probably referred to, or around what time the words 'friendly society' had probably been painted on an old office window. A similar infusion of meaning into the landscapes and townscapes of France came through Richard Cobb, when I got to know him — a scholar who used things like Simenon's novels, or the route of the Tour de France, as means towards understanding French society.

But I learnt most from the man I fell in love with, half-way through my time at Oxford. From the moment I met him I enrolled in his one-person university. He conducted it in pubs, walking the streets, in wonderful letters packed and bursting with knowledge and ideas. He knew about the history of art and about paintings, which were his great passion. But he also knew about model villages, how to play bar billiards, classic French cooking, the early history of Aston Villa, Soviet songs, the history of witchcraft ... He was loud and happy and shabby and vivid, and — impersonal. He and I didn't talk about personal things. It was a challenge to get him to attend to the personal.

He was just leaving Oxford, and I had a year to go. We had absolutely no money. We squatted in a basement and he bought books on account in one bookshop and sold them immediately in a secondhand bookshop to get us cash to drink and eat a bit. It was summer. I happen to have a piece of paper we must have doodled on during some long day talking in a pub. He has drawn a map of England. I've written in the few places whose location I happened to know — London, Liverpool, Crewe, Hull. He has filled in the names of the rest. If we had both been English, things would have been different. But we weren't. However — in 1966 — it didn't matter.

I'll call the ghost who looks like this young man, "Rob". This year I was invited to speak about Ireland at a conference of politicians and bankers and diplomats, in Oxford. The organisers put me up in the Randolph Hotel, in the centre of town. I looked down on the stretch of street I had walked along, when I came to visit the Welshman, in the depths of winter, long ago. We had come up from the station, my hand in his in the warmth of the pocket of his duffle-coat, up Beaumont Street, across into the Broad, past the sculptured heads outside the Sheldonian and the domes of the Sheldonian Theatre and the Radcliffe Camera, all covered in frost, all shimmering in the moonlight. Silent and shining, as I was never to see the place again. The streetscape was no less fine as I looked at it not long ago. But it meant nothing more than itself.

A street away was the spot where I had my first rendezvous with Rob. I needed to work on what I would say at the conference. But his ghost was in my way. Cold rain was spilling down that morning, but I walked out from the hotel to the field beside the Thames called Port Meadow. That night — the night of the day I met him — had been warm and close. We'd lain on the grass on the bank of the river — here? — no, further on. The fishermen had made clinking noises, very quietly, across the sleek river, under the black hedge. Then we needed more privacy and we went back across the meadow and down into the soft, high weeds on the bank of the canal. I followed that path, again. That must have been the spot, I said to myself, standing above the canal, shivering. There. I was wet and cold and bored, that morning. But I was trying to get rid of stubborn memory — to mock it, to force it out to the dim distance it should inhabit.

One swirling, shadowy image somehow sums that time up. It isn't of me or Rob. It was something I saw for a minute, late one winter night, in Paddington Station. I'd been in London with Rob and now I was going back up to Oxford on the last train. The big caverns of the station were dark and full of gusts of wind. A man I knew by sight was talking desperately to a woman, beside the train. He was very beautiful and she — I saw it was his young wife — was beautiful, too. He had his hands in her long hair and he was crying. She was crying, too. She had a white coat on. They kept kissing each other desperately. That romantic sadness is what I was expecting of Oxford, from *Dusty Answer*. But I'm not sure whether that's what I really experienced, in that part of my life. Or whether I imposed it, from my imagination. And if so, whether I imposed it then, or gradually, afterwards.

All I know is that when I left Oxford and went back to Dublin, I faced into the future looking backwards. I was half a girl still. I was half-heartbroken. The place I was leaving had from beginning to end contained feelings so vehement, however silly they were, that even now it is hard to believe they don't live, still, somewhere else as well as in my memory. I looked down at the paving stones as I hurried back to the hotel through the rain, that wet morning this year, and I interrogated the pavement, half as a joke. "You're made of fine big slabs of granite," I said to it. "Are you the same stones I walked on then? And if so, why are you not crying out?"

9

When I came back to Dublin from Oxford the English Department in UCD was more ticking over than being run. I got a job there. Not many years later, when the burst of prosperity that opened things up in the mid-1960s was spent, I would have had to have a publications record. As it was, I was soon commissioned to edit an anthology of Beckett criticism. This came about through being taken up by a very well-known English academic, who came to Dublin to give a lecture. I lived high up above Merrion Square, in an old flat where the servants had once lived, underneath the roof. He came back there, after an increasingly breathless day wandering Dublin, but left dramatically because my bedspread was the same as the one on his son's bed at home. He sent a card from the airport: 'The end of a sensing,' it said, referring with a certain wit to the title of a recent book by the critic Frank Kermode— *The Sense of an Ending*. This man arranged the Beckett commission.

He was one of three or four established academics who took an interest in me in those years. That was how it was, and perhaps is, when you are a young woman in a male-dominated field. The men dispensed patronage. They could tell you where the jobs were, and get you invited to conferences, and endorse you for grants, and mention your name to publishers. This wasn't exactly corrupt, but it wasn't fair, either; they wouldn't do it for you if they didn't like you, or if they didn't feel you were personally grateful. I didn't see any general truths such as that, of course. I was blinded by the habit of translating everything into personal terms. I saw the academic world around me as being comprised of such-and-such a nice man and such-and-such a nasty man and so on — I didn't notice that it was ninety-nine per cent comprised of men. I didn't ask any of them for help. I wanted to be liked, not helped. I had no sense of being at the start of a career. My aim in life was something to do with loving and being loved. That was going to work out, somehow. In the meantime, and on the side, I did the job of lecturing to huge classes of students, on texts which, in UCD in the mid-1960s, no one had ever considered in the light of whether they might interest students.

Pater — I remember talking about Walter Pater in a lecture theatre so long and narrow that in the rows at the back the boys were reading newspapers — studying form, probably — and even smoking, while the nuns at the front wrote down everything I said. I remember giving imploring lectures on Newman. A lot of the students had just come out of Catholic schools and pretended to be pious. If you asked them, they picked something like 'The Hound of Heaven' as their favourite poem, in case the boss-class still wanted that of them. But most of them didn't want to make the serious forays into the moral life that the writers we were teaching asked of them — Shakespeare, Milton, Wordsworth, Newman. I was lecturing on 'The Idea of a University' in 1968 when the students came up with a few of their own ideas about a university. I knew about the anti-Vietnam protests in the USA and the *évènements* in Paris, but I couldn't have been more astonished at an authentic protest happening in UCD.

The student revolution was nothing much in itself, as might be guessed from the fact that its heroes call it the "gentle" revolution. The main hall at UCD became very untidy, because with the students sitting-in it could not be swept. At least one meeting of the Academic Council was blockaded and the worthies couldn't get to the toilets. Unpleasant mimeographed estimates of the teaching staff's capabilities were circulated — at least, the one about me was unpleasant. 'Miss O'Faolain is so authoritarian and sarcastic that many leave her tutorials and will not approach the Department office while she is there': that's what 'Confrontation', the pamphlet of the Students for Democratic Action, said. I deserved that: I did use sarcasm as a weapon to try to smash the students' blandness. And I did believe in laying down the law. But my personality wasn't the problem. The problem was that the college had fallen into decay. The staff/student ratio in the English department was 1 to 250. Students had to make an appointment to talk to someone on the academic staff and they might have to wait two weeks. Examination formats were changed without consultation. And things were worse in other areas, like architecture, than in English. The institution was so inert that no one in authority had perceived that a revolt was inevitable. You could see confusion and even fear in the faces of the older academics, so accustomed were they to docility.

I was a contented product of the old system. And I was too young myself to respect students so young. They were right to complain that they had no more input into the way things were done than they'd had at secondary school. But they weren't very different, themselves, to my eyes, from secondary school pupils. I had a Messianic belief in the capacity of the academic study of English literature to change a person, utterly. But all but a few of the students thought "doing English" was grinding out essays on the three stages of Wordsworth's relationship with nature, or the role of the Fool in *King Lear*. I thought that "doing English" was easy on one level. Yet the student was meant to learn to hold on to the self while going out of the self to enter into the literature that someone else had made — to find a poise between subjectivity and objectivity. This poise would then be rehearsed and made more stable with each access of understanding of a piece of art. The change in the person comes in that: it isn't a matter of learning a technical vocabulary. There is a vocabulary peculiar to the study of literature — literature itself never having asked to be studied. A university English department — a place where the autonomy of a piece of literature is subsumed to the supposedly civilising purpose of the academy — uses that vocabulary. And some smart students picked up this special vocabulary by reading the critics for whom it was really expressive, and they parroted it so well that they thought they understood. But not many of them did understand. They weren't changed in themselves.

The night students, teachers and gardaí and civil servants, coming into Earlsfort Terrace on dark winter nights, shivering in their damp coats, grimly addressing themselves to a most unfriendly syllabus, hardly ever understood. But I admired those people. In fact, I half-loved them. When I lectured at night I used to end the hour as exhausted as a performer, from the effort of trying to show the texts properly to such serious people. The night students were, metaphorically speaking, the proletariat of the student revolution. They hadn't time to revolt. They were only interested in getting what they could from the system. The day students were the middle-classes: they had the leisure and the self-confidence to force change on the authorities.

The professionalising of the college began around then. Before that, it was something of a friendly shambles. The ladies in the front office made a great many bureaucratic decisions. The head porter, Paddy Keogh, ran the teaching operation. If a lecturer with a drink problem rang up from a pub down the street to say — as one did when I was with him — that he was in Bray and cut off by floods — Paddy would rearrange the lecture or find someone else to give it. Professors were such for life. So if someone like the historian Desmond Williams, for instance, found himself uninterested in most aspects of being a university teacher, from very early in his career, no comment was attracted. If Desmond disappeared in mid-lecture series it wouldn't have occurred to anyone to protest. In fact, probably only Paddy Keogh would have known.

On the other hand, the teachers — Desmond among them — were still people you could talk and drink all day with, or go to the afternoon pictures with, or borrow money from, or lend money to. The peer group wasn't defined by status. It was made up of different kinds of people who had in common that they drifted around the Stephen's Green area, trading short-term pleasure for long-term strain and difficulty. I might set out in the morning to do a bit of work but end up drinking whiskey with historians in the Arts Club, or at a Eucharist (brown bread and off-licence Beaujolais — we'd finish the bottle afterwards) organised by Sean Mac Réamoinn in someone's flat, or maybe I'd have bumped into John Montague coming out of a gloomy building in derelict Temple Bar, and drift on with him to the little house in Ballsbridge — its tables covered with bottles of pills — the poet John Berryman was living in. I might have burrowed into a company that had settled down in Hartigan's or O'Dwyers by four in the afternoon. I might head for the National Library and never get closer than Buswell's. Someone might have won money on a horse. Paddy Kavanagh might beckon from a doorway to run to the chemist for him. A lot of people lived in an uncommitted, public, way. If they had home lives, somewhere, they were hardly mentioned. I sometimes went back to Merrion Square to bed with an aquaintance in the afternoons, before he went home to his family. He was almost the only man I knew who, if they had any responsibilities to wife and children, attempted to discharge them.

I think a lot of the people around lacked, like me, the kind of inner balance that young people seem to have now. There had always been a censored literature in Ireland: now, books that truly appalled, like *Last Exit to Brooklyn* were handed around. There had been an unbroken silence about sexuality. Now films like Ingmar Bergman's presented the erotic to Irish people, whom it made shy. The world darkened: the ambulance brigade people stood at the back of the cinema to help anyone in the audience who fainted at the realism of the nuclear horror in *The War Game*. The first drugs other than alcohol were coming in, to a generation who had been treated like infants by de Valera and Archbishop John Charles McQuaid. I went to Morocco with a gay man friend, and we were not able to be anything but madly reckless. The young boys we were with could only either murder us or protect us. We went — stoned — to *Hamlet*, done in classical Arabic, but left it to go back to eat more hash, because we thought we had been at the play for four or five hours. A predatory Italian sailor took us to a disco among pine-trees, where in a divided cage a mangy lion crouched on one side of the partition and a moth-eaten tiger on the other. Frank Sinatra sang 'Strangers in the Night' over and over in the hot dark. The animals smelled as if they were rotting. We obeyed dodgy characters when they told us to follow them to empty hotels with cracked swimming-pools. We abandoned each other for a while. My friend came back with his face bruised. I was sick. In Dublin, he went back to his respectable job: I put on my academic gown and went back to lecturing. The biggest difference among the people who moved around the centre of Dublin was between those who knew something about self-preservation and those who knew nothing.

———————

I am still acquainted with a lot of the people I knew in Dublin around 1970. But most of them are so different now that the past might never have been. I remember the vulnerable, not always dignified, young people who are, now, dignitaries. A judge. A professor. A feared critic. A consultant ... In a more confident culture people like these would claim their youth. In North America people, however powerful they become, are happy to go to reunions to recapture the innocence of youth. But I think middle-aged Irish people feel that they are much more innocent now than they were then.

And middle-aged members of the Irish establishment behave as if there is no history between them. There is a pretence that no feelings are in play between people who have been acquainted with each other for decades. I thought about this a few years ago when I was presenting 'Booklines' on RTÉ television, and the *Field Day Anthology of Irish Literature* came out. Seamus Deane, its general editor, was going to come on the programme to talk about it — to say something, too, about why the modern history of women wasn't part of its account of the history of the island. I often interviewed people I had known. Each of these people came with this flavour or that. The flavour of Seamus Deane was one of the most complex. He was a colleague of mine when I was teaching in UCD, and a most brilliant one. I conducted a post-graduate seminar on Yeats' 'Among Schoolchildren' with him once. I remember the room exactly and the light in it and the faces of the students, and how that great poem seemed to give up its riches. I'd count that among the most exciting couple of hours of my life.

Seamus was a hero to me when we were young teachers. He was a sensationally interesting literary critic, but above all, he was the first Northerner from a nationalist background I had ever known. What he said about how his family in the Bogside was treated under the Stormont and B-Special régime was like something out of a frightening book. He was a very modern man, in some ways. He had just come back from Berkeley, and the house he lived in with Marian and the children was itself like a piece of California. A new friend, an American writer and critic called Leslie Fiedler, came out there with me a couple of times, and the four of us lolled around in the open-plan room with the picture-window, and drank champagne and were lighthearted. But Northern Ireland was where Seamus really stood. He had a complex contempt for

Dublin. He was watching the people around him closely, and judging them. It was as if they were summing up "the South" to him. He would say of someone he didn't like that they had "no speed, no style, no silence," and he'd say about people he admired, like Tom Kilroy and Tom Kinsella, that they were "whole". I was proud to have the position of confidante. He advised me: 'You don't belong in hysteria, wild mobilities, pub-drives (never crawls), promiscuities, endless charities with yourself as donation ... '

That was when we were colleagues. Then I left Dublin and I didn't see Seamus again till a James Joyce conference in Paris a few years later. He barely spoke to me. Leslie Fiedler and his wife looked at me as Seamus innocently waved at us in a café and walked past to join others. "Well, our lives have moved on," I said, and that was of course all that had happened. "We don't even live in the same country," I said.

So there was that little personal history somewhere in my consciousness when we met in the television studio for 'Booklines'. I'd spent the days since I got the anthology studying it. It was a very grand undertaking. We'd been waiting for it for years. It was Seamus' biggest public act: a massive effort at national self-description. But something had happened between women and men in the interval between Seamus' and my youth, and the publication of the anthology. The women's movement had happened. Women had emerged from the silence of the past and had begun to make their marks. I could not find in myself, talking to Seamus about the book, an unemotional response to its omission of women's testimony. The anthology was a history, of course, not a mere collection of literary texts: that's why I expected the momentous change in the condition of women in twentieth-century Ireland to be there. But I wasn't sure myself whether the tiny raw spot left from Paris was not a part of what was almost grief at the absence of women. As if not acknowledging me in the café had been writ large.

The *Field Day* is a wonderful anthology for much of its great length, and we talked about its successes for most of the time we had. Then I brought up the missing women. He said words to the effect that he really hadn't noticed what he was doing. He just hadn't noticed. This helpless tone was entirely accurate, I felt. He was weary and baffled and he didn't want an argument. I overheard Seamus Heaney saying not long afterwards, "Why doesn't Seamus Deane defend himself? There's a perfectly good case to be made for the anthology the way it is." But Seamus Deane let it go, whether from ennui or shame it was up to the world to guess.

When we had finished the interview that day, and we were getting up from our chairs and disentangling microphone cables and saying our thanks, he paused beside me and said, "I'm sorry I hurt you." Did he mean back then, or now? Did he mean "you" as in me, or "you" as in women? And was he sorry? This remark was masterly — it restored the preponderance of power to him, after a brief dip in my favour, when I had turned to the woman question in the interview.

This is an example of the histories that inform the ostensibly purely civic life of a place. They complicate Ireland enormously — North/South, man/woman, then/now. Seamus had a house near mine before he went to America. A few years ago I was walking up his road when a squad car bustled past, ee-aw, ee-aw. Ahead of me I saw Seamus come out and peer up the road after the back of the squad car, the way people do. Then he walked down to his gate and out to his car, and he walked comfortably around the car, his hands in his pockets, kicking a tyre or two. I held back a bit, till he went in. There's not the slightest problem about saying a friendly "hello". But the "hello" for me, anyway, is one of the many in this town and this country that slightly reverberates.

There was a James Joyce conference in Dublin in 1968, and all of us in the UCD English Department were involved. That's where I met Leslie Fiedler. My friend Sean Mac Réamoinn happened to be sitting on the next bar-stool to him in the Lincoln Tavern. Leslie was famous in America at the time for pioneering populist critical works with great titles — *Love and Death in the American Novel* was one; an essay on homosexual feeling in *Huckleberry Finn* called 'Come back to the raft ag'in, Huck Honey!' was another. Leslie was a novelist, too, and a traveller, and he loved food and drink and people. Over the next few years he showed me things like the Jewish side to Joyce's places — the grave in Trieste where Stanislaus Joyce was unobtrusively buried, sidelined as usual, and the little stones that had been left on it by mourners of his wife, who was Jewish. The purification baths and the kosher cafés off the Place Des Vosges in Paris. The synagogue in Rome. Leslie came and rescued me when all my money was stolen in Venice. I went and rescued him, at a party in New York, when a beautiful girl who had been hitting Norman Mailer in the face was getting ready to hit him, too. He looked like Neptune, and he was a proper Jewish patriarch in his personal life. He was a great connoisseur of popular culture, too. We went in and out of the singles bars one night along Second Avenue, to see how quickly we — separately — would be picked up. (Very fast. Both of us.) We went to the movie *Beyond the Valley of the Dolls* and it gave him days of pleasure. I made some kind of contribution with him to a supposedly authoritative seminar on Joyce in 1970, in a palazzo in Trieste. I remember standing on the podium singing "Put another nickel in/ See Our Lady in her skin/ All I want is loving you/ and music, music, music." This school playground ditty was central to some new reading in *Ulysses* we had thought up in a bar.

We were silenced, once. The film director John Huston was interested in making a film based on *The Tempest* and he wanted to talk to Leslie about a script. Huston was at his house in East Galway. Leslie asked whether he could bring me with him, and we headed off on the train to stay a weekend.

Huston's house was a simple, perfect, Georgian manor in a wide landscape of big fields and stone walls. He lived there because it is hunting country. The driveway crossed a stream beside which hawks were caged — I saw a walk-in fridge later, stuffed with the chilled day-old chicks the hawks were fed on. Lovely horses grazed in paddocks across from the hall-door which opened into a beautifully proportioned hall room, full of precious things — I understood Huston had contacts at Shannon Airport who greatly assisted his antique collecting. Some of the staff led us to our rooms. I had a luxurious suite, with the most wonderful bedside things: there were new books and magazines and flowers and a calligraphed card with the house phone numbers of the household staff, and also a little medical kit that included a selection of sleeping tablets. Everything was perfect. The master of the house himself was found in a pitch-dark room, peering at a small television. It was a great moment. *Apollo 11* was just at that moment landing on the moon. We watched the juddering grey-and-white images, as Armstrong stepped onto that unimaginable surface. Huston was a reserved man, and Leslie hid his serious feelings under an impenetrable geniality. But this was a very great moment for America. I stayed quiet behind them. I think they were both very moved.

Later, we moved into a sitting-room and the two of them chatted, sizing each other up. Huston said a very interesting thing about Marilyn Monroe, when he was directing her in *The Misfits*. She thought she would keep her looks if only she got enough sleep, he said. So she took a lot of sleeping tablets, and while half-sedated by them, Paula Strasberg would read her lines to her, over and over. The next day, Marilyn would take barbiturates to counteract the sleeping-tablets, and finally arrive on the set. And she would know her lines. She'd know the main words in them, and how long they were. She would know the exact rhythm of each line. But she would get the tenses all wrong. She wouldn't know whether a given line was in the past tense or the future tense or the present. I have often brooded on that.

I knew nothing about class and America then. If I had, I might have noticed how Jewish Leslie seemed in that ambiance, and how Wasp Huston seemed. Leslie was a nervy, sensitive, rubicund little man from Newark, New Jersey. He didn't suit being taken to lean on a fence by Huston in impeccable tweeds, to discuss the hunters in the field. But we might have stuck it out but for the meals. These — lunch as well as dinner — were formal occasions, served in the dining-room where the wallpaper was handmade eighteenth-century Chinese, or something of the kind. Various silent children, done up like the children of the English aristocracy in white knee-socks and velvet headbands, sat at the table, their meal administered either by a nanny or, in the case of one exquisite little boy, by his equally exquisite mother. She appeared to be a Bolivian from Rome, and to be living out the back, where a stable yard had been converted to residences. Presumably, she was a mistress of Huston's, and the child was his, and so were all the other children. He didn't say. He said little or nothing, at those glacial meals. Leslie, the soul of happy appetite in normal circumstances, withered under the silence. We had dinner the first night: lunch the second day. Then we made a furtive plan around the side of the house, under a window, where no one could see us. Leslie proffered some excuse, and we were driven to the railway halt where the train back to Dublin would pause. We were hours too early. Mind? We didn't mind. The Huston car disappeared and we were left at the little station — just us, in the miles and miles of summery countryside. We jigged up and down the platform shouting and laughing, in transports of relief at getting away from the tension of that household, and Huston's coldness.

——————

My long friendship with Michael had faded away. The important times were when I went to England to see Rob. He took me to the town in Lancashire his family came from. He was such a well of historical knowledge and had such an eye for the way a place has been made and the distinctive things in it, that travelling around with him was a revelation. Sometimes he came over to Dublin on the boat. It came into Dun Laoghaire early in the morning. I'd still be asleep when the bell from the front door jangled in my attic in Merrion Square. I'd stumble to the window in my nightdress. There, four storeys below, on the empty footpath, in the clean morning where nothing moved but the seagulls, would be his upturned face. I'd throw down the keys and jump back into bed and in a minute hear his footsteps coming running up the stairs. I remember those exultant mornings when I pass that corner.

But we fought, too. I was jealous. He was jealous. We didn't know each others' lives. One Christmas he was in London and I was in Dublin. But someone thought he was in Dublin. I came in to the hallway of the house one day and took the post out of my box and ripped open the cards as I went up the stairs. I didn't notice that one letter was addressed to him, and had been sent on. 'Dearest Rob,' I read before I knew what I was doing, 'I have lost our baby...' Who this woman was and what had been happening I never grasped. The huge blaze of jealousy and grief that consumed me —I had never managed to get pregnant by him — wiped everything out. I could walk through the wintry mornings to Earlsfort Terrace to teach — I could manage nothing else. I had rung with shaking hands the hospital in London she'd written from, to try to find out her full name. A suspicious nurse had hung up on me.

In endless, urgent, phonecalls from London he said nonsense; it was nothing, all a mistake, the girl was a fantasist, I was the only one, see — really I was — we would get married. He would get a special licence. He hurried everything up. He got the licence. We were booked into St Pancras registry office and a few friends would join us in Yates' Wine Lodge down the road for wedding drinks. He was lent an old mill house in Somerset for the honeymoon. The time of the registry office was such-and-such. The time of the train, change at Bristol, was such-and-such, and it would connect with the bus. A neighbour would have the house in the country warmed. Bustle bustle. Forget the letter.

So one February night I was in the attic in Merrion Square doing last-minute things so I could go to London in a few days and get married. I was making a list, beside the fire, crouched right in beside the bright wigwam of briquettes. I could hear the gusty wind and the rain it spattered on the slates just over my head. The bell from the front door went. I peered down from the window, and below, where the traffic swished by in the rain, I could see a big car idling, and the man who had got out of it standing on the doorstep. I ran down the stairs and hauled the front door open. "Daughter!" my father greeted me. "Get your coat! We're going to play dominoes in Ringsend." He thrust a big bouquet of flowers into my hands and backed away. He had never called to Merrion Square in the two years I'd been living there. He was on duty — the dominoes would be part of his 'Dubliner's Diary' column the next day. I sometimes bumped into him around town, but I didn't go places with him. "I can't, Da," I began, "I'm up to my eyes..." Then I realised that that wasn't rain on his face. He was crying.

We went off in the car, and he made steady small-talk for the hour or so we were together except once, when he said over his shoulder, waiting to get served at the bar in the crowded pub. "Don't marry him. You'll only have all the trouble of getting divorced." "Well ... " I said. That was the longest private conversation we had in our lives. It carried great weight with me, because he kept at such a distance from all of us. He never offered advice. And I did ring Rob, the Thursday before the Saturday we were to have married. I did say to him that we were only doing this because the worse our rows were, the bigger the gesture of reconciliation had to be. We didn't go to the registry office. We went on our honeymoon, anyway. But we never married. Years later a fellow we'd known around that time passed me in a street in London and recognising me, ran back. "Where were you the day of your wedding?" he called out. "We were all in the Wine Lodge with your presents."

There is another document from the patriarchy I would like to enter here. Someone told my Grandad — who was in the Hospice for the Dying — that I had got engaged. As I had — Rob had run out from Doheny & Nesbitt's and bought a proper diamond ring. It must also have been mentioned that Rob's grandfather was a "Sir" — he had been knighted for his war work. My grandfather sent me the following letter:

Dear Nuala,

I have just heard of your intended marriage, and deplore same. Do you realise what you are doing — you are marrying out of your own circle, a chap who has no religion and in a registry office. Apparently you have nothing in common. By your foolish action you are letting down all who are dear to you. What will your friends say in marrying in a registry office a pagan who I predict will show his true colours after a short time together. He will probably have you keeping him. There are I am sure plenty of his likes in London. I would strongly advise you to see your confessor or clergyman whom you must know and lay all before him. It would only be a half hour to you now, but later a pain that may be yours during life, if you go on with this and bring shame to your father who is so good to you. Please send this to your titled gentleman postponing your mad adventure and as every cloud has a silver lining this might not be an exception. Now, don't come near me again until you have put your house in order.

Your sad Grandad.

1 0

I used to walk along the winter streets from Merrion Square, and leave my washing in the launderette, and go up and talk about the novel to a class of night-students at the People's College in Ballsbridge. There was a hunger then, as it came up to the 1970s, for self-development. A desire for a second chance at education was part of the massive social change that was taking place. In Britain, when Harold Wilson was asked what was the most important achievement of his Labour administration of the 1960s, he said "the Open University". And although it was irredeemably unglamorous, providing "distance learning" opportunities for the masses was a right response to the spirit of that time. And Wilson planned the Open University with generosity. A lot of Labour politicians were personally familiar with the old adult education scene — cold halls, study-notes mimeographed onto cheap paper, men and women trying to improve themselves in rundown libraries. The Open University was going to have glossy colour printing, comfortable summer schools on the best campuses, and above all, it was going to have television and radio programmes made by the BBC to the highest standards of the BBC.

I was so used to England that I didn't think of it as a significant move when I applied for a job at the BBC making Open University programmes. I believed in the OU's mission: I saw it as an extension of what I had been doing at night in the lecture-theatre in Earlsfort Terrace and up at the People's College. When I got the BBC job in 1970, I went to live in London. Rob had a little house in Clapham. We still might get married — I wore my engagement ring. There was a cat called Furriskey. I thought we would be very happy.

The BBC trained us in a labyrinthine building across from Broadcasting House that had once been a hotel, and its winding corridors, its offices that still recalled bedrooms, its false walls and unexpected cupboards and bathrooms with baths and back staircases made it more like a surreal playground than a place of work. It is a hotel again now — an Intercontinental. I went and stood in its glittering foyer recently, in affectionate memory. We were trained exactly as if we were going into a mainstream department of the BBC. But we were to be teachers as well as broadcasters. I would be one of a team working out the components of a course on say, the Renaissance, or say, the nineteenth-century novel, or say, the religions of the world. Around me there would be academic experts on literature, music, political history — all the disciplines that crossed in the subject. My task was to isolate the idea or theme or place or person within the subject-matter that would best suit being treated on television or radio, and best serve the student by being broadcast rather than written or said. Academics are inclined to believe that a lecture — with subject-matter such as would impress their peers — delivered straight to camera by their good selves, is a well-nigh ideal use of broadcasting. The BBC member of the team, however, had to try to win support for a programme idea which would be, certainly, academically worthwhile, but which could also engage an audience used to sophisticated television.

I liked the experience of being trained. I had never been before — and I never was again — part of a group being led to a goal through exercises and competitions and various strategies of induction. I liked belonging. And then, the BBC was a glamorous organisation to me, redolent of Elizabeth Bowen's wartime London of Portland Place and Regent's Park and of black-and-white films about heroically restrained men and women with vaseline tears in their eyes. In the pubs around Fitzroy Square damaged geniuses back from the war had written radio scripts on the back of pieces of paper. The BBC struck me as being more like Oxford as I had imagined it would be than Oxford itself had been. It was stately and hierarchical and proudly separatist. On one level our training was about manners — about becoming a BBC person. Old Corporation gurus came in to talk to us about ethos. The protocols surrounding bounced cheques were explained at length. I began to sense the extent and wealth of the ancient BBC civilisation, to which the coming of television had merely added provinces — to see how the BBC was a parallel world, with its own buildings all over London and Britain, its own libraries, insurers, doctors, travel agents, lawyers, chefs, grandees. We ourselves, sitting in our training room in 1970, were almost a parody of a new era. My friend Tony was the son of a Ghanaian fire-eater, and he was himself a marine biologist who already had a gland in a certain sea-snail named after him: being a scientist was almost as new in the arts-dominated producers' culture we were entering as being black. Some of the other trainees were social scientists, mathematicians, chemists. There was one Scot and one Welshman. I was Irish and a woman. It was confidently assumed that we would become assimilated to BBC ways, not that we and what we represented would in any way change the BBC.

For my first exercise on the course I did a dramatised account, full of thundering Widor organ music and slow dissolves of the Richmond portrait of Cardinal Newman, of the moment when he knew he would have to go over to Rome. Then I did an exercise about Elvis Presley (I faded to black and played a recording of a foetal heartbeat, running it into the first few chords of 'Heartbreak Hotel': I was awarded zero marks as a result, because if a BBC screen ever goes to black for long it will trigger the deployment of the national emergency services). I had knowledge and imagination. But I didn't even listen when we were being taught the technical side of television studio and film production. If I heard words like "focal depth" or "interneg stage" I stopped trying to understand. This turning away from even the possibility of acquiring technical understanding and technical skills did me — and a lot of other women, I imagine — great harm. It was cultural. Men were assumed to be capable of learning about cameras and lighting-plans and transmission frequencies and so on. But it wasn't purely to do with gender. You see a shying-away from technology, too, in men with poor or bookish backgrounds. My problem wasn't quite one of self-confidence. I limited my own intelligence by refusing to take pleasure in abstract problems, or in information that had no human content. The BBC is, or was, so structured that the producer sits at the apex of a pyramid of technical people, each trained to do his or her job as well as possible, for the sake of the job. A producer can be carried, most of the time, by this structure. I was. But technical insecurity is a constant strain and in the end it limits your thinking. I was stacking up trouble for the future.

I did love the training course. But what mattered most to me was my life with Rob. And it was going hopelessly wrong. For a while we would be happy. He worked at home — he was writing two books, one on Keats, one on the Pre-Raphaelites — and in the evening he'd go up to the tube station and wait for me, and we'd saunter down our street, looking over the fences at all the little gardens, before putting a packet of Wall's First Choice sausages on low in the frying-pan, and nipping out to the pub next door for a few drinks and a game of bar billiards. We had friends and a set of matching knives and I was doing the occasional book-review for the London *Times* and he would show me how to do the second draft better than the first. But neither of us knew then how to live with another person. For a while I went in to the training course with a black eye. Sometimes — in bewilderment, and because we drank —

we'd attack each other, physically. We would say horrible things to each other. I was frantic because he liked another woman very much. She was a beauty, and quite grand. I got prescriptions for the sleeping-tablets my mother used, not realising that Mandrax were barbiturates and that I was addicted to them.

No one ran the unhappy house. The cat went away. I came home once from a trip and there was a little piece of desiccated orange peel on the papers on the table and there was dust in the arc of the piece of peel. Where had he been for the last few days? I became expert on cigarette butts, on the charred shapes of things that had been burnt in the stove, on letters that he took straight to his desk. One winter night I went to a country town to see the other woman. I sat across from a pub table with her, as my taxi back to the station waited outside. She was a very nice woman. What was she supposed to do? she said, helplessly. She was certainly going to go on being his friend. What did I expect?

Anyone who has known jealousy will know how all-enveloping it is. I lived in a bubble of it. I could get out of the bubble to work, but then I was trapped again. For a while I didn't even see the world. I didn't notice the curtain going up on Northern Ireland or anything else. I was very thin and shaky. And — heartsore. We must both have been heartsore. In the end, I left.

For the next few years I worked for the BBC in an Edwardian peoples' palace — Alexandra Palace — on top of a hill in a park. On All-Ireland day Irishmen went up there and put their transistor radios up into the trees and strained to hear the commentary from Croke Park. The Open University section of the BBC moved like a pygmy tribe in the vast, dim spaces of the Palace. There was a whole crumbling, plush-and-gold theatre behind a door. There were high, echoing halls full of forgotten scenery. There was a grey pond, with battered row-boats you could rent by the hour, and the vestiges of a race-course. It was a dramatic place to work, and the work we were doing was as fascinating as a drama to us. We producers working in the arts faculty of the OU were pioneers, and we talked all the time about the programmes we were making or wanted to make or had been prevented from making. We watched each other's rough-cuts and made suggestions and wrote bits of script for each other. My colleagues were very talented. I wasn't in the same league. I said that to one of them, not long ago, when I bumped into him at a conference. "I wasn't very good," I said, humbly. "No," he said. "You weren't. But you were a facilitator. You made other people good."

There was a feel of the eighteenth century to the terraced houses and wide pavements and little railed-off greens around the Angel, where I lived. The bus to work rose and fell and rose after it passed the Arsenal football ground, following the contours of the north London hills underneath the crust of the city. The bus the other way, descended to a plain. It was easy to imagine the streets as lanes, full of carts going down into the West End. I passed the graveyard where Shelley made love to Mary Godwin on the grave of Mary Wollstonecraft, halfway down the hill to Euston. I'd be hurrying across the square of grass there, on my way to the Open University at Milton Keynes when I'd hear my own accent. My countrymen, my countrywomen, reeling and nodding, their faces swollen purple with alcohol and rough living. When I saw *Dancing at Lughnasa*, that's where I saw the two aunts who went wandering in England in my mind's eye: in the dreary park outside Euston. But I hardly ever thought about Ireland.

I travelled, by myself. I went to Prague, for instance, when not many people did. I got a bus to Lidice. I knew its name: it had been a village rased by the Nazis in retaliation for an assassination. It was autumn when I went there. There were no other visitors, at all. But the man running the place made me sit in the cinema and watch, alone, the film the Nazi camera-crew shot themselves, as a warning to others, showing the village being tumbled, the men dragged away to death, the women and children herded out separately, dogs being kicked, and hands with guns jumping into frame to shoot dogs in the head. All in rushing, half-lit, black-and-white. Silent. Then I went to the museum. There was a wall of letters — kept, efficiently, by the German postal services, because they had never been delivered. They were from the children to the mothers. The mothers had soon died or been put to death in the camps. But the children didn't know that. 'My dearest Mama, if you could send me some bread ... ' I remember that I sat afterwards to recover on the concrete rim of a dry flowerbed, where a few roses had shrivelled in the autumn frost.

I travelled for work. It was a modern thing to have to learn to do, and for a long time I was bad at it. Losing boarding-cards. Taking subways in the wrong direction. Not understanding how to use the phones. I was always nervous. I got used to the sensation of being held back in hotel bedrooms by fear of the difficulty of going out. Of picking up the phone, and then running out of confidence. But I had to conquer these incapacities, and, gradually, I did. I conquered the gypsies around the station in Florence in winter, and the shared taxis that won't stop to let you out in Teheran, and the men who came up to my bedroom because I'd been talking to them in the bar of a hotel in New York, and the dust and the heat of a village in Israel where no one would speak, and the time my front tooth fell out when I had to record an interview in the morning and only that I was reading *Jane Eyre* and Jane had been so brave I would have succumbed to panic. I see women with briefcases in airports now and it is as if they are a different breed.

Sometimes, I banged the door of the flat behind me and set off for the airport. To go to Florence to collect the material to recreate a Renaissance wedding-festival, or to the USA, to record radio talks on Mazzini or Courbet or the role of concrete in modern architecture, or to Israel to film the Passover among Yemeni Jews, or Scotland, to show how its physical fabric reflects the social history of Gatehouse-of-Fleet. In Cornwall, I recorded Donald Davie, standing in Hardy's places, giving an eloquent, Englishman's readings of Hardy's poems. On the parapet of Thoor Ballylee Denis Donoghue talked about Yeats. I went to Stanford for Rodin and Paris for Tolstoy and Lyons for the revolution of 1848 and Jerusalem for the Greek Orthodox Easter liturgy and Edinburgh for the man who had known John Cornford before he went to the Spanish Civil War. I met scholars and visited libraries and slide-collections and galleries. But there were also the hard, slow, frightening bits. I had to haggle with officials, to cope with difficult camera crews, and strikes, and transport that didn't arrive, and demands for cash on the nail, and lonely hotel rooms and boring meetings and airport terminals late at night with the last plane gone. And bad ideas that turned, humiliatingly, into bad programmes. You paid with every bit of yourself for the job, but it was full of revelations.

One moment stands out from those years. It was a remark about music, or rather — it was prompted by music, and it was said quite casually, one night at the opera, in Covent Garden. It is important that it was made by Arnold Kettle who happened to be the Professor of English at the OU, but who more relevantly was a central figure in the Communist Party of Great Britain, and a colleague of the big international Communist leaders and of James Klugman, who had brought Guy Burgess and the other Cambridge "traitors" into the party. Arnold had given everything a serious man could give to bringing about revolutionary socialism. He and his wife were also passionate opera-lovers. And I had been listening to opera myself, ever since I found a box of records of Maria Callas in *I Puritani*, in a carved, wooden chest, like treasure, in a little medieval house I lived in in Oxford.

This was my first time to see *Fidelio*. Arnold and Margot had seen it in Lisbon, the very night the Salazar dictatorship ended: the soldiers in the plot of the opera, when they had come onto the stage that night, had had red carnations in the barrels of their guns, like the real soldiers of the "bloodless revolution," out on the streets. In the first act there is a quartet, *'Mir ist so wunderbar'*. The four protagonists come down to the footlights, and they do that thing that happens in opera — seemingly unaware of each other, they each sing their line of music out straight to the audience, as if it is not of their doing that the lines intermingle in a complex and perfect harmony that it takes the four of them to make, but that is a separate thing from each of them. I was transfixed, as I always am by ensemble singing. When the curtain came down on the act I wiped the tears from my eyes and I said to Arnold — "Why is ensemble singing so beautiful? What makes it move us so much?" And he said: "People would be like that all the time, if they could."

This remark was full of meaning for me. It was about his Communism, I thought. He must have had in his mind a vision of people perfected — society perfected, free of deformations and oppressions. People so freed would communicate perfectly, as they do when they sing together in opera. Music prefigures whatever there can be of human and social perfection. There is an ideal, perfect, shape, behind the appearance of things. There is the possibility of perfect communication, and to try to establish social justice is a way of moving towards it.

In my real daily life, however, idealism was something quite destructive. It manifested itself as a nostalgia for, or a hankering after, something better and other — something more overwhelming — than even the best things that actually happened. I used to get formlessly depressed. I felt I was not in life: I was looking at it. I'd come back to the flat after being away somewhere. I'd push in the door against a drift of junk mail and the place would be emptier than empty. The air would be thick. I'd push up the window, and the dead brown leaves would rustle down from the lemon-geranium plant. I needed to move on.

11

It takes a novel to describe the subterranean shifts in the relationship between two people. My friend Tony from the training course and I must have seemed amiable friends from the day we met at the BBC. We used to tell each other our troubles, lightly enough. He cared about his family. He was the eldest son, and he felt responsible for the others — including his parents — because though they were gifted and beautiful, they lived on a sad housing-estate, and things didn't go easily for them. He would talk about them and about his girls. I'd talk about Rob. But there was a little event that changed us to being real friends, not long after we met. And it was as unpredictable as an invention in a novel. We went skiing, on a Ski-Train to Austria, and I ruined my part in the holiday by getting horribly drunk on the way, and then injuring my leg, the very first day. Tony was an athlete: he could ski at once, and he looked wonderful, blue-black against the glittering snow. I just hung around, limping.

Then, one night in the hotel, we started talking about poetry. Tony is a scientist. No one had ever taken a poem and analysed it with him. He wanted to know how that is done. So I jotted down Wordsworth's 'A Slumber Did My Spirit Seal' and started to show him how I saw it saying what it says. I remember the warm room — the rough golden wood of the low ceiling, and the check curtains, drawn against the snow. He sat across on his bed and I sat on mine and did the one thing I could do — I gave him a vivacious tutorial on lyric poetry, Romanticism, Wordsworth's "Lucy" poems in general and this little poem in particular. That he immediately and totally understood made this a shining episode to me. I valued myself: the self-disgust I felt at the drinking and the clumsiness was alleviated. And I valued him enormously — the seeking intelligence inside him whose prompts he always followed. I trusted him after that, even though what had happened wasn't about trust.

I followed him to a new part of the BBC, which had decided to set up its first ever "access" television unit. The idea was to have an ordinary terrace house instead of an office, and to staff it with a handful of non-intimidating people, who would help individuals or organisations who felt overlooked or slighted by the BBC to make their own programmes. These would then be broadcast in a slot called 'Open Door'. We applied to work on 'Open Door' and of course we got the jobs. The middle-class, middle-aged white men who ran the BBC not only could not communicate with members of the public — they didn't want to communicate with them, face to face. There was some kind of confused thinking about minorities going on, certainly. There were two bosses and three working producers on that first 'Open Door'. Both the bosses were white men, but the producers were me, Irish and a woman; another woman; and Tony, who is black.

The access idea as it was then was largely a piece of empty rhetoric. Professional broadcasters can hardly bear to put out material as bad as it almost always is, when it has genuinely been made by amateurs. The unseen hand of professionals was everywhere in 'Open Door', picking which applicants got a chance, manipulating the applicants, balancing one sort of material against another. The whole idea was a typical mid-1970s nod in the direction of democracy by an élite organisation just smart enough to have felt the winds of change. I became very doubtful of the value of what we were doing, as we went along. I thought we left a wake of baffled and aggrieved people behind us. The stress of making a programme caused awful rows in groups: I remember an obscure poetry group in Brighton — the mildest of people —

eventually coming to blows. The process of examining themselves so as to plan a programme showed up all the things they had been covering over. Individuals, too, never seemed much happier after they'd said their say than before. They still felt misunderstood.

But the idea behind the whole thing was right. I liked the informal style of it, too. I crossed London in the morning on the rickety old Metropolitan Line and came out into the street market at Goldhawk Road and went round the corner to an ordinary-looking house with a front garden, which was the office. I had splendidly bizarre clients. I made a programme with a rich accountant about over-population: he looking steadily into the wrong camera as it went out, live. I made a film protesting against pornography with the Queen's gynaecologist and his colleagues in 'The Responsible Society'. I made a film with a religious sect whose meetings I had to go to in a pungent basement lined with mauve satin, where the adherents prayed into a battery, which their leader then took — in conditions of some luxury — to California, where he went out in a yacht and lowered the battery into the San Andreas Fault, so that the prayer-power would seep into the very fabric of the planet.

I made a film for transsexuals. One of them insisted on showing me her new vagina, in her hot little flat in Roehampton. It was a kind of hollow, lined with the skin from her former penis. She had been a policeman in South Africa. Another of them was a gentle Yorkshire woman who had been sent down the mines, when, as a boy, a breast had started growing on one side of her chest. The mines were to toughen her up — make a man of her. She'd tried. She married, and her wife had children. But lovemaking gave her migraine and vomiting. The wife, very understandably, left, and the children lived with their "Mum" whom they sometimes called "Dad" without noticing. There was also a melancholy electrolysist, and a woman who had become a man — an Italian waiter, to be exact. When I took the men who had become women into the BBC Club in Shepherd's Bush they loved going into the Ladies. But they did things subtly wrong. In front of the mirrors, they'd hoick up their skirts to fix their tights. I'd never seen born women do anything like it.

By far the most important programme I made was in Derry, for the Bogside Community Association — the effective negotiating body for the Bogside at that time, after the British army had moved in to end the "Free Derry" stand-off. I knew nothing about Northern Ireland. I had been in Derry once, for one day, when I was twelve. But because I was Irish I got the assignment — just as Tony would have got Turks or Somalians because of the colour of his skin, though he was born in west London.

When I went to Derry I saw for the first time a town in the process of being ravaged, and I met for the first time people completely alienated from the state that was supposed to claim their allegiance. It is a measure of the English establishment's ignorance still, in 1973, that an account of the grave political and social revolution in Northern Ireland, and its life-and-death war, was being handled by a nobody from the tiny "access" unit. But it was an extraordinary experience for me. I was like most foreign reporters — I was thrilled, not horrified, by the place. The bullet-marked high flats, the patches of waste ground swept by fleeing boys after impromptu riots, the terraces of tiny houses in places like the Brandywell where mutual defence had only welded the people more completely together, the slow river, the armoured cars and helicopters and soldiers running backwards into laneways behind burnt-out buildings, the people living on their nerves — I had never been anywhere so exotic.

And so impressive. The Bogside Community Association had men in it — women were not at all noticeable in those early days — who had evolved under pressure into activists of a kind I had never imagined could exist. Paddy Doherty was the most visible individual in the organisation at the time, but there was almost an oversupply of men of intelligence and passion. The BCA had a Portakabin which was on one level an incubator for ideas about the organisation of society. On another level, an old lady might come in looking for a community activist to put in a light-bulb for her. Children came to call their fathers home to their tea.

I had no right to be there — an uninformed person, sent by an uncomprehending institution. I had power over the representation of these people. But they weren't yet known, much less respected. Only through 'Open Door' could they even get their voice heard. I did make a film for them — working out of BBC Belfast — that caught something of the intensities of the place. Gunfire broke out across us when we were filming one day. This was commonplace. Yet BBC Belfast was an outpost of the BBC that had been mouldering away for decades. Some of the people there had been beneficiaries of the lifeless *status quo* in the province. They were quite unable to rise, intellectually or even physically, to the demands of the new situation. They hated everything that had happened since 1969, anyway, and they either couldn't or, in protest, wouldn't, raise their levels of competence.

I noted these things, yet when I went back to England, I didn't go on thinking or learning about what I had seen. It was just another exotic war, like Vietnam or Algeria. When I went back to Northern Ireland, two or three years later, I was still as ignorant as most English media people. I had moved on from the 'Open Door' programme and was now working in a general educational part of the BBC. I was given the chance of making two Irish film "portraits". One was to be of Crossmaglen, and one of the Shankill

134

Road. This was for a series that was to be about ordinary life in places that seen from London were on the fringe — Scotland, Wales, Northern Ireland — though words like "fringe" were tactfully avoided. These were the last programmes I made for the BBC. Again, I unpacked my bag — in the Rio Guesthouse, Crossmaglen, in the Windsor Bed & Breakfast, Belfast — and walked out to start making decisions with nothing but the names of a few people I might talk to, and the eyes in my head. And of course this wasn't enough. There was no ordinary life in these places. But you couldn't explain why there wasn't without going into politics, which it was my explicit brief not to do. I had no option but to make the most noncommittal of films. They looked terrific. Tanks reared through the heat-distorted air behind burning gorse. Silver motes of dust danced in the air where the sun came in around the shutters of a Shankill drinking club. But since they hardly touched on politics, they were like those old cinema travelogues on Bournemouth, gone mad. Not that I fully realised that, then.

When I came back to Ireland towards the end of the 1970s, and got a job in RTÉ, I innocently showed my Crossmaglen programme to Nicky Coffey, an old television hand himself, and from Dundalk, just down the — highly dangerous — road. I slipped the video into the machine in a corner of the office and went off to my desk behind a partition. I heard him begin to laugh. He was laughing uproariously by the end. He stood up, when the end credits began to roll, and walked off, never saying one word to me. That laughter was the beginning of real watchfulness in me. I paid attention, about the North, after that.

1 2

Rob and I came back together, in a way, in the tenth year of knowing each other, the same year I worked in access television. All unexpectedly, it was a year of great happiness. I liked working on 'Open Door'. And I loved time off from work. And the reason for that was a place called Wrabness.

Wrabness sounds Scandinavian. I suppose that Vikings did sail past where Harwich is now, and press on up the wide and beautiful estuary which divides Suffolk from Essex. Wrabness was a hamlet on the south bank of the estuary — nothing more than a railway halt and a pub and a few houses, and then a sweep of woods and fields going down to the wide water's edge — a lush and secret countryside, a corner of the most hidden England. Rob had been writing a book on Picasso, but he had fallen behind, because he spent so much time wandering London, dropping in a book-review here, collecting the fee for a lecture there. So one day his publisher, who was also a friend, told him he'd borrowed a country cottage for him. He put Rob and his cooking gear and his books into a van, and drove to Wrabness, and left him there. He was to stay there until he had finished the book.

On many of the Fridays of that year I hurried from work to squeeze myself into a packed tube-train to go to Liverpool Street, where I ran through the great echoing station weighed down by my bag full of treats, and jumped into an express train that went north to Ipswich or Norwich. In an hour or so it came to a junction and I got out, and so did a few commuters, and they'd go down into the station carpark and I'd hear their cars drive away, and I'd be left on the platform in the quiet summer evening, or in winter, in wind or rain. And then the little train would come in, that tut-tutted down the branch line to Harwich, stopping every few minutes. It stopped at Wrabness and I'd see, as I waited to open the door, that Rob was waiting in the station yard, beside the hedge sprawling with dog-roses or, if it was cold, that he was passing under the pool of light of the street-lamp, hurrying down from the pub at the sound of the train. There was hardly ever anyone else. When the train went off there was only evening birdsong, or the noise of a winter night. We'd run up to the pub, and the quiet drinkers in there would look up and say "Allo, Nooly." The nest Rob had left would be there in the corner — his half-drunk pint of beer, his papers and books, the bit of shopping he'd done in the village shop. We'd have a chat with everybody — how the runner-beans were doing, whether there was a fête in the next village on Sunday, the pros and cons of getting an electric heater for the bar. It was easeful talk, such as had gone on in that little bar for decades. Lots of the people in Wrabness a quarter-of-century ago had never been to London.

Then we'd buy our take-away bottles and head off. We went home by a pathway along the edge of the fields, then by the side of a thick beech wood, and then we ducked in to the wood and went across the soft forest floor parting the boughs until we came out into a clearing in the middle of the wood and there, in a patch of grass, like a thing of magic, stood the cottage. In spring there was a sea of bluebells under the sharp sweet green of the new beech leaves. Every season was beautiful. In summer, the golden cubes of straw glowed in the stubble fields and the woods were blackish-green. In autumn, the searchlights of ferris-wheel harvesters played and replayed on the blank wall of the trees as they whirled and thumped up and down the big fields, chewing up whole pea-plants, and spitting the mulch out behind. Winter was most wonderful of all. First there was a season when the leaves fell so thickly in the wood that there was silence. The mist rolled up from the estuary and the bare twigs of the trees were covered in a cold sweat. Then it would freeze, and when we came out of the pub and started along the path to home we'd be breaking the skin of ice that had begun to form on the puddles when it got dark. We'd turn in to the skeletal woods. And there, in its little clearing crisp with frost would be our cottage, the light glowing from the warm kitchen, the dinner ready in the stove. We had no bathroom, no television, no telephone. We had everything.

Most of the time, nobody came to the woods. There was a deserted stone farm, covered in ivies and brambles, down in a meadow that led to the shore where brown water whispered. Across the wide river, a greensward swept up to the handsome portico of some big house. Those were the only signs of humankind. We were alone with the birds and the flowers and the changing trees. At night, I'd run out into the clearing to pee. If it was winter, my warm feet would melt feet shapes in the powder of frost. I'd run back, and snuggle down, quick, quick behind Rob's back, in the welcoming channel in the centre of the old bed.

We never exchanged a disagreeable word, Rob and I, the year he had this place. Even when, one weekend, I came down and found that the clothes and other things I kept at the cottage had all been hidden away. He had had someone else there, and not wanted her to know about me. Any woman, I thought bitterly, would have put the things back exactly as they had been. He forgot. I went into the scullery and stood at the stone sink and for the first time in my life, I controlled my response to pain. The place was actually teaching me proportion.

In the end, the owner took the cottage back. Rob had also lost his London house, while he'd been away. We tried to live together in my dark basement flat. It was hopeless. One day he left a note saying 'Back Tuesday' and disappeared, and though I saw him again for a while, he never really came back. But what happened afterwards hardly matters. That year of 'Open Door' and Wrabness was a culmination. All kinds of accidents had had to happen for it to happen. It wasn't like real life. It couldn't have gone on. But it was wonderful to have it, and especially to have known, while I had it, that it was out of this world.

1 3

On the first of the huge 1970s marches for women's liberation young men jeered at us as we shuffled along Oxford Street chanting our slogans. That was how things were, then. Nothing on earth would have stopped me going on that march. But though I knew I needed to be there, I didn't know why. Blatant injustice to women was everywhere, especially in employment. But I had a great job. If someone had come up to me, in my floor-length hippie coat, and asked me why I was there, I'd have said I was there for other women. It never occurred to me that I needed to interrogate myself. That I'd spent my whole adult life on the errand that smoothed the way to being a woman in the home — a search for a man, for love, for the one man to love and be loved by and have babies with — without wanting to be a woman in the home. I could see sexism in operation everywhere in society: once your consciousness goes "ping", you can never again stop seeing that. But I was quite unaware of how consistently I put the responsibility for my personal happiness off onto men. If I'd been asked why I was often unhappy I'd have said, "Oh, I'm having a bad time with X," and mentioned some man's name.

Relationships were the hardest things to think and feel anew. I never joined a women's group, so I never picked up other women's insights. One remark, made by a sister of mine who was a serious feminist, did give me a flash of self-knowledge. It was a sneer at a — relationship is too strong a word — a one-sided crush I was having at the time. I fondly called this womaniser a "poor man". My sister said, "Poor man, indeed." That was all — but it moved me on.

He was one of two men I had sporadic relationships with during the 1970s, which are worth mentioning because they are almost case studies in the limitations of my supposedly raised and feminised consciousness. And in the limitations of any change in man/woman relationships, at least among people who were not young. The first man was not honest or faithful, but he was exceptionally sweet and gentle, and for the very reason that he was so sweet, women — myself included — allowed him to behave in ways that hurt them. The second man was as intelligent and subtle as a person can well be. Except in his dealings with women, myself included.

I had met, through an Englishman I knew, a tragic American middle-aged beauty called Peggy Craig, who lived in a big flat in Rome, moving around its rooms in a dressing-gown, reading art history, and brooding about where her husband, a Hollywood script-writer, might be. The husband was an Irishman called Harry Craig, who since he had come up from his father's quiet parsonage in County Limerick to go to Trinity — and probably before that — had been a dedicated, heartfelt, womaniser. He was charming, by all accounts, and an idealist — a trade union organiser — and a lover of poetry. He turns up in Maurice Harmon's *Sean O'Faolain: A Life*, helping on *The Bell* magazine: '...the assistant editor, Harry L. Craig, a student at Trinity College, who was well known for the lack of order in his life and his sexual pursuits ... Craig attributed his success with women to having a double duct in his penis...' He moved on London to cut a swathe through the post-war BBC — he was said to write the Royal Christmas message. David Thomson's widow — Harry had known the "Phoebe" of *Woodbrook* — told me recently that the bed in Harry's flat in Hampstead was said to have black satin sheets, which in austere 1950s London was near-legendary.

The Englishman and Peggy were close. He and she came up from Rome to Paris once, to the suite reserved for Harry's party at the Ritz for the gala premiere of *Waterloo*, a film — Rod Steiger was Napoleon — which Harry **wrote**. Peggy hadn't seen Harry for weeks. But Harry didn't turn up.

I met Peggy in Paris that time. I waited with her in a bar while the Englishman got the car from a distant garage to begin the drive back to Rome. She was a woman of powerful charm when she was well and she was, that day, and her golden beauty came back for a few hours as she sat in her black velvet coat in the tacky plastic bar. By the time we set out to drive south — I was going part of the way with them — I worshipped her. We stopped that night in Vezelay. It was winter. Burgundy was as black as the sea as we drove across it. There was a cold fog in the lanes that led up to the great grey abbey. The village was deserted. I remember that the hotel was in an ancient building, and that we drank a lot of wine beside the fire, and that there was a wide staircase of polished black wood, and at the landing it divided, with narrower flights going to right, where my room was, and to the left. I didn't know which way the Englishman would go, when the three of us went up together on the way to bed. I didn't know what the understanding was between himself and Peggy.

I would have been content to be her friend. I would have been more honoured by her than by Harry's interest. But she was only interested in him. He, as soon as I met him, enrolled me — it was a reflex action — among his lesser women. Then we had to behave like lovers when we would have been perfectly content to have had long lunches. I was less interesting to him than any man because I was a woman, and he knew with weary exactness how to make the low-voiced phone-calls, to have the car sent around, to order the Chablis chilled and sent up to the room. Peggy and Harry and I were unable to climb out of the deep grooves of conventional behaviour, even though the women's movement had genuinely begun to change the world.

Harry had such a splendid physical presence, and was at the same time so silly, that he wasn't easily judged. He used to assure us little coven of expatriates who were his guests in Roman restaurants that he was going to do something about Northern Ireland. "I'm going to go to the border! I'm going to stand there and throw my arms wide and say to them — 'Listen!' And then I will read Yeats to them ... " Then he'd read us the bits of Yeats he was going to read to them, if he ever had time to go to Ireland, with tears of emotion in his eyes. Sometimes it was North African politics he was excited about. He was somehow acceptable to the Muslim film industry, though he drank with gusto. We were enrolled as admirers of Muhammad, of course, and — in modern times — "the lion of the desert" — the Libyan hero of the war of independence against Italy, as depicted by Harry's friend Anthony Quinn. Empathy was his great gift. But it also meant he was a complete moral empiricist. No one could rely on him. His *maîtresse en titre* was an American journalist and in her recently published autobiography she talks about Harry, and the terrible shock of hearing he was dead, and ringing Marlon Brando to tell him, and how she couldn't stop talking to her mother, obsessively, about her grief for him. The account ends with her mother's judgement on Harry: "I've been trying hard to sum him up, in a single sentence, and I think I've found it ...

He never quite made it."

Harry, in fact, was too personally successful. He implicitly offered the gift of his charm in exchange for being allowed to do what he liked. I accepted this deal. When I was chattering to my sister about how the poor man had to juggle his passports to escape his women and she said "Poor man, indeed!" I did see what I was doing. But I didn't want to respond to the feminist call to self-respect. I wanted to know Harry, and the conditions of knowing him were not negotiable.

During those same years I knew another man, a renowned American art critic called Clement Greenberg, who made an absolutely exceptional effort to be honest. But he was no better than Harry at breaking through to some kind of new communicativeness. And I was no more authentic with him than I was with Harry. If intelligence could do it, Clem and I would have had a truthful intimate relationship. But intelligence seems to have had little influence on pre-modern habits of self-abasement, furtiveness, falseness.

Clem was old when I met him. He looked very Jewish and very much a New Yorker: he moved his heavy-lidded eyes and his bald head slowly, like a tortoise, and dressed like a bookish Bronx boy's idea of an English gentleman. And he was formidable. In his circles, he was considered a very great cultural historian — this century's Matthew Arnold, even, a lineage he saluted in the title of his collection of essays, *Art and Culture*. He had championed Matisse before anyone else, and changed perceptions of modern painting, and named and promoted the abstract expressionism of his friend Jackson Pollock. He was Rothko's friend and executor among others. By the time I knew him he was paid to walk around galleries and lend his prestige to the art just by looking at it. He was an immensely serious and original thinker, and in the circumstances of the mid-century USA and the role of art within it, this had made him rich and famous. The nexus of art, art criticism and wealth to which he was central was later savaged by Tom Wolfe in the essay 'The Painted Word'. Not that savagery bothered Clem: he was pretty combative himself.

However, when I met him in a Dublin, when he came to the first ROSC exhibition of contemporary art, in 1972, I knew nothing about this. I just recognised one of those dominant, difficult personalities whose attention it is gratifying to attract. We went off to the West in a chauffeur-driven car with John Elderfield, a young art historian. At Lord Mountbatten's castle at Mullaghmore Clem bribed a caretaker to let us in, because he had a simple, fervent crush on Princess Margaret, and he wanted to ogle the photos of her among all the photos propped on pianos and mantelpieces. In Galway there was a little show of amateur oil-paintings in Salthill, and we went to that. "You'll see," Clem growled to John as we went in, "there'll be more people here with a really painterly feel for oils than in the whole of the States." We went to Cork. "Have you got something kinda acid?" he asked the wine-waiter, seriously. "Something that would cut the phlegm?"

I knew him for five or six years and visited him in America and saw him when he was in London. We wrote. He expressed himself with crudeness, but I knew that he was trying to do what he done in his intellectual life — he was trying ' to cut the crap'. He continually tried to know himself, and to be honest in relationships with women: 'How to live? Find out how to let yr. intuitions come through, and how to tell them from the whisperings of the Devil. Some kind of desperation came over me about women. Now I'm in training ... ' Or again, '... Only one out of seven or eight people in the Western world is kosher (which I say flatly on the basis of sixty-eight years of living). But as Kant says you can only find what you look for; something turns over inside you, after a long while, and then somehow you eliminate the un-kosher ones, as many as they are, and more of the kosher ones come into your ken ... ' He encouraged me. '...You'll come into your own. Maybe the longer you delay, the more indolent you are, the better whatever it is you have in yourself to write will come out. The only thing I have over you, I think, is that I've implicit faith in my outcome. But that's only the advantage of a male — certainly in my case, without balls I'd be a cripple ... ' 'All females in the British Isles seem brought up to be petitioners,' he wrote. And 'in hopes of another orgasm,' he candidly signed himself, once.

But I knew, though I couldn't articulate it to myself, that he did not, as a matter of fact, like me. We did not really mean anything to each other. I didn't appreciate him. So why, one winter, did I fly from New York to his house up country, on a snow-and-ice-bound lake, where there was no food, and he sniffed cocaine and jitterbugged frantically to the swing music of his youth when it came on the radio, and I was miserable? I went to Edinburgh with him once, and we walked around the National Gallery of Scotland. Hundreds of people would have given anything for the privilege. But I didn't know enough about the history of painting, or have a good enough eye for the painting before me, to be thrilled by his commentary. And he — for all his "eye" — did he see the living me at all? Did he think I found him physically attractive? Why did he treat me as if I had as much money as he did? He told me to fly from New York to his house upstate: why didn't I say "I can't afford this"? He might have thought I was begging. He mightn't have wanted me at all, if I was troublesome. Above all — how much of an acquaintanceship would there have been, if I hadn't slept with him?

The gap between us once visibly gaped. I annoyed him, and he attacked me. "You're a loser," he rasped at me, with pure contempt in his voice. "All you Irish are losers ... " And he went into a rant full of physical distaste for me and people like me — people (as I understood it) who had no edge, who weren't in the game, who were unimportant, who were soft and melancholy and depressed instead of out there in the bright, hard world, fighting towards success. (This is a reaction to the Irish I came across again in other successful Americans. Mary McCarthy told me once that she feared the sogginess of the Irish so much that even when the plane stopped over in Shannon she wouldn't get out, in case she was sucked into the bog. The night Dukakis lost the US presidential election to George Bush I watched the results in Boston, sitting beside Murray Kempton, a much admired American columnist and author. "I've never wanted to go to your country," he said to me. "The very thought of it gives me fatigue.") Clem was marking a difference that does exist, I think, between New York Jews and Irish Catholics. But he was marking it with such vigour because he was angry with me. He was enmeshed in dishonesty with me, but he couldn't quite identify it. I know. I knew it then.

Maybe he, like me, knew on some level that we were lessened by each encounter. But it seemed like such a good idea that we should know each other. Maybe he, like me, was pressing on out of a mixture of insecurity and vanity. And out of the desire not to give up —to keep trying things — to go on living and learning. Again, as with Harry, the relationship was too embedded in an old culture to be invigorated by women's movement thinking. That old culture had come crashing down, but we were wandering among its ruins, picking through its fragments.

14

During those years in London I never forgot the family —
the household in Clontarf — for long. I never stood back
and estimated them. I called myself in letters 'your London
branch'. I don't remember being surprised, even, when my
parents sent my youngest brother to me, for me to get him
through his difficult adolescence. He was in trouble with
the law in Dublin. My brother wrote to me about that time:
'My father suggested to the justice that if only I could be
given the chance of vacating the area there'd be no more
trouble (for him!). The problem would literally go away. I
got to Lime Street Station in Liverpool at 2 a.m. No idea
where I was, how to use the phone what platform, etc. I
just panicked, started crying. A policeman took me to the
station, cup of tea, calm down, etc.' This brother used to be
taken along by my father 'when I was nine or ten to visit
Auntie Carmel, who was always "sick in bed". He'd leave
me with a young boy in the living-room to play with his
train set,' my brother says. 'It seems vaguely strange to
me that (a) I never saw Auntie Carmel and (b) I never
sussed the connection between the young boy and the rest
of my family. "Here you are, son — half a crown. Don't tell
your mother about Auntie Carmel. She'd only be upset ..."'
This brother hadn't much of a childhood: 'My father was
never there. My mother usually drunk. The old man would
occasionally come back from some far-flung location and
hearing of some indiscretion beat the shit out of me (his
army belt, a bamboo cane, his walking stick.) Once, after
one of these incidents, I stayed out for three days in a
cardboard "hut" in a dump at the back of the Clontarf Road.
The Ma found me on the fourth morning. "Come home,
son," she said, wearily. "Just come home. He's gone."'

This brother was an exceptionally gentle, and a very intelligent boy — I remember him reading Thomas Hardy, and saying, "He's a miserable git, but I can relate to him." But he had the marks of neglect on him. I remember the look on a friend's face, when my brother, who was newly arrived in London, stubbed out his cigarette on a plate which still had the runny yellow of an egg on it.

I wish I could have that time back. If it were now, I would push and pull my brother with all my energy towards some kind of goal. But as it was, I was absorbed in myself, and I paid him only intermittent attention. The next few years are punctuated by interviews with bad schools and busts at rock-concerts and probation officers and looking for my brother in squats. He was the only important responsibility I ever had. There must be huge amounts of a particular hopeless pain in the world, that no one seems to mention — the pain of someone who didn't do their best for a young person, and can never make it up.

Sometime during those years, I accepted that Rob was gone. I saw him for what was to be the last time for decades at a dinner at St Antony's in Oxford — it turned out he'd gone back to Oxford — given in honour of Conor Cruise O'Brien. Dinner was dominated by Lord Goodman, who only stopped telling self-congratulatory anecdotes when Conor forced in an anecdote about himself. Rob and I slept uncomfortably that night in the single bed in his little room. In the morning he walked me to Oxford station. Same place: ten years later. That was the real end of that. But on the level of the incorrigible imagination, I hardly moved on.

I have a notebook that I sometimes wrote to myself in, when I was sitting at night in my flat in Islington, listening to the Third Programme and drinking wine. 'If you came the shorter way, across the wheat-field ploughed entirely in October, you walked for maybe three minutes beside the thin hedge of the Old Rectory ... ' I was writing about lost Wrabness. There is the beginning of a short story: a man and his half-drunk wife are hurrying across a field, with their children, to the Christmas party in the landlady's big house. The wife is trying to find out where he has been all day .... Childhood was still haunting me.

In real life, I was at a loss. Love seemed to have failed. I went on a binge with another Irish woman journalist whom I met at a lunch-party. We went on drinking, during the afternoon. We found ourselves in a very Cockney, very criminal pub in Kentish Town. There was a house nearby we went back to with men from the pub. I went home the next day, sick, and sick with myself. That was one of the episodes that made me, in the end, hardly go out. Not many people came in.

An Irish writer I knew came to see me one hot summer night and stayed for a few days, lying on the floor of the bedroom, watching Wimbledon. The difference between coming home from work, down the hot street, to him, and coming home to my usual no one ... I wrote to that man in the notebook, too. Outpourings, full of longing. And full of lies I was telling even myself. I assured him I wasn't needy or lonely. I took a wise person's tone. Even though, the previous Sunday, I'd gone to Mass in Westminster Cathedral in the mad hope of seeing him from the bus, because he lived in that area. Even though I'd have done anything — short of tell him any of this — to have him back.

But I also had friends and suitors. I had two sisters living near me, and I had my brother. I travelled. It was so easy to get cheap tickets out of London that I could go to Rome for the weekend. I worked in Teheran for a few months. And there was the growing light shed by the woman's movement.

Ireland and England were in a different relation now, in the mid-1970s, than they'd been in even a few years earlier, when I could say intimate things to Rob, or talk to my colleagues at work, without knowing that they heard the accent before the words. Not long before Rob left, the IRA murdered twenty-one people and injured more than a hundred, in the Birmingham bombing. It was bad enough that, at work, the cleaning ladies backed me up against the wall, in the toilet, and heaped angry questions on me. But Rob turned to me in my own kitchen. "Your friends are murdering my friends," he spat at me. Even though he knew me. He knew I couldn't possibly have known anyone in the IRA. I'd been away from Ireland for seven of the preceding ten years. I knew hardly anyone there, except my family and Sean Mac Réamoinn. I was so uninterested in Ireland — or in public life in England — that I hadn't even taken in things like Bloody Sunday in Derry. I didn't feel Irish in anything, except that I still often went to Sunday Mass. I liked nineteenth-century England — provincial, working-class, football-club England. I knew a lot about England — I knew the literature, for instance, all the way back to Anglo-Saxon. But I knew almost nothing about Ireland.

My old friend Sean Mac Réamoinn came to see me when he was in London. We whipped up his favourite supper of the time — spaghetti carbonara, accompanied by large amounts of sparkling Veuve du Vernay. Sean told me that I must come to the Merriman Summer School on my holidays. He'd helped to found the school. I'd "done" the opening lines of Merriman's *Cúirt an Mheán Oíche*, where he throws off an accomplished description of his native landscape in East Clare, in Irish class at school. *"Ba gnáth mé ag siúl le ciumhais na habhann..."*, we had chanted. In the effort of transferring this passage to my memory without knowing what half the words meant, I picked up nothing about it. I didn't know it was the opening of a long satirical poem about the lustiness of human beings and their rejection of the Catholic clerics who tried to control them. I didn't know it was by a real person, a hedge-schoolmaster called Merriman. Sean had been one of a group of people who wanted to rescue the Irish language from being a grim thing taught in schools and to reaffirm it in every area of life — in comedy, sex, cursing, drinking — everything. These men started the Merriman School so that for one week a year, anyone who wanted to could go to Clare to learn and talk and listen and sing and dance, in Irish or English, but anyway in the old Gaelic spirit.

It was a turning-point in my life, when I went to my first Merriman. It was 1973. I flew to Shannon one August day and got myself across the county to the grey stone market-village of Scariff, in a mild, turquoise landscape of wooded hills and water-meadows and lakes and broad reaches of the Shannon River. I had never been in rural Clare before. I could number on my fingers the days I'd spent anywhere in rural Ireland. It was so beautiful, after the grey streets and the dirty tube stations I walked through in London every day. The voices of the people were so expressive. At that School, I fell completely in love with an Ireland which turned out not to exist. Yet this visionary Ireland gave me the impetus to break my links with England. And it pointed me in the direction of the real Ireland I am getting to know now. If I hadn't encountered modern Ireland late in life, and if I hadn't — because of my ignorance and because of being away — thought it was magically interesting, I wouldn't have been so eager to learn about it. And learning about it has meant more and more to me with every passing year. A new concept of "home" came into my life when I realised that Ireland, in all its aspects, present and past, was mine. That I belong to Ireland, just because I am Irish.

The people, mostly from Dublin, who were in Scariff for the school — academics and artists and journalists and diplomats — were just what I needed. I needed the format of lectures and seminars. It wouldn't have been enough just to have found some lovely little corner of Ireland to go to on my holidays. I needed a crash course in roots. That first time, after so long away, I was shocked and delighted by the lavish amount of personality around. The great bearded figure of the scholar and teacher David Greene is an example of a person who by any standard was remarkable. Soon after I got to Scariff I was walking along in the company of him and his wife, the sculptor Hilary Heron. She murmured, "Montbretia," as we passed clumps of the slender flame-coloured wild-flower twined in a grassy bank. I had first seen that flower twenty years before, when I was a child in the Gaeltacht. Now, at last, I knew what it was called. That something I had never known the name of was named for me, that first day, is symbolic to me of all that happened because I went to the Merriman in Clare.

The people who were figures at the school seemed larger than life to me. And every event seemed freighted with significance. Liam de Paor was in Scariff because he was actually living there, excavating a mediaeval site of pilgrimage on Inis Cealtra in Lough Derg. I went to the site on a wonderful mild and blowy day when Liam had brought a grand-daughter of de Valera's, an archaeologist, out to the island, to talk to the students about some of the skeletons they'd found. We went out to the island in a boat and stood in a little bower of green with the wind stroking the grass, and looked down at the skeletons laid out on the grass. They were very small. One was a skeleton of a woman with the skeleton of a baby still jammed in her pelvis. The de Valera grand-daughter bent down to show us our ancestors' teeth worn down to the gum. "It was the chewing on hard grains," she said. "And the honey." That brought them close. I was so moved at being in the sequence: ordinary people who had died in the Middle Ages; de Valera's flesh and blood; and me, allowed to stand there and be part of it.

I didn't see the Merriman people as themselves. I saw them as walking treasures. I was stage-struck. I cried my eyes out at almost everything. I heard for the first time accounts of some of the big Irish songs. I heard Diarmuid Breathnach singing 'Na Connerys' and a Clare school-teacher sing 'Sliabh na mBan' and someone sing 'Príosún Chluain Meala'. There was a late-night club in the hotel ballroom but it was for dancing. The singing would just burst, you could never tell when, from an individual with a drink in the hand. These things were new to me. I'd only ever been to a couple of Fleadhanna and that was more than a decade before. When I was young I'd gone to the pictures on a few afternoons with a lonely Connemara man I met in O'Donoghue's. That was Joe Heaney. But he never mentioned singing.

I heard people chat away in Irish. Or — better — not even noticing whether they were chatting in English or Irish! These people were like a new species, compared to the Londoners I was used to. They were each so distinct. There was so little grey. I moved in a daze of happiness around the small spaces of the town of Scariff. I might go to a lecture down in the Tech, or across the street in the little cinema. I might go to one of a number of pubs, for example, Johnny Maloney's pub, where Johnny sat cross-legged at his tailoring in the window, while he conducted a commentary on the affairs of the pub and the nation. I might go a few doors down to Maire Melody's, where I'd be taken into the kitchen for sandwiches of thick slices of ham between chunks of fresh-baked bread. We might even, in the evening, play a game of cards. By the time I stumbled home to my B&B — it was a bungalow so new that they were still digging around it, and every night I fell into a trench — I was a walking swamp of emotion.

I did it all wrong, I realise now. I was much too soppy and gushing for the ironic people concerned. Also, I wore cheesecloth smocks at the time and long Indian skirts and didn't wear a bra. But the innocence of my enthusiasm must have saved me. I thought all the people I met, every single one of them, visitors and locals, were wonderful. I thought everything about Clare was wonderful. We went on a bus-trip to Doolin and sat in the sunshine outside Gussy O'Connor's pub and a girl who'd just won the flute competition at Fleadh Cheoil na hEireann played. After a week of ecstasy and drink I was poured into a taxi to Shannon, and I wept all the way back to my dreary London flat and for days afterwards; and during the year I had to wait till I could go back again, I often dreamed of the golden men and women who went to the school, and the lovely contours of Clare.

When the venue of the school changed to Ennis, and then to West Clare, I fell even more thoroughly for the county. I began to rent a house south of Lahinch, on the Miltown Malbay road. Some of my sisters and their children started to go there too. These were our first ever family holidays. We were there when I heard a thump in the night from my little sister's room — she'd just heard on her tranny that Elvis was dead. (She wrote to her pal first thing in the morning: 'R. I. P.' was inscribed all over the envelope.) We were there when Mountbatten was murdered. We were there when the Anglo-Irish agreement was signed. We go there now. Some of my sisters — I can hardly believe it — are set dancers in London and Dublin. That came from Merriman: I literally never heard of set dancing till I was in my thirties. That particular corner of Clare — the stone and grass, the cattle coming to the whitewashed milking-parlour out on the bright windy, road past the caravan site, the little beach, divided by the stream that comes down through the boulders — has been the ground on which we now stand, constructing a relationship with Ireland that is more than simply accidental.

I decided to come home, of course, now that I saw Ireland as home. I had bought a small house in a slum in Dublin for £4,000 a few years before. Squatters had been living in it, but they left. I came back to Dublin, after seven years away, with nothing but a suitcase-full of letters I had somehow hung on to during this part of my life (and which I've used, writing this piece).

I started off my life in Ireland again on the first of January 1977. I got a temporary job as a producer with RTÉ. In the job, I went around Ireland all the time with presenters who knew all the ins-and-outs of the country. I remember my first time in West Cork, with Doireann Ní Bhriain. I remember, with her in Donegal, going out on a half-decker from Magheraroarty pier to the scoured stones of the houses on Inishbofin, silent and barricaded against the cruel winter. I remember the lordly rocks in Glenbarrow in the Slieve Blooms — the very core of this place lately called Ireland. I remember going down through Kilkenny to Enniscorthy with Paddy Gallagher, stopping at pub after pub, on the trail of the designer Eileen Grey, for 'Folio'. Inis Meáin, the first time I was ever on Aran, in spring, had wild flowers in profusion in the cracks of the stone, and hens scratching on the grassy street. RTÉ crews stayed in every second-class hotel in every town in Ireland. Bailieborough. Youghal. Birr. Dungarvan. Loughrea. Listowel. Cavan. Each of these names — every name in the country — evokes a whole complex of memories and impressions, has a distinct taste, calls up an atmosphere as definite as a colour.

I was extremely naïve about Irish social groups. The shock of finding that out was, in the long term, a blessing: I'm interested at looking behind surfaces, now. I realised as time went on that the Merriman School, for instance, like most Irish events, had a core of insiders and people perceived to be "important", and a periphery of people perceived to be less important, and that that pecking-order was a matter of difficulty and, often, hurt. I saw that the school, as one of the very few venues where adult men and women were together outside their ordinary Irish lives, could reflect the awkwardness and shyness and sudden cruelties that continue to deform social intercourse between the sexes here. I think, over time, that the school changed and that now it is more accessible than it was. And it is less forgiving of "characters". I went into a packed and happy pub, with Nell McCafferty, the first night of one Merriman, and a Merriman "character" — John A. Murphy — sent over a note saying 'no Provo-lovers wanted here'. I don't forgive him for that. I don't forgive myself for fawning on the same man later in the evening to get him to sing. I don't blame the Merriman School, of course. It is valuable exactly because it is one of the few events in the year where opposites — Northern and Southern, nationalist and unionist, being one — do meet in a social setting. But it is not an easy event, on many levels. Nothing that attracts so many egos could be.

RTÉ wasn't easy, either. Going around the country was one thing, but working back in Montrose was another. The same larger-than-life personality I admired in Irish people compared to English people was a burden if you had to negotiate with it day after day in colleagues. Yet it was an immense exhilaration to come back from England and be free of its rigid class structure. It was wonderful to be with people who were what they were, not cowed and classified from birth. At the BBC in the early 1970s, when I was working on location, the technical staff ate at a different table from the producer and presenter. The electrician might be called "Sparks" instead of by his proper name. It was an enormous relief to be away from that. But an agreed social hierarchy, such as there is in England, helps organisations to work smoothly. Some of the people in RTÉ, compared to the BBC, seemed to want to be charmed or amused or pushed by superior force of will into doing their job. They were brilliantly good at it, often. But doing it well for its own sake didn't satisfy them. If someone was bored, they'd obstruct everyone else, and if they were in a good mood they'd help with unsettling lavishness. And there was the usual problem of men who disliked working with women. This was expressed in a particular Irish way. Women were put down by endless recall of the golden era of RTÉ television production where "great nights" — usually drinking escapades — had been had by this or that group of men. It was being made clear that the present situation was a come-down.

Women were also excluded by the rough, macho, management style often in play just underneath the good manners of formal management. The place was run by men — not all of them nominally bosses — who had "strength". The "strength" would be personal, or political. Hardly ever professional. Some producers and managers didn't really know what they were doing, technically speaking. But they didn't care. Real passions were ideological or political, though these are words too grand for the very limited aim of the dominant ideology, which was to keep anyone with any sympathy for Northern nationalism as far as possible from any influence.

I've heard it said that RTÉ television hasn't come into its own, so to speak, because its development has been checked by the Troubles. But other organisations in the media — The Irish Times, for example — developed perfectly well, while covering Northern Ireland in a competent and honourable way. In RTÉ, two things connected with Northern Ireland seemed to me to be happening. Direct, public, personal abuse of anyone deemed to be either nationalist or insufficiently anti-nationalist was allowable. Meetings about Section 31 of the Broadcasting Act were particularly vile. Perhaps it was because RTÉ television is such a young organisation, but there seemed to be no governing standard of professional or personal conduct. The second effect of the energy poured into anti-nationalism was that no programmes mattered except political and current affairs programmes. In the BBC, people of energy and talent worked in arts and features. In RTÉ, those areas were often moribund.

I myself benefitted enormously from a different aspect of those times — the new interest in women. In the 1980s, I worked a lot on women's programmes. I did a series, inspired by the 'Late, Late' audience, called 'Women Talking'. Doireann Ní Bhriain and I went around the country and sat down with almost random collections of local women and recorded the ebb and flow of the talk as they discussed subjects that interested them. Then I worked on 'The Women's Programme', where Clare Duignan and Marian Finucane and Doireann and I did pioneering programmes on incest, prostitution, abortion, women's pay and employment, contemplative nuns, health issues, Unionist women and their views on Southern women, the fall-out within their families of the activities of "supergrasses" both Loyalist and Republican (protest from an anti-nationalist to management about that: we shouldn't have included the Republicans), world issues for women, the HRT debate, how to run a 10K race, where in Ireland there are most unmarried men (Ballaghdereen, at the time) and so on. It was serious, and it was fun. Nell McCafferty used to do a marvellous script about women in the week's newspapers. She would take something — for example, an ad for thermal underwear, based on testimony from a priest about how comfortable he was saying Mass in this thermal underwear on various mountain peaks, and she'd weave an extravaganza from it. Between the five of us, we were approaching women's issues from every angle and in every mood. At an EC weekend conference once, in Brussels, on women and broadcasting in the Community, after Clare's report from Ireland — which included 'Women Today', then running on radio — broadcasters from all over Europe came up and congratulated us. They thought RTÉ must be really progressive. And it was a place where opportunities could suddenly appear. This was the good thing about the lack of hierarchy: a person could take an idea to a manager, and if the idea was good, and the manager a powerful enough patron, they could cut through the usual structures and make their programme. That's how I got to make the series on older women called 'Plain Tales'.

I started and ended my RTÉ career on "magazine" programmes. These are the ones whose titles no one can ever remember: they go out early in the evening and consist of four or five harmless items presented by reasonably good-looking presenters sitting on sofas. These magazines cost a great deal to produce in terms of human effort. The last one I was on had people like Cian O hEigeartaigh, who is a true scholar and aesthete, and Richard Crowley, an exceptionally gifted newsman, and David Blake-Knox, a real expert on television comedy, and myself, and perhaps ten other production staff, all churning out six-minute items on things like female bodybuilders. It isn't easy to manage Irish talent. A lot of people who work in RTÉ are almost by definition dissatisfied. I was. It was a stroke of the greatest luck, to get the chance of going to *The Irish Times*.

———————

By then — in 1986 — I was well on my feet. But the first few years back in Ireland from London — the years leading up to 1980 — were in most ways my life's lowest ebb. I was back with my family again. I couldn't cope with physical things. My basic lack of skill in directing in the television studio kept me terribly anxious. And I was unskilled at everything. I couldn't drive. I couldn't type. I didn't know how anything worked. My house in the slum was beyond me. A big grey rat jumped out of the press. Plaster fell in chunks from the ceiling. I had never run a house, and even hiring workman after workman, things got worse. I didn't understand Ireland. One summer afternoon, when I was in bed, four or five big men shouldered their way in downstairs. They were Special Branch, they said. They wouldn't talk to me as they began going through my bag of coal and taking up the floorboards. Then their leader saw that I had some books in Irish. "Can you read Irish?" he said, obviously impressed. He stopped the search. I didn't know that they couldn't do that — they couldn't just walk in and push a citizen around like that.

Things happened to me, at that time, instead of my choosing what would happen. The worst was getting pregnant. I was thirty-nine. I was so completely stunned by this turn of events that I was quite unable to think about it. When I miscarried, quite painfully, all one night in a room by myself in Holles Street Hospital, I still didn't know how I felt. I still don't know.

You can never get everything together, if you're drinking too much. You can only do a bare minimum of things. But there are also good sides to drinking. A pub always has a company of regulars. People who drink in the afternoons belong to a company of people who also drink in the afternoons. Pub life is an undemanding, floating way of life, unjudgmental, and full of small incident. People who are as shaky as I was then are very kind to each other. I had thin relationships with other people who drank too much. I was never well. It was hard enough coming to terms with RTÉ, but it was a self-imposed handicap, doing that on a diet of hangovers and take-away Chinese. My former friend Michael, with whom I had discovered sexual bliss when I was twenty, took me out a few times. But we had nothing left to say. I was just going through the motions, with the relationships I had.

Yet that seemingly waste time, just before I was forty, when I was on the edge of alcoholism, was in some deep way rewarding. An aspect of being vulnerable is that you are very open. I used to lie on the bed and look at the sky as it very, very slowly got dark on summer evenings. There was a kind of perfection of melancholy. On Sunday mornings, or on Bank Holiday weekends, I had absolutely nothing to do but feel the quiet. In a way, I was with my self very fully. Afterwards, I used to miss that feeling of being held within pure, empty, space.

I thought nothing was happening, then. But my head was filling with riches. The mosaic of the country was being assembled inside it. The mysterious valleys between Leitrim and the sea with their oily black rivers full of fat trout. The stretch of plain — deepest, silkiest green — out beyond Lissadell with its abrupt end at the fierce beaches, as indifferently beautiful as when the little curled ships of the Armada foundered on their rocks. The Shannon welling up silently into its round pot, and then changing character, discovering youth, prancing out towards Dowra to begin its long slide down the country. Down through the silvery-greys of the water-meadows, down past what were stone hotels, corn mills, old canal buildings, past the swans waiting beside half-submerged alder trees. In winter, when you get the train that crosses the Shannon river, it seems to go across the surface of a huge water into low country. In the wintry light, the train goes into the water and the water is steel, and carries the train. But Ireland isn't just landscape, but history, and present society. There was famine and brutality and emptiness in the country. And the damaged underclass I was part of in the afternoon pubs was as much part of Ireland as its beauty.

1 5

Most memoirists in Ireland write about their fathers in a sweetly one-dimensional way, as if there were no unconscious. The older man I knew when I was a young woman — the doctor who helped me get through college — was wary of my relationship with my father. He used to hint to me that my father preferred me semi-derelict — that when I found strength, for example, to take my mother for help without his knowledge, it threatened him. But I wasn't aware of anything except that my feelings about my father were (and still are) contradictory. I feel a pang, for example, every time I remember that the last he knew of me was those drinking years. He'd be so proud of me now. Yet I also believe that it is not a coincidence — though there were other reasons — that I started getting healthy when death took him, and a few years later my mother, away from me.

The others — my sisters and brothers and even my mother — must have been as ambivalent about him as I was. No matter how, on paper, he most certainly let us down, he didn't abandon us. We mattered to him. And none of us could ever be even for a moment genuinely indifferent to him. Just when you thought it was safe to hate him, he'd make some loving and sensitive gesture. He was particularly kind to the daughter who most resembled his own mother — my sister Deirdre, who married young, is a truly religious Catholic, and who with her husband has reared a large family in a modest and happy home. The thought of that household must have often comforted my father (as it has all of us). Daddy called to Deirdre in the hospital when she had her first girl after three boys — a hand came around the door, holding a silver cup, then another hand, holding a bottle of champagne. That was the sort of gesture he'd make for any of us. But he offered Deirdre in particular, steady, important, kindness. He was a different father to each of the nine of us. Some of us hardly had parents at all. Some, when my father was getting older and milder, used to have a lavish supper and play cards once a week in the small flat he and my mother and my little sister had ended up in. Not that Mammy played cards: she wafted woozily in and out of the bedroom in her nightdress, looking like Miss Havisham.

One of the things that tormented my mother was that my father would tell her nothing. She never knew what exactly the financial position was. A few times the poor woman even went into town, and trembling, braved whoever his paymaster was at the time to ask that his money be given to her directly. Nothing was ever sorted out. His life was ideal for concealment. No one felt any obligation to her.

She did get some leverage when my father sold the only house he had ever had a mortgage on, as opposed to renting. He murmured, "Your mother really cannot be trusted with stairs ... ", a remark calculated to win him sympathy for the step forced on him by her drunkenness. But in fact he was in some kind of worse-than-usual cash crisis. He moved my mother and my little sister, who were the only family members he still took responsibility for, into what turned out to have been the flat of his mistress. She, presumably, had been moved somewhere else. My mother discovered this one quiet night, when she was alone, reading in bed, and the mistress burst through the bedroom door and attacked her with the bedside lamp. It would be funny, if both women hadn't been so desperately unhappy.

I gather from Michael O'Toole's reminiscences that my father's mistress was a public fixture. O'Toole refers to my mother in half a sentence as a very intelligent woman who had a problem with drink, but goes on to tell an anecdote about my father's companion of long standing, who was apparently well-enough known around town to have a nick-name — "the lady". I didn't know this until I read O'Toole's book, and I was shamed for my mother. The anecdote had to do with my father arriving at an antique fair bleeding from the head where the mistress — apparently unable to hold her drink— had attacked him in the back of the car. The man from the welcoming committee was lost for words at their appearance, and asked my father—for something to say—whether he was interested in antiques. My father makes a quip about never travelling without one.

I can't say I find this funny. But I do admire my father's fast thinking on another occasion. Mammy told me, when my little sister was born, that Daddy had visited her in hospital and suggested the baby be called Carmel. "Carmel?" my mother said. "Why?" "I've always had a devotion to Our Lady of Mount Carmel," he told her. I knew, though my mother did not, that the mistress — I presume the same one as in Michael O'Toole's anecdote — was called Carmel.

After the bedside-lamp incident my mother got herself to Clontarf Garda station, where she received first aid and prepared to lay charges against the mistress. My father came hot-foot from whatever part of town he was gracing. He begged my mother not to disgrace them all in public. In exchange, he offered her information. She would know how much he earned, how much he owed, and how much he'd got for the house in Clontarf. She settled for that.

He was a very disciplined man, and extremely reserved. The public carry-on with Carmel, if it was Carmel, and Carmel did hit him, was a decline in his standards. The years of trusting no one but himself must have told on him. He had no partner, no peers, no friends, when it came to it. The day he could not, finally, go to his work, he made his own arrangements. His driver was waiting outside to take him on the usual social round. He was too weary to knot his tie. 'He sat thoughtfully awhile on a stool beside the phone,' my sister wrote in a letter, 'little finger hooked between his teeth, head tilted sideways as though listening.' Then he picked up the phone and cancelled his appointments. He booked himself into hospital that day and packed his own bag and went in there for good.

My sister Deirdre recalls how my mother and he reached for each other, at the moment he knew he was going to die. My father had leukaemia, and on a certain day, after two months of horrible chemotherapy, the consultant was to say whether the treatment had worked. 'At 3 o'clock the consultant arrived up at the far end of the floor, and proceeded on a leisurely tour through the wards,' my sister wrote. 'Isolated inside Dad's room, we chattered desperately in low voices while we waited, petering into silence when we heard his brisk steps approaching. There was a slight pause, then a quickening of his gait, as he hurried past the door, down the corridor, then clattered down the stairs. My father's piercing blue eyes opened wide, and caught mother's brimming eyes in his. He stretched out his hand to her. Neither spoke. Some time later, my Dad chuckled wistfully, and, turning his face to the wall, embraced the waiting coma ... '

We "children" were not so important in those last months. But my brothers, in particular, whose young lives he had made desperately hard, threw up everything to be near him in the hospital. I understand their still reaching for him. I don't understand his neglect of them. I see fathers all around me and they love their sons with a practical passion. But my father dumbly refused the ordinary effort of being a father. My brothers were loving and bright, but there was no tolerance for the difficulties of their growing up. One of them was no trouble, but he was almost punished for that, and let sink into unskilled casual jobs, where he wasted years of his life. One of them, after a saga of desperation, had ended up starving in the England to which his father had bought him a one-way ticket. He joined the British army, which hurt my father as deeply as anything could — the man who had changed his name from Phelan! Yet my brother did it in part to impress him, being too young to know that nostalgia for the Irish Army was quite a different thing from being pleased that your son is a squaddie. A sister who was only a teenager, working as a bank clerk, tried to promise her wages in advance to raise the money to buy the brother out. My father said he would buy him out — that when a certain insurance policy matured, he would pay the sum necessary. But nobody bought the brother out. And then my parents deported the youngest brother to me in London. My mother was drunk when she put him on the boat. My father wasn't even there.

How do you forgive these things?

My father acquired a companion, Frank, late in life. A large, benign, almost completely speechless man, who for a couple of years went everywhere with my father. When Frank died, I wrote a letter of condolence to my father. He replied. 'I find it impossible to believe in the living and the dead and the resurrection, though I stand up in St Gabriel's and say all this,' part of his letter read. 'Another surrender of reason is due, I suppose. Unreasonable is the thought that there is no point in looking forward to the resurrection and the life unless your friends and neighbours and all you loved on earth are there ... but that to me conjures up a vision of a non-stop press reception ... for all eternity ... and I don't want to interview my grandfather who was an RIC sergeant and who left me his eyebrows, or to be interviewed ... We buried uncle Frank dacent. He had no next of kin and he left me all his massive wardrobe. I gave it to the Men's Night Shelter in Tara Street and the Norfolk Home for Unfortunates and some gigantic tramps and drop-outs are now magnificently dressed by O'Callaghans of Dame Street ... As you will understand,' he says, 'the loss of Frank Finn hurts much more than that of my brother. One was a lonely man all his

life, and I know that towards the end ... this huge and
gentle man depended on me as none of my children did,
and I am glad I was with him every night till a few hours
before he died with dignity ... ' My father is telling the truth
here. He did love Frank. But the phrase leaps out at me —
that Frank needed him 'as none of my children did'. My
brothers needed him. We all needed him.

At the end of his dying of leukaemia, when he had
shrivelled and discoloured and was like a terrifying brown
boy, hunched in his nappy on the mattress of his bed in the
hot room, we still looked up to him. It was terrible to all of
us to lose him. My brother whom he had not saved from
the British army came home and joined the vigil in the
tobacco-smokey room at the end of the hospital corridor —
even though this brother had been tormented, in
childhood, by the sounds of my father beating my mother.
And even though — and he said in a recent letter that it
hurts him still — 'on at least two occasions, when I was a
child, my father forgot my name.'

There was nothing we wouldn't do. I went to Confession
for the first time in twenty years, to prepare for a Mass
beside his bed. My brothers and sisters didn't sleep, didn't
eat. I could not read, for the only time in my life. I went
back over and over to the same poem — the Tenth of the
Duino Elegies, where Rilke praises suffering. 'We wasters
of sorrows!' he says:

> How we stare away into sad endurance beyond
>   them,
> trying to foresee their end! Whereas they are nothing
>   else
> than our winter foliage, our sombre evergreen, one
> of the seasons of our interior year, — not only
> season — they're also place, settlement, camp, soil,
>   dwelling...

This elegy, and the last part of Mahler's *Lied Von Der
Erde* — I had the Kathleen Ferrier record — forced
themselves on me. I'd go back from the hospital to my cold

house in the slum, not wanting anything on earth, and too tired and sober to dramatise myself. But these two pieces of work did quite straightforwardly console me. They are both full of perceptions — vague, but compelling — of ultimate meaning. The promises of Christianity meant nothing to me. This German romanticism was all I had to oppose to the anguish of pity I felt for my father. That God wouldn't let him keep his aloofness to the end, but forced him to beg! "Take me out of here. Take me out." His eyes becoming round and filmed exactly like his mother's when she was very old. "Just take me home ... " On his gravestone we had carved, '...*ar ball, gheoaimíd radharc, aghaidh go h-aghaidh*'. In the end, we will see, not as through a glass darkly, but clearly, face to face. I don't expect, of course, to understand life and death. But I might understand some day what kind of a father my father thought he was. What kinds of fathers there are.

———

He was very lonely. And my mother was lonely. But I think they had a middle-of-the-night understanding that only they knew about. She often boasted to me, shyly, of what confident lovers they were. Perhaps she felt she was altogether there, when they made love. Perhaps sex was her best experience of wholeness.

I was at a horrifying Sunday lunch once in a house in Hampstead, with the actor Robert Shaw and his then wife, the actress Mary Ure. He abused her loudly and steadily from the beginning of the meal. If anyone said anything, he, watching her all the time, would say something like, "Do you hear that, you stupid woman? Are you listening to what intelligent conversation is? Or are you too stupid to know what an intelligent conversation is?" After five minutes or so she ran out of the room choking with sobs. He relaxed immediately, and began to tuck into his meal, smiling cheerfully at us shellshocked fellow-guests. "Sorry about that," he said. "But I have to do it. She doesn't know she exists unless I put the work in ... "

The arrangements between my father and my mother were almost as hard on us, the bystanders. They would be cruel to each other. Then, for no reason we knew, they'd forget that, and get on well. For decades, he referred to Mammy's drink problem as if it were a wryly amusing habit of hers. He took her on holidays, and faced down the criticism he must have encountered. Silently, he would not allow us to discuss her with him. When she was falling down in the street! Getting sick in public! It was a vast denial. But it kept a kind of dignity possible between them. "Oh, Katherine! I've always loved your smile!" I remember him flattering her with his last strength, in his hospital room, not many weeks before he died, even though to anyone else her smile was a half-tranquillised, half-terrified rictus.

After he died, she looked around absently for him, the way you might glance around a room if the light in it suddenly changed. Every so often, my sisters would with heroic effort get her into a home to dry out for a while and get some treatment for her malnutrition. Mammy was like a child in there — afraid of the authorities, keeping clear of the other patients, hiding in her room, lonely as ever. She would ask me plaintively, "What's wrong with your sisters? Why is everyone so cross with me?" She didn't even remember the awful episodes my sisters were dealing with all the time. And she'd say, with honest petulance, "*Why* did your father die and leave me here?"

She didn't even totter down to the pub any more. She stayed in the flat. She kept the amount of time she had to be conscious as short as she could manage. When she got up, sick from gin and sleeping-tablets, she would start drinking again. If she got her doses right she could be slack-faced and unreachable by late afternoon.

I drove out to see her every week or so. I would ring beforehand, my stomach cramping. I often put the phone down, half-way through dialling. But then I would work up my courage again, knowing that if I was lucky I'd get her in the interval between her being too sick to talk and too drunk to talk. If she seemed lucid enough on the phone, I would hurry out to the flat. Sometimes she was ready for me, sitting on her chair in her crumpled coat, her handbag clutched to her chest with pallid, shaky fingers. In my relief my heart would open to the pathos of her. The lipstick swiped on with unforgotten expertise. The blobs of mascara. The dabs of pink powder. When under the make-up her skin was grey, and bristles were breaking through on her upper lip.

If you fed her the cues for one of her little reminiscences going along in the car, and if you linked her up the steps into the library, and the librarian quickly got her four or five books she would like, and if you sat her then at a sunny window in some hotel lounge with a double gin, she would radiate happiness. She would take on the mannerisms of a pampered, pretty, woman. She would beam, in a blurred kind of way, at any people around. The flowering might last half-an-hour. An hour.

One Sunday I phoned before going out to her. She seemed all right. But she didn't pick her way to the door to unlock it when I rang the bell. I stood on the doorstep, afraid she was dead. I went around to the window and peered through the slats of the blind. She was sprawled on the floor. Her legs were wide. She seemed to be snoring. She had her coat on, so she had been ready for me, but she had overdone whatever drink it was she had glugged down or whatever pills she had gobbled from her palm. I stood outside and banged and banged on the window and shouted at her to get up, get up, raging with grief and anger, and furious with a lifetime's fury at her doing this to me.

Soon after that, I was driving to the West, and as usual I was writing her a letter in my head. You did this, you did that, you didn't do that ... And suddenly I felt a single sharp sensation: the vibration of a single heavy twang. And it was the parting from her. It was completely unexpected. Breaking-point. From that moment on I was at a little distance from her. So when a few years later she intimated to me that she was going to die soon — though there was nothing particularly wrong with her — looking up at me as I stood at the end of her bed, and giving me a wonderfully frank smile — when she said "Nuala, this can't go on," I just said, "That's right." I admired her from the bottom of my heart at that moment, looking down on her poor face, all discoloured by falls. She was at her stoic best. She wasn't looking for sympathy, or even comment. She was merely remarking — in quite good humour — that she was finished.

When they rang me a few weeks later and told me she was dead — that she had died in the bathroom, and they had found her on the floor, I was almost prepared. I had seen her sprawled on a floor. Her dead body was only the same as the body that had shut me out, that day I shouted at her through the window.

I remember her through windows. Standing at her bedroom window when she was young, a sheet wrapped hurriedly under her ivory shoulders, in the bungalow we lived in then. She was shouting at us children to go and play, to stay out, not to come in till we were called. Then she turned back in to the bedroom, where my father would have been waiting.

She left her clothes, a wedding-ring, and an estate which totalled £1000. She left the biscuit-tin, with her scribbled book-reviews in it, and the letter from my father, from Donegal. And she left us nine people, her children. None of us had mattered very much to her. Once, when we all happened to be in Dublin, six of us adults got together and took our courage in our hands to go and see her and ask

172

her to allow us to get help for her. She threw us out of the flat with a few venomous words. We were only "the children".

One of my younger sisters lives in a town down the country, and not long ago the women there organised a "Woman's Day" and I went down to report on it. "I'll have to go to a workshop for the morning," I said to my sister when I bumped into her in the crowded hall. And my sister gave me a glimpse of herself — I hardly know her — when she said, "Well, I'm going to one called 'Adult Children of an Alcoholic'." It was extraordinary to sit beside this sister in a circle of women in a small room, with Mammy back from the dead between us, in all her power. At one point, the woman running the workshop asked everyone to draw the floor-plan of the house they had grown up in. I drew the flat instead, that our mother died in. Two little boxes of rooms, and the bathroom where liquid gushed into her lungs, and the breath was choked out of her, and weight bore down and down onto her heart until the last beat could not labour on, and life emptied out of the empty thing on the floor.

In the workshop my sister and I said almost nothing, The most terrible stories were being told by some of the others. When we came out after the morning I said to my sister, "She wasn't that bad, was she? Compared to what some of those in there had to put up with, we had it easy. Didn't we?" But my sister just looked at me, and turned away, and left me to hear for myself the eagerness in my voice. And the falseness.

16

There is one broken-down hotel in Mopti, a little Malian river town on the Niger, on the edge of the southern Sahara, thousands of miles into Africa. Nell McCafferty and I had stumbled off the ten-hour bus from the capital, Bamako, when it got into Mopti in the steaming, insect-humming dark. The boy who had carried our rucksacks from the bus didn't want us to go to the hotel. It was "*trop cher*". So it was: in the dim foyer with its empty display cases a woman got up from the tangle of staff lolling on mildewed sofas for long enough to give us a key and tell us the unbelievably expensive rates. Fleets of velvety green frogs scuttled before us as we felt our way down a dark path to our room. They hopped against our door. Inside, the erratic air-conditioner dripped water on the floor and stirred the air in the stagnant room. The concrete walls were covered with smears of dead mosquitoes. We had not been able to eat the brown messes the other bus-passengers bought at roadside stalls, but the hotel had no food. I had been sick all day from a reaction to anti-malaria tablets. We turned out the light. The heat thickened. Odours of mould rose in the terrible little room. Dogs howled outside. The night was going to be awful.

We lay on our stained beds, sweat trickling down our faces. I heard Nell light a cigarette. Then she said out of the dark, "Do you know what?"

"What?"

"I don't care what Bishop Casey did. He shouldn't be made stay in the tropics. They should let him come home."

I did the planning of our holidays. I had great ideas — we were in Mopti, for example, on our way to Timbuktu.

I'd heard the phrase "from here to Timbuktu" all through my childhood, and Timbuktu was the most exotic place I could think of. Now, for Nell's fiftieth birthday, I'd surprised her with tickets to go there. But my ideas would often land us in trouble, and I'd fall into despair. Nell kept us going, then. She pulled laughter out of the hat. We were in the Peloponnese once, living in a hut on a beach, just north of the Mani. The first day we set off to walk through olive groves to the village, not realising how hot it was. After a while we were panting, purple in the face, hardly able to breathe. I was afraid I'd collapse. And then we saw a water-trough, with a pipe trickling into it! We threw ourselves into the cool mud around it and soaked ourselves in the water. When we finally crawled upright, our hair and clothes stuck to our bodies, covered in mud and moss and leaves, Nell said — as one writing a caption to a photo — "Irish models take a break from the catwalk."

She never blamed, no matter what we got into — bamboozling a travel agent in Bologna to sell us train tickets home on an expired Access card, being threatened by Serb men we'd been drinking cherry-brandy with in a hotel bar in Belgrade, trying to climb a glacier in Norway with an ice-axe, because the man in charge of our walking holiday liked to frighten. There wasn't anything Nell couldn't lighten. Even after Timbuktu, when she was rushed to the fever hospital with life-threatening malaria, she stopped me being tragic. Half-delirious, with a temperature of 104°, she managed to whisper, as they were putting her into the ambulance, "For my sixtieth, I'll arrange the surprises myself."

But I don't know whether we'll be in touch on her sixtieth birthday. We lived together for nearly fifteen years, and it was by far the most life-giving relationship of my life. But we were made helpless by our angers, in the end. I don't know why. In *Hamlet*, when the ghost of his father comes back to harass him, Hamlet jumps from spot to spot, bending his ear to the ground. "Art thou there ...?"

he calls. "Old Mole!" he calls, trying to pin him down. The old moles of my childhood come, malevolently, to the surface of the ground I try to stand on.

When I was a child, in Athlone, once, there was a festival on. The song of the day was 'On Top of Old Smokey', so it was that year. There was to be a parade, with music and fancy dress, and then soft drinks and sandwiches in a hall. The thing is — I was a helper. I was a trusted lieutenant. I wore myself out in an ecstasy of helping — running here, running there, carrying messages, tacking up crepe paper, being responsible — being part of the indescribable glamour of it. I remember running down the rainy street, past the lights of the shop-windows to the hall where the lady I helped would be needing me. I've never been absorbed in anything as much again. That is my ideal. That is what I imagine good relationships are like. But I have never wanted to help a partner, since I grew up, with my whole being, the way I wanted to help that lady.

Deeper than heart, primitive feelings would stir, when Nell made any real demand on me. "Why can't she look after herself? I don't ask her for anything. And if I'm not asking her for anything, why is she asking me? I mind my self. She can mind herself ... " I hear that voice and I think — I've heard that voice before. Is that not the primitive hostility my mother expressed in her drinking?

Our two lives became involved with each other around the time my father died. I was physically and mentally at the end of something. I went into St Patrick's psychiatric hospital on the morning of Christmas Day, in 1980. We had buried my father a fortnight before. I was in shock. I had hardly slept since his death. I had nowhere to live, either. I'd sold my little slum house sometime that year because I couldn't cope with it. A friend was putting me up. I wasn't easy to have around. I drank all the time and couldn't get drunk. In the end I asked the friend to get me into hospital and he did.

It was exciting, that breakdown. I thought I was having huge insights. I kept scribbling writings down, that I was sure would be of the utmost importance when I had time to study them. I was swept with tides of emotion. I lay in my bed one night, listening to the rain on the window, thinking of it lashing onto my father's new grave on the hill in Sutton, and seeping down on to his lonely corpse, as I wept for myself, in the guise of weeping for him. Then I heard his voice! His voice! Someone on the radio murmuring in the corner had played a tape of an old interview with him, in memory of him. I was a mourner ambushed. Thinking of his voice, silenced, reminded me of all the voices that had been silent all their lives, down the centuries. I wept for the millions and millions of anonymous women who might never have been, for all we know of them. I wrote a kind of paean to them. I still couldn't sleep.

But Nell came back from her family Christmas in Derry and a friend lent us a place in Sandymount, and I began to mend. She was exactly as ready to bustle bossily and warmly and unselfconsciously into someone else's life as I was not. She looked after me. Slowly, I began to drink less. I ate a bit. Six months after I met her, I threw away the last of the sleeping-tablets. I remember one glorious spring morning coming out of the flat and going down onto the sand and dancing with the purest delight.

I began to be able to stand back and see the world, and manage it a little. I tried to buy a solid little house, even though a mortgage was hard to get at the time, because I didn't have a permanent job. I did have a job, though — I was teaching, on a year's break from RTÉ. One day, I had to go to a man in the bureaucracy of the place I taught, to ask him for a letter saying that though I was not on the staff, a permanent position might ensue. I needed this letter quite desperately: if I had it I could get a mortgage. I believed that if I had a house and my clothes were hung up, I could sort myself out. This man had a big office. He sat at his desk. I sat opposite. He looked at me with open contempt. "What makes you think you'll be kept on here? I have no evidence that you have performed your duties satisfactorily. I'm sorry my dear, but I am certainly not signing any letter ... " And so on and so forth. He gloated, because my employment record for the year was so bad. And he knew how to do it — he'd been on top of the heap, because he was a middle-class man, all his life. I crawled to him. I had to, to get the letter. When I got home, I was glad to be living in an all-woman household. (And I often was again.)

I went back to RTÉ, this time to 'Féach'. This once-powerful Irish-language programme had a complex history, and its standing in RTÉ was a complex matter. So much I understood; otherwise I was an outsider. I didn't mind. I'd become like most workers — the real focus of my life was my home. I could hardly believe it. We had a house. We went to a sale and bought dishes. I couldn't believe how rewarding order was, and cleanliness, and making a home. Once I came back from a few days working down the country. Nell was all hot and bothered. She had a towel wrapped around her jeans as an apron. She had been making pizza dough, and had it in a bowl in front of the fireplace and it wasn't expanding the way it was meant to. I had never known anything like this simple crisis. It gave me the deepest pleasure. I never wanted to go to a pub again. I felt as if I had come in from being on the road almost since I was born. I felt we belonged. We knew a couple who were equal friends of the two of us. When they had a little girl we were the joint godmother. I planted a white lilac in the little square of earth outside the front window of the house. On the first warm Saturday of that summer, our first year, we sat out there, eating our breakfast. An old lady who lived further up the cul-de-sac leaned over our gate and said, "It's lovely to see people enjoying themselves. You're very welcome to the street." The more we made a life that was regular and ordinary, the more I was freed. The public world became my interest and entertainment, because my private world was secure.

Yet Nell and I were not alike. We didn't agree on very much. It was only when we were abroad that we relaxed with each other. On our holidays, the rough edges of our personalities were smoothed. We were never more than tourists, but we were that with the intensity of travellers. We went to the Communist-run European countries, not knowing that the Iron Curtain would one day be raised. Because those countries were cheap, we could leave huge tips. The old women in cloakrooms used to kiss us. We had duck and black cherries and a whole gypsy orchestra in Gundel in Budapest, and a box at the opera, where everyone applauded the arias so heartily that the singers repeated them, even if they had to come back from being shot or stabbed to death to do it. We went east, and the thunder and lightning caught us out walking across the endless Hungarian plain and the sky turned black and cracked open and we held on to each other crouched into the earth as lightning crackled around us. Outside the austere Calvinist meeting-house in Debrecen the first refugees from Romania were gathering: borders were becoming porous. When we came to the wide river that divided us from the Soviet Union, Nell stood on the gravelly bank and sang, to the thick woods on the other side, 'Lara's Theme', from the film of Doctor Zhivago, to show that we were friendly.

We got to know Iron Curtain food, before the Wall came down. Dry pork. Balls of gristle. In Warsaw the gallant people — the women so dainty in their home-made frocks — got up from the tables and danced to the shabby band, while they ate the bits and pieces of cheap meals. In Prague the people in the packed Christmas streets talked in such low voices that there was a surreal absence of noise. We were the only people having Christmas dinner inside the perfect marquetry box of the panelled dining-room of the Europe Hotel. We wore our coats. The kitchen had made a great effort, for those times. There was a little pattern of gherkins around the meat. The waiter was as cold as we were. We propped our books on the ornate table silver, and shivered. Prague was sad, but in Budapest, another Christmas, we heard the people answer back to Moscow, at Mass in the Cathedral. There were soloists from the opera and players from the orchestra up in the balcony, and after the service they had bounced the Hallelujah Chorus off the great dome of the church. And then, the congregation — the solid men in their belted loden coats, the women in neat astrakhan hats — had launched into a hymn in Magyar, singing it out with such fervour that we knew it was their equivalent of 'Faith of Our Fathers'. We came out so affected that we had run, half-laughing, half still crying, to pull ourselves together in the Ladies of the Hilton. We heard the first sounds of the end of the Soviet empire. We were in Austria, cycling down a stretch of the Danube. Hungary had begun to allow East Germans to get out across its border and their road to West Germany ran parallel with the river. At night, when the countryside was very still, we would hear the rattle of the overloaded Trabants as they — the first to be released from the socialist experiment — made their way to new lives.

"This is the life," one of us would say fervently, settling back in the chair in a café in the warm Mediterranean night air. The feeling of lightness — the being freshly showered, lightly dressed, at leisure. Lobster and candlelight on the quay at Fethiye. The lunch we had every day at the two-table café behind a scraggly hedge in Sperlonga with little golden chips and greenish, ice-cold wine. We'd be just finishing the wine when the afternoon shower would come and we'd run across the road, and peel off our T-shirts on the rain-pitted sand and whoosh down into the foamy sea through the warm rain. We went into a *fin-de-siecle* tobacconist shop where they sold loose, oval cigarettes wrapped in old sheets of Arabic newspapers, in Aswan, and hired a barouche pulled by a malodorous horse, and ate ice-cream in the street, smug at our adventurousness compared to the English below decks in the cruise-ship, moored on the exquisite Nile. We swam unexpectedly in our bras and pants in the turquoise Atlantic waves that rolled into a rocky cove near Lisbon. We walked through the hot dusk, in a village south of Kalamata, to take our ouzo and saucer of titbits at the outdoors taverna where the men of the village argued and laughed under the lights strung from the plane trees, and flocks of noisy birds rose and fell from tree to tree as they tried to settle, and the election vans went up and down playing tinny music. "This is the life," one of us would say.

Fleeing the video bars east of Corfu — we took the boat across the Adriatic to Ancona, to go up through peach orchards to arrive at last in the honey-coloured stone piazza in Urbino and watch stately parents and their tumbling infants, out for the evening stroll. We got drunk on hot sake with the proprietors when we were the only people in the Chinese restaurant, in Ely, on a freezing New Year's Eve, when we were wandering a deserted and beautiful England. The ilex woods above Spoleto, the sushi bar in New York, the rushing green river that went down to the fjord in Norway, dancing *paso dobles* in the seedy ballroom in Barcelona, eating a trout in Salzburg because we knew the name from Schubert, swimming in the hot springs full of classical debris in Pammukale — "this really, really is the life." On a slope of scree in the Agrafa mountains in Greece or when I was frozen by vertigo to the edge of a ravine in the Vercors Nell talked to me and got me through. She showed me how to be courageous. When I got tired she told me the plots of films to keep me going the last few miles. *The Magnificent Seven. Bad Day at Black Rock.* In Rome, she knew the Colosseum already from the movies: "Victor Mature came out of that archway there." In Sicily we could see Don Corleone everywhere, even in the businessmen having lunch beside us in the chic café near the Fountain of Arethusa, where we ate pasta with cream and shrimp in January, fifteen years after we met, the door open to the sunshine and the boisterous sea... I said, "This is the life," tentatively, that day, but we couldn't smile, because we were leaving each other.

We would come home to Ireland, close. Then the messages, the tensions of free-lance journalism, the snapping at each other .... Yet I loved the way she always woke up happy, swimming up to the surface, babbling away about her dreams and slurping up, half-asleep still, the tea and the bread I'd bring up. I'd hear her singing in the shower every morning. When she was sick, she was so humble. And I'd see her coming towards me in the street, a formidable woman in her jeans and little worn shoes. Once, she and I went to Belfast for a night, and walked through carnival streets down to the docks, where the Tall Ships were visiting, and the whole city had come out to look. We fell in with some Unionist women who had seen Nell on television — Protestant or not, they knew their 'Late, Late Show'. We sauntered along, happy to be together, them interested in Nell, she fascinated by them. They were ahead of me — four or five middle-aged women in pastel cardigans and big beige shoes, their heads turned to Nell, the small, delighted one in the middle. Most of us just take what we're given. But "Look at her," I thought, "full of energy and argument, because there are women here to talk to, and politics to talk about. She'd argue with the world. She *has* argued with the world."

In Nell's family house, the visitor would sit on the sofa in the back room, the big telly grimacing in its corner, while her mother wandered in and out from her tasks in the scullery, patting her pinny down, regaling the company with a stream of anecdotes and ideas and tales tragic and humourous and questions about the world and sayings and disquisitions on this and that. I had never met such a charmer. She played on the sofa with her grandchildren and taught them hymns and songs and how to show courtesy to neighbours, especially the elderly, and inducted them into how things are done and were always done. The tea, for example, of "red fish" and great bags of chips, wouldn't be right unless served on the table with sliced pan and butter, pickled onions, beetroot.

I sometimes came back early to this house — needing a bit of solitude — maybe from a daughter's house to which the whole family — granny, daughters, in-laws, friends, grandchildren — had decamped and were settled talking in front of the television with their drop of tea. I'd fish the key up through the letter flap and walk down the brown tunnel of the hall past the holy water font, into the little ticking room, where the table-cloth was folded on the corner of the table, ready for spreading; the mother's apron was hung on the back of the door, her slippers lined up under the rocking-chair, the cuckoo-clock whirring on the wall. I would stand in this rich, eloquent silence, knowing that the family knew where exactly everything was and had always been — this ornament, that bottle of pills, Lily's purse, the Padre Pio prayer-card. At first, I sentimentalised it all. Then I felt an outsider to it.

There was one night in particular when the McCafferty family's courtesy mattered to me. There was a debate in the Guildhall around 1994 on the subject of feminism and nationalism, and it came down to a stand-off between Bernadette MacAliskey and myself. The hall was packed with a partisan crowd. They were egged on by Bernadette who prowled up and down on the platform behind me, rolling pieces of paper into balls and flicking them sharply at my back, while I spoke. I said feminism was about human development and was therefore incompatible with killing. I said the armed struggle was one of the reasons there was no all-Ireland sisterhood — that Southern women, in my opinion, had little or no sympathy with

Northern nationalist women. That the men of Sinn Féin were just another layer of patriarchs among the many in Northern Ireland that oppressed women. That women who lived on tea and biscuits brought steak to their husbands in jail and the men took it without apology. I bitterly regret making that last insensitive point. But otherwise, I bore with being excoriated by Bernadette and by fierily eloquent speakers from the floor. I was spat at on my way out of the Guildhall. It matters a lot to me that when I went back to the little house in the Bogside the McCaffertys were the soul of tact. Because they don't understand why I am what I am, any more than I understand them. We have been formed by completely different historical experiences. Yet they don't retreat into righteousness, and they don't ostracise.

Nell and I disagreed about many things — especially the politics of the island — and after a while we hardly talked about them at all, for fear of fighting. Not many people came to the house. We didn't talk much at home. Gradually, I seemed to myself to lose the ability to talk naturally at all. I didn't notice at first. I liked not talking. But when I got the chance of working on the 'Booklines' programme in RTÉ, I discovered that I was so rusty at ordinary communication that I used almost practise how to go into the room where the production team met, and how to talk, because I had forgotten how to behave in a group. I'd come away sometimes with tears of chagrin in my eyes because I'd got it wrong, again — been too loud or too sulky or too flippant. I was ridiculously sensitive to hurts from other people and not sensitive enough to whether I was hurting them. I hardly knew how to sit calmly and let a bit of talk ebb and flow.

Abroad, we chatted about all the little things of each day. We walked from Volterra to Siena one warm, rainy May. We stood in under dripping trees while the rain soaked the heads of poppies till they bent, and the bright drops made the banks of violets sparkle. At night, we tried to dry our boots with the hair-dryer. One day, deep in a valley of vivid green grasses we came to a river. 'Cross by the stepping stones,' the instructions said. The rains had swollen the river far beyond stepping stones. We took off our boots and trousers and put on our runners, and waded through, even our panties getting soaked at the deepest bit. And we stayed that way to climb up through the wet undergrowth on the other side, until we came to a village. Two half-naked women of a certain age with their legs pink from the cold and plastered with grasses and seed-heads and leaves, laughing like lunatics. That night, the two of us squashed into four-inches of bath water. We started laughing again, snorting helplessly.

Abroad, it didn't matter that we didn't talk much. We read. We read the same paperbacks at the same time, me speeding along, and tearing out the pages as I finished them, for her. I remember in Opatija — which we'd gone to on the coastal ferry from Trieste, because of Nabokov and a story of his I'd once loved — we sat in our hot little room behind the metal 'J' of the Hotel Opatija sign and solemnly read a novelette called *The Rich and the Beautiful*, passing each page across. We read all the time, meals included. We read local newspapers and children's schoolbooks and left-behind thrillers in French if there was nothing else.

In my best memory of the two of us, we are reading: one in a little bed under the slanting wooden roof of an attic, one in a little bed tucked into an alcove opposite. We are in a B&B in Bergen, on our first night in Norway. We have wandered the town, deserted in the soft, implacable rain on this late September night. We were not the rich ones now. We'd stood outside a restaurant, watching through the window as people got a bottle of wine put on their table. "£20, minimum," we'd breathed. We'd had a Chinese meal, and tea. Now we were propped in our beds, hearing the rain on the roof, seeing the rain sliding down the little dormer windows. Warm and companionable. Our Irish troubles forgotten. And surrounded by little lamps. The landlady seemed to have a thing about lamps, and we'd lit them all, and the rain-sounding attic was full of lights and shadows, and felt as if it were sailing through the night.

1 7

And did you get what
you wanted from this life, even so?
I did.
And what did you want?
To call myself beloved, to feel myself
beloved on the earth.

Raymond Carver, Late Fragment

I didn't have to give this account of myself at all. I don't
know why this story insisted on being told. Partly, I think
something was dislodged in me by the evidence given about
his childhood at Brendan O'Donnell's trial for the murder
of Father Walsh and Imelda Riney and her little boy. His
sister told of the brutality Brendan saw — he saw his
father smash his mother's false teeth with a blow, and the
mother trying to jump from the car and Brendan
screaming at her not to jump. He saw the father's incessant
beatings. His mother — who was well until her marriage
— broke down. Mother and son huddled together so close
that she went to school with him: to stand in the corridor,
until Brendan could let her go. This evidence wasn't even
printed in the *Clare Champion*, the local paper. The waters
closed over yet another Irish family. My two brothers in
England had their life's chances taken from them in
childhood, as surely as Brendan O'Donnell had. Maybe
that trial brought me into the presence of my own sorrow
and anger.

Or — maybe that's just fanciful. Maybe what matters is
that it was a few days before last Christmas when I
surprised myself by offering to write an introduction to this

selection of columns. Christmas is a time when powerful
feelings are stirring. And this was going to be my first
Christmas completely on my own. Ever. There wasn't even
a special person whom circumstances had prevented me
from sharing the day with. Since Nell and I had parted,
there was no such person. I wasn't absolutely alone, of
course — I'd be speaking to some of my sisters on the
phone, and people would ring me. But I had no person of
my own. In my fifties. I kept coming up to this blank fact
and looking at it. It wasn't that I was unhappy. But I kept
on thinking — sometimes surprised, sometimes just
making a note of it, sometimes panic-stricken — "You're
on your own. You're on your own."

What happened?

I know this isn't a tragedy. On Christmas morning, I was
in Clare, driving up the coast to meet a friend who would
give me a lift further up, to Ballyvaughan. I was going to
spend the day walking back over the Burren to my own car.
Suddenly, I heard myself on the radio. I'd recorded a little
piece for that morning's 'Miscellany' about the wonderful
light and colour of Christmas when I was a child, and how
that magic had infused the phrase 'and may perpetual
light shine upon them' for me ever since. And so it has. But
my beautiful god-daughter died when she was eight. I
imagine her held somewhere in some golden radiance. And
the word "perpetual" means that she is gone off into that
light forever. Her suffering, her pointless bravery — all for
nothing. What she went through, and what was lost when
she died — that's what tragedy is. Or my brother, who was
sent to me to mind in London so long ago (there's no getting
through Christmas Day without going over the family in
your mind). He's a grown man now, with a life of his own.
But I see a suffering child in him. He ended a letter to me
about the pain of his childhood: 'I don't blame anyone or
hate anybody. Just me.' Just himself. That's tragedy. And
he is only one of the Irish who might come stumbling out
of England rubbing their eyes if there was a way of taking

the past back. And in the world — I'd just a few weeks before Christmas come back from Manila where I'd been writing about sex-tourism, and children used for sex. I was still full of all that.

I do know perfectly well that I don't deserve any pity in such a world. And I'd planned the day so as to eliminate creeping self-pity. But why should I devalue what was wrong, either? Millions and millions of people besides me have thought that another person is what you need to complete yourself and to offer completion — that together you can unlock the best of the world, and the best of yourself. I was in Holland not long ago and I went on the train to an open-air museum, with ducks and apple-trees and old fishermen's cottages. Suddenly, the most fine rain was borne across the place, on a satiny breeze. "I want to be with someone!" I cried out inside myself. "It is ridiculous to go around open-air museums on your own!" I feel chock-full of experience that it is now too late to share. Until I met Nell I had no right companion to marvel at the world with. I heard her footsteps stop, once, behind me on the forestry road above Glendalough. When I went back she was immobile, open-mouthed, looking at a bird smash the snail in its beak off a rock. In Paris, we found the doorstep where the baby Edith Piaf was born. Nell walked away backward down the street, like a child, unable to pull herself away. I saw things through her absorption in them. I could tell her how I'd seen things when she wasn't there: 'The boat to Paros swung in and out of other islands just casually, as if it was a milk-van dropping a few bottles off...'

How brave widows and widowers are! How resourceful people are, and how many secrets they carry around with them! It is not about sex, the desire to share with another person. But it is about creation. Even though what "together" means is a mystery. I stayed in a village in the Pyrenees last autumn. It was small, quiet. In the evenings, in the square outside the church, a few teenage boys and girls played a kind of badminton. They played as the dusk came down, calling out softly, until it was too dark to make out the glimmering white shuttlecock. The event wouldn't have been different if there had been a person with me, glancing out through the windows of the hotel. But it would have been a whole: us there; it happening. Instead of a fractured thing with me, by myself, knowing that my solitary self was observing this lovely scene.

When I stay with the couple who are my closest friends, I hear them laughing and talking in bed, and sometimes in the middle of the night one of them goes down and makes tea, and when the clock goes off in the morning, they're at it again, talking away.

What happened to me?

My Christmas Day was cleverly arranged. I made luxury sandwiches — avocado and bacon. I packed them and a flask of coffee for myself, and a bottle of water and a carton of gourmet dog-food for Molly, my mongrel collie. When my friend dropped us off at the green road that goes around the flank of the hill above Ballyvaughan, the dog leapt and bounded into the landscape crackling with frost, brilliantly bright in the winter sun. It isn't possible not to be thankful with all your heart for such a high blue sky and such a sweep of sparkling valley. How wise I was to be there! But underneath — I didn't believe in my own wisdom. While loving what I was doing, I didn't believe in it. "How can I be so sensible?" I thought. "Will I be able to keep all this positive stuff up? What will happen next year?"

What happened, to make contentment so precarious? I've been trying here to understand the way things have worked out in my life. And though what I've written is personal, part of my predicament is general. The challenges of middle-age, and the challenges of loneliness — which I know exist even within relationships — confront many more people than me. Just as the same place I grew up in and the same influences I came under affected more people than me. Teachers used to say, "Miss Noticebox!

You're nothing but a noticebox!" But when adults slap children down, and tell them not to be drawing attention to themselves, what are the adults doing? Why do they want the child to stay quiet and go away? Single middle-aged women aren't supposed to kick up, either. Who wants to know about them? If no companion depends on them? If they're nobody's mother? Nobody's wife? Nobody's lover? If they're not famous or powerful? My problems are banal only because so many people share them.

The time and the culture I grew up in proposed to me that somewhere in the creation there was another person — my other half — walking towards me. That person would catch sight of me. But a woman, past the age where she might be contemplated as a sexual partner, is hardly seen. She turns into a silhouette. Nobody scrutinises her detail. She could become a "character" — in Ireland, anyway. But being avidly watched, because you might at any minute make everyone laugh, is a parody of being watched because you are desired. I met two old ladies in a train in California, on the first leg of a long journey. They were on a frank, not to say raucous, quest for husbands. In Ireland you're not meant to mention love, after a certain age. Yet life teaches you to value love more and more. Human love, if you can secure it. And if you can't, you must hope that other loves will bring you through to the end — for a house or a garden, or a country, or a job increasingly well done, or money, or animals ... But how can you confer on those the status that loving a person has?

The dog makes me tender. She couldn't believe her luck that Christmas Day. She'd run up the path ahead of me, and then turn and crouch, looking up at my face in her mild and hopeful way, checking that we were still committed to this heavenly activity. We went along behind Newtown Castle, under the flank of the hill, and then we climbed with the little road up to the ridge where there's an old fort and we sat among stones glittering with ice and had our picnic. That night, I would look around the room of the cottage — Molly deeply asleep on her back, her legs sticking straight up, her pink tummy offered to the air — Hodge, the cat, staring, immobile, at the flame of the Christmas candle. I love these animals much more than I want to say. But they are not children.

Rob has a child. He rang me from time to time over the years, usually when someone we'd both known had died. "I couldn't go to the funeral because I was picking my boy up from school," he might say, or "I last saw him when I was taking my boy for a spin on the bike." One day last year when I was in London he asked me to lunch. I wanted to see him again while I still had my own teeth. So I went to his house and chatted in the big family kitchen with him while he got things ready, and then some friends came and he opened bottles of wine, and then his wife came home from her office and was warmly welcoming to everyone and eventually, nobody wanted to go back to work. Then he and his wife bowed their heads to each other in a quick murmur about domestic arrangements. Then she disappeared for a while. I saw that Rob was watching the door. Then — it was as if the density of the air in the room had changed. A small fair-haired boy in a scuffed school uniform hung in the doorway. He lifted his face to his father in the hope that he wouldn't have to say hello to all of us. This person, waiting to be released to run up to the television, was of a different order from us adults around the table. His head, his soft hair, the school tie badly knotted around his thin neck — the more you looked at him, the more you saw why his father would want to mention him in every sentence — would want to say "My boy, my boy." He told us — in a whisper, but confident — that Arsenal would win the Cup. Then his father gave him the nod and he slipped away.

I would have been a very bad mother, during most of my life. But I'd be a good mother, now. Too late. Sometimes I have to look away from small children — hopping where they stand as their mothers try to put on their little jumpers, or talking to themselves pressed against the window in the seat in front of me in the bus. They are too beautiful to bear. Then again, I see what is done to them. Last year, on an elegant beach in the south of France, I saw a father dangle a terrified little boy at the water's edge, ducking him into the waves. Sometimes, after an episode like that, exhausted by my own cowardice as well as by pity and anger, I think, truthfully, "I just want to be finished with everything." But mostly, the life-force inside cries out. The world looks at middle-aged women and talks about sexual frustration. But, what is it that has been frustrated? Is it that a woman's life is bracketed by two hormonal tides, and that one goes out, in middle-age, and she runs down the beach after it? Is it that the children she hasn't had are calling out within her? It feels so like the body asking for something to begin. It doesn't feel like a farewell. People say without thinking, "Oh, what she needs is sex." That would be a fine distraction. But the longing is in the head and the heart as well as the body.

The body is where it expresses itself. A while ago I tapped out the opening paragraph of something I called "novel". There were just a few lines:

> Sometimes when she wakes up during the night and straightens her limbs her hands slide across her breasts and she is ambushed by a sensation of their softness before she can guard herself against it. Then she sees herself as if from above. A middle-aged woman under a duvet on a bed in her space on the surface of the spinning planet, pressing a face twisted with the anguish of a lonely body down into her own shoulder. She clenches her eyes in shame, as if there were someone to hear her groan. Sometimes she smoothes her sides and her belly and rubs her thighs with her useless hands. She has a roll of fat around her hips. But she is flexible, still. "I'm still a woman!" she says. "Use me! Find someone to use me. Or let me get old — quick, quick!"

She is pleading, I think, not for excitement, but not to become invisible to God.

The remembered fluency with another person, the remembered ease with the self, the complexities of the imagination at last in perfect balance — that's what there is to regret. I went through a time, three or four years ago, when I saw love everywhere. I saw two handsome, middle-aged tourists —Italians, perhaps — in white macs, start to run, laughing, with their arms around each other, when a shower of rain blew down Nassau Street. I saw a middle-aged man I work with drop a kiss on the top of the head of his middle-aged wife as they waited to cross Eden Quay. I wanted someone who had known me when I was young to trace the lines that had come on my face with tender familiarity. And, as well, I wanted to be mad about someone. I wanted more time! And I wanted time to be wiped out, the way it used to be!

Time. I note every day the physical detail of middle-age. The transparent polyps that have formed on the skin of my neck. The first white hair in my eyebrows. Pigment spots on my midriff, which will never tan again. I see people my age cherishing their parents. No service they can offer is too much. If my mother had got old and I had been able to love her, would I be able to love my own ageing body now? If I had had children? How do people arrange to love their ageing selves?

How can you persuade yourself to accept your fortune? I was as fortunate as anyone in the country last Christmas Day, and I knew it. We came down from the ridge, the dog and I, slipping and sliding on the icy track, and we crossed the rushing river at the bottom of the valley and then we set off up the other side through crisp, squeaky snow that had caught behind the ruined walls and stands of trees, there, where there was shelter. In that perfect air, we hummed with energy. We were half-way home. As I am. *'Nel mezzo del camin'*. And back in the cottage, as darkness fell, I piled turf on the range. I tickled the little circular cushion of velvet that is Hodge and woke him up. I opened the wine. My neighbours saw my light go on and at the signal sent a daughter up with a Christmas dinner to me, on a plate, wrapped in tea-towels. I had saved up a Henry James story I'd never read before to have with the meal. There wasn't anyone on earth, as a matter of fact, that I would have preferred to be talking to, rather than reading 'Madame de Mauves'. I was warm. If I cried at the Christmas music on the radio — well, that's almost what it's for. And I was sleepy: that's why I'd walked so far. I had everything. All I needed was to be able to convince myself that I wasn't pitiable because I was alone. And that there was nothing wrong with having so much.

"I don't want to live like this!" I shouted at Nell once, during a row. "I want to live like Colette!" Even in the crisis, we both started to laugh. I'm no Colette. But I long to pick up some small bit of her gift for living, now, when I need it so badly. Colette was in her seventies when she wrote: 'Love, one of the great commonplaces of existence, is slowly leaving mine. The maternal instinct is another great commonplace. Once we've left these behind, we find that all the rest is gay and varied. But one doesn't leave all that behind as and when one pleases ... '

I can't agree with her (not yet, not yet) that life without love is "gay and varied". The new genre of middle-aged women's writing insists in a hectic way on the delights of the post-menopausal condition. We are to become benign witches. But this is meaningless to me. I went to a talk Germaine Greer gave in Dublin a few years ago, hoping to be inspired by her vision of new access to vitality around the age of fifty. The lecture-theatre was packed with women, just as eager as I was, I presume, to listen to someone who spoke to our biological and cultural condition. It was worth going, if only to look at her, because she is so handsome and assured. But she chose, as prima donnas do, to confound expectation. She gave a rather dull academic talk. I want a more plausible prophet. I want to believe that old age is not to be dreaded.

Luckily, in real life, little things make people very content. I see it in the languor with which they answer the door, because they've been curled up in front of the television, or the eagerness with which they reach up to the shelf in a newsagent for the latest *Gardening Weekly* or *The Gramophone*, opening it even as they queue to pay. People do not live in single states of mind. I'm as often happy as not. And whatever it is I am lonely for, it is not for company. I have Yeats' 'company of friends' in my head. I have imaginary companions as real as the girls at the Dunnes Stores checkouts, or the man next door, coming out onto his step for a smoke. "Bookworm," they used to say at school. That's right. I've wormed my way in to what I've read and no one can ever shake me out.

Music is, however, a more dangerous element. It can surprise me, getting at me before I can stop it. Especially the human voice, and especially voices intertwining in sestets, quartets, duets. Voices imploring each other, resting on each other, playing with each other. Even in pop music it is the unison of voices — Dolly Parton and Kenny Rogers, Sarah Brightman and Jose Carreras — that starts a response. I listen in what Martin Amis would call "a miasma of spinst" to pearlfishers, madame butterflies, Rusalkas imploring the moon, countesses grieving for past love. This romantic commentary comes out of the culture around me, reaching for me, trying to ruin me. The trio at the end of *Der Rosenkavalier*, where the older woman gives up on love and sings her line of acceptance and renunciation in intricate relationship with the ecstatic lines sung by Octavian and his new young love strikes me down with sorrow, every time. Except once, when a small, strange cat put its head around the door when it was playing. The cat did nothing but peer in, alertly. Yet it was so other to the music, so here and now — it brought so different a world into the same place as the world of human emotion and human art and human performance — that it distanced the power of the music.

Last Christmas Day I had all my resources marshalled. Health. Landscape. Friends. Food and drink. A book, and music. And my cat and my dog. And those little beings are saving me much more directly than by their company, or by being graceful and amusing. They have given me the measure by which I find my parents wanting. I don't like my mother and father, when I think about them and these animals. Hodge who sits folded into himself and perfectly still, gazing with narrow golden eyes into the mid-distance — a tiny, plushy sphinx. He has a ball of a head, a body like a plump velvet teardrop, wide and innocent paws, a fat tail. "Mrkgnao!" he cries, like the cat in Molly Bloom's basement, when he's hungry. He flops into sleep. "Eck?" he says softly, if he half-wakes, "eck?" "Get that cat out of here," is all my mother or father would have said.

I took it for granted that they had little tenderness for us. They made me accept that, for myself and my brothers and sisters. But I can stop being passive when I think — they would have had no tenderness for Molly! They would have said: "You're not expecting me to mind that dog, are you?" Molly, who when something out in the street frightens her, runs in to where I'm standing, maybe at the sink or the cooker, and presses her thin body against my legs for protection. And I think for the first time — I let myself feel it — how did my mother and my father not care more for the small children around them? How did they not pick them up, not comfort them? How did my father strap his defenseless sons with his army belt? The dog gets her bits of stick and stone and arranges them between her paws so that she can guard them when she's asleep. These animals give me my first measure of what is owed to helpless beings. When I come home, the dog is sometimes waiting against the inside of the front door. The cat slides into the hallway when he hears the key, and looks up at me bravely, and mewls. As I come in I feel that the place has an air of pain, the way the home in Clontarf had. Mammy got the messages when she made her quick visit to the pub at lunchtime to steel herself for Daddy getting up in the afternoon. The children at home, powerless, had to wait for the messages. If I wanted to torment the dog and the cat, there would be nothing they could do.

The thing to do is: go out. That Christmas Day I did what my parents did on Bray Head and on Howth and in Inishowen when they were young and handsome and everything was going to be good. I sat on a headland, and looked out at the world. The dog and I sat against a wall above Fanore and commanded, like conquerors, the prospect where this island ends in a shimmering haze of sea and sky. The turquoise shapes of Aran lay calm out on the horizon. There is always somewhere further to go. Each time I set off from Dublin in the direction of Naas or Maynooth or Swords — starting off to find something out, on my own, no one to worry about but myself, radio on, petrol in the tank and money in my bag — that is the best there is. I'm conscious of it always, and full of inarticulate thanks. And I often wonder whether it is by accident or unconscious design that I'm doing exactly what my father did. He used to disappear every week to write a page from around Ireland for the back of *The Sunday Press* called 'On the Road, with Terry O'Sullivan'. And later, when he was doing 'Dubliner's Diary', he didn't stick to Dublin. He built in the events he made his milieu — the Rose of Tralee Festival, the Galway Oyster Festival, the Castlebar Song Festival. When honorary secretaries hurried forward across hotel lobbies to greet him with the utmost servility, snapping their fingers for Terry's bag to be taken, Terry's Paddy to be poured, it looked as if he needed to be bribed to be there. But for all his jaunty, impersonal tone, he was there out of love. He had an intemperate love for the fabric of Ireland. And I reap the harvest he sowed for me, in that, as in other things.

There are things to see. I happened on an art-work that had been installed in a deserted house up a quiet country road between Belturbet and Clones, in that mysterious country where you don't know where the border is. The late-autumn day, when I was there, was silent and brown. The house had been left unlocked for whoever would come. With beating heart I pushed the door back and went in to the stillness of the rooms. The artist had covered the wall of the kitchen with shoes — worn shoes — and let blue dust accumulate in them. The marks on the shoes — the heels unevenly worn, the bulges toes had made, the cracks where foot and leather had accommodated each other — were pathetically faithful to the fleshiness and weight of the humans that had worn them. There were marks on the rough plaster walls, and up the pitch-pine stairs, envelopes from old letters, and emigrants' luggage labels. A bedroom was hung with sheets like the sails of a ship. The sedgy fields outside and rushes and willow scrub, and all the people gone ... When I started the car going away a Bach tape came on, and I turned it off — quickly — because such elegance and attack isn't right. Not for this Ireland. But is it not wonderful that what was in the house was shaped and artful, not incoherent, like suffering? These sudden transformations happen all the time in Ireland: they are out there for me.

I'll go out to see such things. Or rather — things will make themselves seen. I might want to remember perfectly the stained-glass at Chartres, but actually remember, with perfection, the sticky surface of a table in a café near the station. I was in Dubrovnik on my own, in a season of torrential rain. I remember the look of the city well enough. But what I really saw, as I waited at a bus-stop near a patch of waste ground, was — fully — the rain hit the puddle in front of me. I went up north of Toronto once, on a bus, to a small town. I spent a weekend there, on my way to somewhere else. I got a room in the usual, deathly businessman's hotel — sealed picture windows, a dark and empty restaurant off the lobby echoing to the tinny sound of Musak, a chlorine-smelling pool, with a salesman or two through the glass wall silently pumping at the Stairmaster. This was a town of two or three streets, a place which had served nineteenth-century settlers and pre-war farmers and has no real role now. The weather was dull and cold. There was nothing for me to do. But I walked those streets of small houses in their grey winter shuttering, contented. The place had no significance. But it seemed to have meaning. And sometimes there is so much meaning that it gives an electric shock — like my first time in Athens, when I threw open the shutters of the hotel-room and there, floating on the skyline, was the Parthenon, a complete surprise, golden against navy-blue.

Perhaps places are for me what books were for my mother? They are altogether full of promise. They assuage some of the regret for all the lives I never had.

What is out there will be my partner. What I write about it will be the record of the relationship. Where I sat above the Atlantic, last Christmas afternoon, turns out to be almost an illustration. Behind me, up in the Burren, nothing knitted together. There's a pre-historic burial site. There's a village abandoned in the Famine. There's a tiny twelfth-century church. There's a holy well. There's a mound of shells near a cooking-pit. Each thing is itself, discrete. Near each other, and made from the same material, but never flowing into each other. That's how the life I have described here has been. There has been no steady accumulation: it has all been in moments.

But in front of me there is a vista — empty, but inexpressibly spacious. Between those two — landscape of stone, and wide blue air — is where I am.

SELECTED
JOURNALISM

With thanks, to Conor Brady

PEOPLE

Birth

The streets are so empty in the first wash of light that seagulls inhabit them, tearing at food, high-stepping down the middle of Fitzwilliam Street. In the whole long Georgian vista down to Holles Street Hospital, nothing moves in the dawn. But see that sash window high up at the back of the hospital, pushed up to let in the summer morning?

Inside that room, the radio plays cha-cha-cha music, and on the bed a young woman with sweat in her hair is trying to push her first baby into the world. Her man has red hair and an earring, and he is bent in to her shoulder. He's holding her lovely, strong hand. "Oh Jesus," she says. "Oh fuck." The midwife is listening to the heartbeat through a little rubber thing that she moves around the big belly. The midwife feels another pain coming. "Ah, it's only a little one," Patricia says, laughing a bit. But sometimes she swears again, not even knowing she's doing it, utterly absorbed in her huge effort, as the lounge-bar music plays imperturbably, on and on.

Just after 5 a.m. it was when Patricia went into labour. Now it is 6 a.m., a most beautiful morning of rose and pearl. Sometimes they whisper a little joke to each other, the young woman and man. The nurse is swabbing between Patricia's legs. I can see the top of the baby's head. But it goes back in again, then peeks again, then disappears again.

Patricia's face goes purple with the effort of pushing. She braces her feet against the bodies of the nurse and the midwife. "Ten more minutes," the midwife says to her, working with her, urging her, praising her. Time is not like time anywhere else — there is only the pace of the event, nothing can make it go faster, or slower, once the birth begins. There is nothing in the world but this.

The midwife picks up a scissors. Patricia starts to pant and grabs the gas mask. You could faint with the intensity of the scene.

Then, most amazingly, the baby slides out to be one of the human beings in the room. All purple and covered in slime, but perfect, perfect. Little Tony, from Wicklow. The nurse puts him on his mother's stomach and big Tony, overcome, runs out of the room.

"Oh, I don't believe it," Patricia says. Her face is completely simplified. Everything here is more real and true than anything else imaginable. She takes the tiny naked being and bends and kisses his silky head with ecstatic tenderness. "I don't believe it," she says, over and over again. And she says to the nurse and midwife who have been with her all night, "Oh, thank you, thank you!"

"Sure you did all the work," the midwife says.

They're like goddesses, those midwives and nurses. In simple pastel shifts, white shoes on their tanned legs, supple and fit and bright-eyed — they could do anything. Four babies they've delivered since midnight, each delivery an absolute event. They don't get tired because they don't get bored. And because the delivery ward is such a place of joy. Outside, in rows of beds, the new mothers sleep like felled oxen, exhausted. Babies wail in their cots. But that is for the future. When a healthy baby is born, the most fundamental event there is has happened.

Night or day, it makes no difference to the delivery ward. Elsewhere, the business of a big hospital is beginning. At 5 a.m., the newspapers arrive. The cook comes in. Sliced pans are delivered, great stacks of them. Night sister prepares her morning report for matron. Matron — on that day — was gathering her papers for a trip to Brussels, as an adviser to an EC committee on biomedical and health research. The Master was in his office. It was almost a shock to see him, so overwhelmingly a world of women is a maternity hospital at night.

Up on the top floor is the other place where there is no night or day. In the intensive-care ward, you hear the silence of the babies. You long for them to cry but they can't cry, because they are sedated. Tiny little starfish things, literal scraps of life. The nurses watch the respirators, adjust the dials, move the tubes. Somewhere the radio news was talking about Bosnia. Here, the parents of the sickest baby had just left after a night beside its cot. Sister did not think that that baby would live.

Still, when you looked out the window, and tried to believe in the outside world, there was hardly any traffic. The ordinary day had not begun. The quietness — the sense of beginning — made the scene back in the delivery ward even more precious.

Patricia had been tidied up and washed, and she had a mug of tea. Tony was sitting beside the bed in the calm sunshine that flooded the room. Little Tony — pink and beautiful now — was between them in his cot. They gazed at him. He slept. Sparrows skittered across the roofs outside. A new family; a new day.

On Ireland

The year I started writing for *The Irish Times*, I met a woman who had had enough of living without hope. She emigrated once before, but came back in the early 1970s because her husband had a rare specialisation which he wanted to put at the service of Ireland. But now they were off again, to Canada, because they were tired of having no money. "Sure you could go easily too," she said to me. "You must be mad to stay here."

I took this comment very much amiss, I can tell you. I'm not mad at all, and neither are a great many people who choose to live here, come what may. It is a bit embarrassing to say so, but there is such a thing as loving Ireland. There are good reasons for sticking it out in this damp little shambles of a democracy on the edge of the Western world.

My reasons may seem trivial or insufficient to you, but I hope that you're not going to suppose me either ignorant or uncaring of the bitterer elements in the mix that living in Ireland is.

To begin with a commonplace: I like the way people behave here. I lived in an England so poisoned by class distinction that I never get tired of the exuberance of personality here which refuses to be bound by notions of status. People don't "know their place". Of course, this makes for indiscipline, but what the hell.

I also like the way charm is thrown around, not husbanded for special occasions. I like the way everyone bows to strength of personality and grace of personality. There are whole cultures where being dull is an asset. Not here, it isn't, not here.

There is also a great deal of civility around. When you get into trouble in Ireland, usually as a result of an almost florid national inefficiency, you get rescued by an equally florid display of kindness. And daily life is packed with courtesies, from the number of "pleases" and "thank-yous" involved in buying the newspaper, to staying for the proffered cup of tea even though you haven't time, to dropping some important ideological quarrel because your opponent's father went into hospital that morning.

I worked here for an English boss who never made head nor tail of anything in Irish life because he didn't like us and so wasn't interested in cracking these codes. I, personally, enjoy them no end, and envy the exquisitely subtle people who decipher them faultlessly — such a person is just as likely to be a night porter as a statesman, I might add.

I like the sounds of Ireland, especially of people talking or singing in Irish, but also the amazing level of individual articulateness in English, irrespective of social background. I like accents — they're a form of richness. The ease with which people talk well is not just a decoration or a flavour: it bespeaks minds and hearts which are still alive and supple; it is an unconscious affirmation of dignity.

Because words are still meaningful here there are very high standards of expression in journalism and in RTÉ. I tried living in Southern California once, where there was no form of intelligent media life. For me, anyway, the perfect climate didn't recompense.

Which brings me to the physical Ireland, which it is easy to love. The weather is interesting. So is the landscape. I miss the churches and lovely villages of places like Suffolk or Bavaria or Umbria, but instead we have holy wells and Iron-Age forts and rushy lakes and magnificent beaches.

And we have pubs. There is hardly a spot in the country that doesn't have, near enough to hand, a nice, quiet, dim bar with the glasses all shiny and a peaceful barman. In those numinous spaces love-affairs are begun and ended, family crises are faced, criminals conspire, deals are done. I don't know how they manage these things in Iran, or Turkey, or Outer Mongolia. I don't know how anyone who doesn't use pubs can enjoy living here, or even be said to live here at all. I'm going to live in one as soon as I get the old-age pension. Old ladies are always treated with great respect in pubs.

From the pub to the church ... It is said that Ireland is a religious country, and I have met many excellent people who for that reason wouldn't dream of living here. They find the whole thing distasteful — the crowded churches, the shrines and statues and ubiquitous Catholic paraphernalia, the bishops in their palaces, the priests running schools, etc. etc. But I like it that the Irish people, or a great many of them, anyway, have a vivid spiritual life.

Faith is in itself extraordinary, but it is part of the ordinary here. I myself look for the separation of Church and State, but not for an irreligious society. However dimmed or demeaned by the Catholic Church as an institution, the general message of the New Testament is alive in this country, and so is the mystery of the Incarnation.

People go to Mass because they like it and love it and feel the need for it. This repeated, intimate contact with mystery is no small thing. That we largely believe we have souls, deepens the level on which every debate in Ireland is conducted and makes each smallest social change acquire momentous overtones. To want to change Ireland is a serious business, not just a fad of youth.

And this, finally, is a reason for staying here. It is a serious place. Very few people are able or willing to drop out of this society, to just accept it as it is and live for themselves. We're too small, too poor and too well-informed. Almost everyone has strong political views and they are the result of experience and analysis on however crude a plane.

They're not unexamined ideological positions. We go on and on to each other about morality and taxation and farmers and Dublin 4 and all the rest of it, and tedious as this self-examination gets it is a form of real political life, it is a forum, and in it lie the grounds for hope that we might make a better country.

Neither the issues nor the people and factions debating them are trivial. Nobody is in it for the money or publicity or out of sheer cynical energy. If you or I moved in the morning to Canada or somewhere, and there were an election here in the spring, could either of us bear not to know the results? I couldn't, myself.

I don't know how we all got into the position of simultaneously feeling responsible for Ireland and not being able to do anything about it. But that is the nature of the dilemma that makes us a fretful, conscious citizenry. We suffer for each other. To me, that has more value than cultivating my own garden. But the real challenge will be, when things get better, to be able to rejoice with each other too. I'd hate to feel that the woman who says we're all mad to stay here is right, and that it is a desire for suffering, a death-in-life, that really makes Ireland the seductress she is.

Because I am seduced by Ireland. I know that 1986 began grey, and became black. I know that we've lost the belief that something is going to make something better, a Fianna Fáil Government, an Atlantic oil-find, or the Anglo-Irish Agreement. I am frightened by the fears that lay behind the rejection of divorce.

But, sometimes an absolute flashes out. In the past year, on television, I've seen the faces of two men — Peadar O'Donnell and Noel Browne — who led noble lives here. For as long as Ireland can solicit such lives, it can certainly solicit mine.

On Human Dignity

I was walking past O'Connell Bridge House the other day when this man stopped me. He showed me a piece of paper with 'Driver Testing Centre, O'Connell Bridge House' written on it. "Could you tell me where that is?" he said. "You're standing in front of it," I said. "Look, it's written on the door." "Oh, is it?" he said. "The thing is, I can't read."

I went on my way, idly wondering whether people who can't read should be allowed to drive cars. How many road signs are symbols, and how many depend on words? And also wondering, as always, how *anybody* learns to read. How does the miracle work? What happens? I remember the exact moment myself, and it was the only transcendent thing that ever happened to me. There were still words in the sentence I was looking at that I couldn't understand, and they were like black holes. But light seemed to jump from each word I could understand to the next word I could understand, so that I could grasp the general meaning of the whole shape. I ran all the way to the shop, to tell them all there. There was no one much to show off to at home.

The miracle doesn't happen to everyone. Last week, I went to a little event in a room in Mountjoy Square in Dublin. Men and women who have been learning to read and write, through the Dublin Literacy Scheme, were reading their first pieces of work in public. Need I say that the atmosphere of first-night nerves was intense, that people were standing outside on the steps, dragging desperately on cigarettes, that in the room, practically every pair of hands you could see were shaking. Yet, they did it. Haltingly, or helter-skelter. "I have a dog called Max." "Being un-em-ployed is very bor-ing." "Christ-mas is a happy occ-asion for fam-il-ies." All ages and accents. All kinds of faces. As each person read aloud, the others followed the words in a booklet. Some of them followed the lines with their fingers: adults, using the gestures of children.

Nobody went out and found these people. They came to look for literacy themselves, most of them in fear and trembling. When you can't read or write, they were telling me afterwards, you think you're nobody. You have no confidence. You lie and deceive to cover up. So you have to face your whole self when you go to enquire about classes. It is much more than just seeking a skill.

And it isn't easy to acquire the skill at the wrong time of your life. These were adults, who talk and think with all the sophistication of adults, yet they had to go back to being like children. They could only express themselves in writing like six-year-olds, yet what they wanted to express had to do with jobs, journeys, Nelson Mandela, bringing up children, Shamrock Rovers, money. This must be the hardest thing — to be able to run like a hare in your mind, but be hobbled by words.

As they read, you could hear that their mouths were dry with nervousness. When they'd come to a shaky stop, the others would applaud and applaud. There were three women who were more or less holding each other's hands to keep each other going. That's how they must have learnt, too: together. These particular women were from a notoriously deprived area of the North inner-city. Usually, they would be described as under-privileged. So they are, on many levels. But not that night. When you saw their courage and determination, and the resource they have in each other, and the amount of laughs they were getting out of the situation, you couldn't but see them as privileged. Other people leave school and never face another challenge in their lives.

Not that literacy is just a problem of the poor, or of women. Most students are men, as a matter of fact, probably because the scheme — relying as it does on voluntary labour — can offer one-to-one tuition, so you don't have to face a group to start with. A learner gets two hours tuition a week for thirty weeks and that, even though it is only the equivalent of two weeks at school, is enough to get them started. But three-quarters of all the people who turn up at Mountjoy Square are unemployed. They could easily do a full-time course, and that's what they want to do. The Dublin Literacy Scheme, however, doesn't have the funds or staff to run full-time courses. Even though it has almost as much funding as the rest of the country's literacy schemes put together.

One woman read out a piece about being able to understand her Christmas cards for the first time. She had kept all her cards over the years, but only now can she read them. This is the least of the pains of illiteracy. You can't read instructions so you're afraid, say, giving medicine to a child, that you're making a mistake. You can't read the signs in railway stations, so you're not sure of your stop. You can't hope for promotion in your work. You can't write letters home. You can't help your children with their schoolwork. You can't buy own-brand goods, because there are no pictures on the labels. The National Adult Literacy Agency has an information pack about its work, and it quotes a few sentences that sum up a social tragedy. 'Any time the AGM came up I was put forward as secretary and I could never take it. Then they'd say "There are people in the club for many years and they get a lot of pleasure out of it, but they're not willing to put anything into it." Now I was willing and I'd love to but I couldn't, and I couldn't turn around and say: "I can't spell, I can't read."'

Chance, or ill-luck, kept these people back. They were put down the back of the class and forgotten, or they were out of school a lot with sickness, or they'd had to help at home, or they had worked from childhood and been too tired to learn. One beautiful girl had been to a very fashionable school. Her English teacher, infuriated by her slowness, had slapped her head, and this girl wouldn't even try after that. As it turns out, she's dyslexic. But nobody understood that, or cared. She left school unable to read.

But she can read now. I heard her. Her tutor sat beside her, beaming and nodding, like a hen with a chick.

There is no fee for being taught to read or write. The scheme takes the view that literacy is a right, and you shouldn't have to pay for your rights. But this means that it just barely survives. It has one full-time paid organiser, and one assistant. Between them, they have to test and train the voluntary tutors, compile teaching materials, administer all the meetings of the students and the teachers, do what research they can, and try to develop outlets for the students who master literacy and are now longing to go on to more learning. If one of those two people gets sick, I don't know what happens. Even so, the Dublin scheme is much the most fortunate in the country. You can get some help in most places through the VECs. But there is no real State scheme: of 1,224 literacy tutors in the country in 1990, 1,154 were completely unpaid.

More and more people are looking for help with reading and writing. The Altrusa/VEC scheme in Cork, for example, has 150 working couples "and more coming all the time". Presumably, life has become impossible to manage without literacy. Presumably, too, this is one problem which a single big push would almost solve. It is a legacy of the past — of school classes of fifty or sixty children, of unkindness towards children, of a time when if the family failed the child, there were no other sources of help. The Department of Education could increase its small grant towards literacy provision for, say, five years: perhaps the teachers' unions — some of whose predecessors short-changed these people — would care to lobby?

There was nothing at all dramatic about the reading in Mountjoy Square. We were all squashed in on plastic chairs, and someone had to run out for milk for the paper cups of tea. It wasn't even funny. There was too much tension in the room for that. But look at all that was happening in that room. Here were human beings who had been denied their birthright of literacy, and who had sturdily set out to retrieve it. They were the last people you'd be sorry for. So, if the reading threatened to move the spectator to tears, it wasn't from pity. It was because you don't often see, overcoming all the awkwardness, such a display of human dignity.

The Language of
the Dispossessed

When the schools opened in September, 1993, there was a piece in *The Irish Times* about little children, on their first day ever in a new primary school, which for the moment is camping out in a sports centre, at Poppintree, near Ballymun, Dublin. As always, how the children reacted to school was very funny. And a bit sad and wistful, too, for adults. What was unusual — not that they know it — about their school was that it is all-Irish, and that it has been started to cope with the overflow from another all-Irish school — Scoil an tSeachtar Laoch, in the middle of Ballymun.

Parents who couldn't get their kids in there could have sent them to one of the excellent local English-language schools. But they wouldn't. Rather than educate them through English, they raised money and borrowed a site and got a teacher themselves, got recognition from the Department of Education, and now there are twenty-one children starting off. In time, it'll thrive like its parent school. It'll have a past-pupils' club and a champion hurling team, and some little person who is four now will be back, as a former pupil is back in Ballymun this year, to do teacher-training practice. For the time being, however, it's more like a hedge school than anything else.

That first day, some of the mothers explained why they'd chosen to take this trouble for their children. "He's Irish, and he's entitled to have the language," one of them said. And another — "I just want him to speak Irish. That's all."

How, I wondered to myself, had these ideals survived? How could it be that they are apparently alive in one of the most disadvantaged areas of Ireland, when for years, well-heeled, privileged people, and extremely influential people, such as certain educational so-called philosophers, have done everything they could to characterise learning Irish as useless and anti-progressive?

Because if there is one place in Ireland where people have little time for intellectual luxuries, it is Ballymun. I went out there, and I saw the children from the new school being left back to groups of mammies, blown about by the wind as they waited for the battered minibus at the entrances to the tower blocks. Some of the blocks have been beautifully done up. But most of the public space in Ballymun is still horrible. Outside one urine-reeking entrance, there were spills of oil, for example, where someone had thrown a deep-fat fryer over a balcony. All kinds of people are put in Ballymun. The community has to cope with problems that would destroy somewhere less resilient. I saw two drug deals, myself, within minutes, in the cheerless shopping centre. At 10 o'clock in the morning.

Yet a few hundred yards away, in the playgrounds of Scoil an tSeachtar Laoch (the seven heroes of 1916, after whom the highest tower-blocks are named), 250 little children, each more spotless than the next in their neat uniforms, played and studied in the language of their forebears. As the free choice of their parents.

Twenty years ago, it was a matter of sit-ins and arrests and unshakeable determination to get this school going. "A parish priest that was there at the time said it to me straight," a woman who was involved told me. "He said, 'No working-class person can afford to give their child an academic career, and Irish is academic'." He surely just wanted his disadvantaged parishioners to do the best for themselves. The stunning thing — the thing unimaginable when I was young — is that the Ballymun parents think Irish is the best. They are quite sure that education through Irish is the most useful thing they could possibly give their kids.

And they've never heard of Professor Joe Lee. The day I was out with the parents, Dublin City University, just down the road, announced its B.Sc. degree in finance, computing and enterprise, to be taught entirely in Irish. Part of the thinking behind that initiative is that enterprise depends on confidence, and confidence depends on a secure sense of self-identity, and Irish identity is affirmed by the language which is unique to Ireland and which contains Ireland's history. Joe Lee is famously associated with those propositions.

The woman put them a little differently. "I want my young fella to have his own language. English isn't our language." Or — "Look at the poor aborigines. Look at the state they're in because their own things were taken away from them." Or — "Like you're sitting there and Nuacht comes on the telly and it's desperate, it's a disgrace, an Irish person not knowing what they're saying. I want my kids to have their own language." Or — "If they start out with the two languages, it'll be no bother to them some day to learn German, or anything else they want to." Or — "It gives them that bit extra, having Irish. My two are fluent. They're only working in McDonald's in Phibsboro at the moment. But they'll have that at the back of them when they go for an interview."

They're striving to say that it gives their children something to be proud of, because it is native and distinctive, to have Irish. The children will have that pride. The pride is the weapon in trying to succeed in the world, not the Irish in itself. Having Irish makes you just that bit superior: that's what's believed. The man in a shop-van leaned over to serve a little boy and asked him where he went to school. "Oh — you're at the *posh* school," he said, not particularly pleased, when he was told "the Irish school". It's a far cry, is it not, from the old attitude that Irish is "no good to you"?

Fluency in the language is a badge of *enhanced* opportunity in Ballymun. People put their children down for the Irish school soon after they're born. One woman who did that said to me: "I used to pass this school on the way to my own school, and I felt that the kids here were — well, not better than us, but more educated, like. And I thought they were happier coming out at dinner-time ... " These are not "Irish language enthusiasts", these parents. Any bit of Irish they know themselves, they learnt recently. They're not trying to convert anybody. They couldn't care less if other people in Ireland speak Irish or not. They wouldn't know the difference between one Irish-language organisation and another. They've far less experience, even, than middle-class people, of sending their children off to Coláistí Samhraidh, because nobody around has the money to pay for those. These people, by themselves, somehow saw the whole thing with a new-born clarity. "All the English schools there are in Ireland!" a parent from the new little school said to me. "Isn't it unbelievable that we had to fight for an Irish one?"

How did it live in them, this patriotism? Where did the spores lurk, while official Ireland was exterminating this kind of thing in case it led to sympathy with the IRA? I asked them all, looking for a clue. Why does Irish matter to you? Was it your father? Your mother? Did someone tell you? Was it your school? Is it political? But there was nothing you could put your finger on. "We were taught to hate the language," one person said. "The teachers hated it themselves. But I always knew that there was something behind it all ... " And another man — a man who's been instrumental in getting both schools going — explained how he got involved. "My mother went down the country with the neighbours and the neighbours were from the Gaeltacht. And I came back from England and went down to see my mother. And there was an oul' dog there and it wouldn't come when I called it and they told me it only came if you called it in Irish. So I started calling it in Irish ... "

The mystery of it. This isn't the way Irish was supposed to survive. But it is surviving. "When Ballymun was built," this man says, "there wouldn't have been more than three or four people in the flats who could have a conversation in Irish. Now, there are more than a thousand."

Of course, it's a long way between that and being able to do, say, the fabulous new DCU B.Sc. in finance, computing and enterprise. Some of Scoil an tSeachtar Laoch's pupils are going to RTCs, and some are clerks in the Civil Service. But none is obviously poised to achieve great things. Ballymun families just don't have the resources to send boys and girls to third-level. It would be better for the language, you might think, if it were Clongowes parents, or Gonzaga's, who felt so strongly about Irish. But then, no one would have thought — to take an example — about the Moriarty brothers,' P. J. of the ESB and the broadcaster Miceál O Muircheartaigh, when they were children in very humble circumstances in Co Kerry, that they would rise to positions of huge influence in Ireland, and use that influence for the language. Ballymun may make a mark yet. As long as there are people who speak the language, some of those people will be exceptional.

The kids are on their way to bilingualism. They squirm in a scrum at the back of the minibus. A tiny, cheerful, Paul McGrath-coloured fellow surfaces. "Srón," he says, pointing to his nose. "Súile," and he squinches up his eyes. He leaps off the bus. "Slán!" they all call. Douglas Hyde and all those, leaning over the bar of heaven, must be weeping with joy.

"It's because of multi-channel television," someone suggested. "It's because we're in the EC. They see that other people speak their own languages. So why not us?" But where did they pick up the conviction that Irish is more ours than the English we speak?

Did all the gestures towards the language, that seemed so hypocritical at the time — the cúpla focail, the Croke Park programmes, familiar names like Aras an Uachtaráin — did those little things keep it going? Whatever — the undertakers had better not bury Irish yet. Life is flowing back into its extremities.

Ireland's Class Act

Let's change the subject from politics for a minute. Let's consider the resonances, in Ireland, of Mrs Alan Clark's remark about her husband's talkative lovers that, quite frankly, if you bed "below-stairs" people you can expect trouble. "Nobody would say that kind of thing here," an Irish patriot said to me.

But they would — they do — say exactly those kinds of things at dinner parties in Georgian houses. It's just that the people in Ireland who would consider themselves upper-class the way Jane Clark — a lieutenant's daughter, I believe — considers herself upper-class do not figure in public life in the Republic. Their Don Juans, unfortunately, do not go into politics here. They may behave in private much the same as Alan Clark does, but since private life is all they have, their diaries are not offered for publication. Apart from a bit of aimless sycophanctic journalism when the odd alcoholic or otherwise déclassé Big House person is unwise enough to talk to some cheap Sunday newspaper reporter, the doings of such people are hardly reported.

What's to report? The former landlord class don't run businesses or industries much, and they don't enter into national debates, and they don't seek national roles. They don't even come to Dublin if they can help it, the capital of the Republic being so much more alien to them than their own country towns. They don't write memoirs like Alan Clark's, because outside a memorable day on Lough Corrib, say, or a try scored dusty decades ago, or a medal brought home from the RDS, or the achievements of a hunter famed in three provinces, there is little to write about. The gossip columns which in England are filled by trivia about the aristocracy are filled in this country by trivia about our own handful of *nouveaux riches*. But that doesn't mean that Ireland doesn't contain people who, in their own eyes, form a quasi-aristocracy. In such circles, Mrs Clark's remark is the least that would be said if one of their own were to have an affair with the mother and daughters of an ordinary Irish family.

Of course, this snobbery is hidden. An example is the discussion in the letters page of *The Irish Times* recently about the position of Protestants in the Republic. Class issues were never mentioned. It was suggested that the decline in the Protestant population here was due to the Catholic Church's divisive marriage laws, as if everyone concerned were high-minded to a degree. Of course *Ne Temere* did its bit of harm. But many Irish Protestants of a certain class would sooner marry a monkey than an Irish Catholic. The servants — the "below stairs people" — were always Catholics.

Irish society does indeed contain a class that considers itself superior to every other class. But it contains no class that considers itself inferior to that class. The assumption of superiority causes no pain or resentment. They live their way: we live ours. No matter how upwardly mobile Irish peasants may be, they can never become Anglo-Irish. It is not possible.

The old gentry don't even set the standards of good taste. Mr Haughey, for example, put together a highly original, eclectic, personal style, and so did Dr Tony O'Reilly. Both use elements of old-money style — who would not, given how wonderful the old houses and gardens are? — but they include other elements as well. There are no titles here, and Irish people are free to invent themselves, instead of being expected, like our European neighbours, to imitate the leathery old aristos whose funerals get into *Hello!*.

Any cross-over between classes is so very, very unlikely that it does not even have to be guarded against. The old families — well, nobodies like myself are old stock, too, no doubt, but have nothing to prove it with — go to school and university in England, if possible. So though we all meet at point-to-points, we do not mix at that dangerous period of our lives when the hormones are active and young men and women believe that their love can overleap such petty things as rank. We don't therefore have Montague and Capulet scenarios where little girls from Darndale are taken up the beech-lined drive-way to be introduced to Mama who is dead-heading roses in the walled garden. Long ago, when UCD was in Earlsfort Terrace, and Unionist sprigs came down to Trinity, such misalliances were possible. But accidents can hardly happen now. The young ones photographed at hunt balls and the like for the "society" pages of magazines are homogeneous: you hardly ever see one called Sharon or Maolíosa or Jason.

Most of us have never been to a hunt ball. But little as we know about Dungarvan-in-the-rain people, they know even less about us. They don't understand the endless, fine gradations that utterly divide, say, a periwinkle-picker from a girl "in the bank". We *all* look like nobodies to the former landlord class. The absolute differences between 60 acres, 150 acres and no acres are lost on them. If they surveyed the bronzed bodies of Irish kids on a Greek beach, they wouldn't know that the ones who work in a hairdresser are as distant from the ones who go to college as all of them are from an Irish-based Sloane. We have no journalism, much less literature, to guide the inquirer in this subject. I have never seen a study, for example, of the significance of announcing your engagement in a newspaper. No one I know has ever done it. A family must at some point in its evolution *decide* to do it for the first time.

Tom Flanagan, who wrote *The Year of the French*, has been a keen student of the Irish scene for a very long time. He once remarked that the English have a complicated class system and they never tire of describing it, and the Americans have a complicated class system, though they pretend they haven't. "And the Irish have a complicated class system," he said, *but they won't tell you what it is.*"

That is true. The *easy* part of the Irish class system is that the gentry are supposed to be on top and no one cares. Their manners are a separate issue — being a paying guest in their homes can be made hideous by a kind of talking that is more like shrieking. But one can always stay in some smeary, rasher-smelling, nylon-sheeted B&B if being shouted at in an Anglo-Irish accent is too much to take. That's not class resentment.

It is the rest of the social map that is the minefield. I don't know how Mrs Alan Clark would find her way around it. It is not always clear who is tacky and naff and who isn't, and it isn't signified, in Ireland, by accent. A great many servant-class Irish girls, for instance — the sweet girls who do humble jobs like waitressing with great charm and earnestness — are far too good for Alan Clark. He's vulgar compared with them. He's fun, of course, but he's shop-soiled.

Quite frankly, as Mrs Clark might say, people are better off sticking to their own kind. Difficult as it may be, in a country where most people seem much the same, to get to the bottom of the mystery of who exactly their own kind are.

The Gold Coast of
County Down

On a soft, grey summer Saturday there was a fête in the grounds of the big house. In the ruins of an abbey, on the lower lawn, a group sang madrigals, and old ladies, perched on their shooting sticks in the soaked turf, read out the epitaphs on the family tombstones to each other. Hundreds of years of the same name, stretching back. Babies for the Bonny Baby competition were being pushed in lacy buggies past the flowerbeds and along the great beech paths. In the village pub, nestling in the picturesque square beside the entrance-gates to the estate, high tea was being served.

Down the road, on the outskirts of town, the whites of the cricketers stood out on the vivid green of the pitch. Inland, a fat little girl clopped past the antique shops of a village street on her pony. Out at the seaside resort, it was gusty enough for raincoats. Elderly couples sat in their coats in the ice-cream parlours. BMWs criss-crossed neat roads between village and town heading for a game of tennis here, a sailing club there. In the car-parks of shopping centres the bags from Marks and Spencer and Boots and Mothercare were being stowed in spotless car-boots. Sussex-beyond-the-sea. North County Down.

It was the weekend Mary Robinson shook Gerry Adam's hand. "The stupid, stupid woman," the young woman at a charity lunch spat out. "Not just stupid," the young woman's husband added, "but silly." "That's the end of her, here," their friend said. Ancient reactions, coming from the mouths of coolly amusing young people, gleaming and modern, like models in an advertisement. They hadn't meant to let their anger show: this old stuff is uncool. Had they talked to each other about the President's visit before I brought it up? "Oh, *no*. It's bor-ing," they chanted. "Boring." "Boring." "Boring." The four of them round the table softly batted the word around.

In a beautifully decorated old house in Holywood, all pine and dried flowers, a present from him to her is on the wall. A painting of their other place, in France. They get away to it quite a bit. "A wee mortar bomb in Poleglass woke me up the other morning," the wife says. "You can hear explosions across the Lough. I do wonder, sometimes, why we're so fortunate, when they're so unfortunate. But then, I'm a blow-in."

She sends her children — Catholics — to the Church of Ireland school. "Why should they be segregated from their friends on the basis of where they worship on a Sunday?" Their Presbyterian and Anglican playmates came to their First Holy Communions. When Catholics are about three per cent of the population, and everyone shares the same social scene to the point of getting the same party eats from Tony at the delicatessen, separatist gestures, one understands, would be crass. "You make it as a Catholic," a watchful insider once said, "by behaving like a Protestant."

"We could have lived in Manchester, but this is a far safer place to bring up the children." That seems to her the basis on which she has chosen to live in north Down. Sunlight spills across the lovely rooms of the house — a house half the price of a comparable one in Manchester. The children play in the middle of the road in this leafy cul-de-sac. The consultant surgeon next door is trimming his hedge.

"The wealth around here is amazing," she says. "The mansions are hidden away, but you can look down on them when you're flying into Belfast city airport. And everyone has a second home. Lots of them go to Donegal because it's not *really* in the South. And we were at a party the other night with a couple — a young couple — and they've a second home in America. And he drives a Porsche and she has an Audi Estate." What does the Porsche driver do? He's a barrister.

Sometimes just like England, north Down is. Sometimes like wealthy America, where the highway out from Belfast runs past Atlantic Homecare and the Kart Stadium and the shopping mall. But off the roundabout, down into Bangor, sturdy, Victorian Northern Ireland reappears. The road cuts down through respectable streets, past the British Legion Hall — foundation laid by Maude, Lady Clanmorris: opened by Viscount Bangor — to the harbour front, where, under the clock-tower, on summer evenings, the evangelists preach. "On this Father's Day you can embrace the eternal Father in heaven. Tonight you can have eternal life. You will be a god in heaven, and thank you for your attention ... " They pack their unsold videos and the cardboard box with their jar of instant coffee into their van. As it gets dark, bouncers take up position along the harbour front outside the chip-shops and pubs.

A fight broke out, that Saturday night, and one boy was kicking another around the tarmac of the marina parking lot, against a backdrop of £70,000 yachts. "One of the reasons I love Northern Ireland," a woman had said to me that day, "is because we don't bother so much about class here. We're more cultured, really, than the same kind of people in England." Someone else had said that rich and poor are not as far apart in north Down as in other places. Certainly the servant class, who come out on the stopping train from East Belfast, or over from the wrong side of the Belfast-Bangor highway to do the heavy cleaning and the gardening, are unique. They are not only the same colour and creed as their employers, but they identify, in a shared defensiveness, with the people for whom they work.

But within the middle-class, the tiniest nuances of social standing count. Cars matter. "A Jaguar for him and a Mercedes sports for her is the top thing," I'm told, though one young woman proposes a status symbol long faded in

England — a Citroen 2CV with a Great Dane sticking out the top. Clothes matter. The women are impeccable in the Mondis and Laurels and Marellas they buy in Bloomfield Avenue. "I once knew some Dublin girls," a woman said to me in confidence, "and to see them out in their Hermes scarves and their make-up, you'd think they were — you know, really nice. But if you went to their houses — well, you got such a land. Untidy, they'd be. Dirty, even. I mean, the impression you got of those girls — there was nothing behind it." In Northern Ireland, a woman's appearance is soundly expressive of a whole range of attributes. Conformism. Cleanliness. Prosperity. Navy and white will have navy-and-white accessories. The white leisure-wear of a sporty society will be dazzling white.

"There's a lot of disposable income in Northern Ireland, you know," a businessman says. "After all, a civil servant here is getting paid the same as in London, but he has nothing like the same mortgage. And an awful lot of it goes on boats." The sailing people form syndicates and race seriously. Or they cruise with friends and family, maybe along the coast of Scotland, visible on the horizon, no further away than one side of Dublin Bay from another. "Or" — the tone is contemptuous — "you get a certain sort of people who buy big motorboats, and they use them like caravans."

Sailing is presented as an activity that transcends the usual differences. "We sailing people are all friends," they say, "north or south. Makes no difference. We're all pals." For some reason, the same claims are not made for golf. The Royal Belfast Golf Club has no name-plate, I'm told. The Royal County Down Golf Club is equally security-conscious. "You're only in it if you know you're in it. All the big Northern Ireland Office men, and the judges, play there. You'd never get a list of members." But these references to the abnormality underlying ordinary life are made almost accidentally, and quickly passed over. It seems that one way to deal with danger is by refusing to react to it — refusing to dignify it, in public at least, with more than exasperation.

And by turning inwards, and making almost a fetish of the home. "I have a wonderful woman who comes in," the North Down ladies say. "I don't know what I'd do without her." But even the rich are not idle in this society, and most women do their own fine baking, and home decorating, at the least. These are key elements in an "Ulster" self-image.

And wives, in general, are key figures in a way of life both ultra-respectable and highly competitive. They run part of the show, in home and tea-shop and tennis-court; the husband runs his part in business and club. Husband and wife together are the social unit: this is not a society secure enough to tolerate alternatives to monogamy. "Ark parties, I call the parties I go to," a mildly bohemian woman says. "They come in two-by-two."

A man who has lived in the Republic and in Brussels has chosen to marry in, and to settle in, Bangor. He sits with his wife and his in-laws and gives his opinion. "Pound for pound," he says, "we have a higher standard of living here than anywhere else in Europe. You can get a nice house for, say £40,000. Within half-an-hour of here there's any sport you want, at a reasonable price. You can leave the house at 8.00 in the morning and catch the 8.30 plane to London. And from the point of view of business — there's real money here and it's *stable* money, because about a third of people in jobs are directly employed by the government." But he sees drawbacks. "It's a bit isolated here, too," he says. "We can be a bit insular."

That weekend, Mary Robinson's visit to west Belfast had brought out the isolation. "I thought she understood us. I thought she was the one person who understood us." This woman added bitterly, "Now there's no one to trust." The conversation had already touched on the South, and its potholed roads, general expensiveness, and dirtiness. Its untrustworthiness went without saying. Whether the kind of Catholic who lives next door and is in the same sailing club is trustworthy is an open question. "We're inclined to say among ourselves, 'he's one of the other'," a Protestant businessman said to me, "but that's because we think that's what the Catholics are saying too." The DUP are out of the question, of course. But even some Unionist politicians are untrustworthy. "I vote Alliance," an unlikely number of people say. Or, "In the local elections, I just voted for the one who wants a swimming pool for Holywood."

There are things that are unsayable, except late at night. Whether Westminster can be trusted, for example. In Scotland, or in Wales, criticism of central government is the stuff of conversation. Not in north Down. "Do you ever get annoyed at the quality of the politicians sent over from Westminster?" I asked. "You do get a few idiots, don't you?" "Your own politicians are fairly idiotic too if I may say so," someone says. "Yes," I say, thoughtlessly, "but at least they're our own idiots." There's a tiny silence before someone says stiffly that their government is their own, too.

Loyalism is one thing on the Shankill Road, where the photos of the royal family are on the walls, and another thing in Down, where they get the knighthoods. The suffering and bitterness is as deep, but much more quiet. Nobody talks directly about nephews or cousins murdered or maimed; a person will tell you about their neighbour's loss, and not mention their own. They talk brightly about their children at college in England or working in England, but never discuss that emigration. Hopes and fears are hidden behind a perfect blandness.

Except, that weekend, for the woman so shaken by Mary Robinson's meeting Gerry Adams. "Really," she burst out, "the way those people in west Belfast *whinge*. They were at it again in the speech welcoming her. We don't have this. We don't have that. It's disgusting. They get everything they ask for, so *I* don't know what they're whinging about now. Even my son — and he's only a young boy — he said 'Turn the telly off, Mum. I can't stand listening to that lot again.'" What did she think it was all about, then? If the nationalists have no grievances, why do they vote Sinn Féin? "For the money, of course," she said. "There's a lot of money in terrorism."

Later that day, the subject of money arose again. A tennis tournament had been abandoned because of muddy conditions, and everyone had crowded into the club-house. "There's a huge amount of perfectly legitimate money being made out of the war," a man said quietly. "In this room, to my knowledge," he said, "there is a loss-adjuster, two building contractors who repair as well as build, and four or five lawyers. They're coining money. Then there are the accountants and the travel-agents and a landscape gardener, making money out of their money," he said. "And the others — the teachers and the civil servants and so on — they're the ones who make Northern Ireland recession-proof. Nothing ever happens to government money."   •

"The Gold Coast," the southern edge of Belfast Lough is called. You can see the money more clearly than elsewhere in Ireland because the shops in the villages of north Down sell the luxuries — fitted kitchens, patchwork quilts, garden lighting — which the wealthy of Dublin and Cork go into their cities to buy. Otherwise, the bourgeoisie of that coast are the same as the bourgeoisie of Dun Laoghaire or Kinsale: none of them go anywhere near the areas where poverty and crime and alienation might hurt them. None of them take responsibility for their respective west Belfasts.

What makes the privileged people of North Down different, however, is that they see the upholding of their way of life as a duty, as a bulwark raised against anarchy, as a moral imperative. "We must go on," a woman says. "We can't let the terrorists win. We must do what we always did. We must look after our families and live a normal life and enjoy ourselves, because otherwise they'll think they're getting the upper hand." When a way of life is represented as heroic, it is above criticism.

As for a united Ireland .... At a fund-raising brunch in a pottery-cum-café in Holywood on a sunny Sunday morning, there was Bucks Fizz and freshly baked cinnamon rolls and savoury scrambled eggs. The people there were friends and neighbours, lively and chatty and beautifully dressed. Volunteers in the kitchen served delicious breakfasts: and at the end, after a jolly morning which raised a lot of money, they tidied up, jumped into their cars, and arranged to meet again in twenty minutes or so, down at the sailing club. Within half-an-hour they'd be out on the Lough.

There are maybe 70,000 people in the north Down area, the great majority of them comfortable with themselves and comfortably off. What possible need have these people of a united Ireland? It would have been madness to disturb the pleasant atmosphere of the brunch by mentioning such a thing. Even to raise the subject of the future, as if it is more problematic in a Northern Ireland town than in Harrogate or Tonbridge, would have been offensive.

The nearest thing to political discussion was the assertion, repeatedly made in private conversations, that the South would have to be completely different — it would have to become in every way what it is not — before any kind of co-operation could be even contemplated. "The South would have to steady up, you know," one man said heartily. The implicit condescension was quite unconscious. One society often consoles and defines itself by a conscious superiority to a neighbouring society, and there's nothing unusual about Northern distaste for the South. It is unusual, however, for the distaste to come armed. "We're very proud to have the Paras here in Holywood," a furiously smiling woman said, pouring me a glass of sherry. "Very, *very* proud."

THE TIMES

An Ugly Little War

I know a woman who is getting on in years but still, until recently, she held down a part-time job, played bridge and took an active interest in life. Then, at a traffic light one day, a boy threw a rock through her passenger window and snatched her handbag. And it's no exaggeration to say that she has become old since then. She's shaky and she falls silent all the time. And it wasn't the shock of the incident that did that to her. It was losing her belongings. She just can't get over that.

Handbags are actually part of people. When my grandmother was dying, she was calm and happy, but her hand used to stray across the bedclothes to check that her handbag was still there. It had everything in it — her pension book, photos, memoriam cards, old letters, her purse, her glasses, her receipts from the landlord. The bag was by far her most intimate possession. No one else would dream of opening it. She would never say to us children: "Take a shilling from my bag." She'd say: "Hand me over my bag," and extract the money from its depths herself.

Old ladies, particularly old ladies of no property, like her, keep everything they've got in their bags. All their money, all their valuables. Words can't easily describe what it means to them to have their bag stolen. And even modern women, whose money is in the bank, always have other things in there that are special and worth carrying around. A love letter or a Mass card or a diary or a child's birth-tag. These things are of no value to the robbers. But then, you realise, neither are you yourself. They don't care about you. You are shaken in your own humanity, you feel cold and lonely when you have to stand there and realise that you

237

are nothing to someone else, that they will throw your precious bits and pieces into a ditch.

Old ladies are not being used for their sentiment value here. They are, in fact, the people whose bags mean most to them and who are simultaneously most vulnerable to being robbed. Still, worse could happen to them: they could be raped. The existence of rape changes the structure of the world for women — it literally shrinks the world, since women cannot, for instance, walk on their own after dark. Property crime does not have such far-reaching effects. But it does change and colour the quality of life. People in cities are warier now than they used to be. Hatred is nearer to the surface. And a lot of people are walking around with wounds inside them that no one knows about. Because society doesn't allow you to mourn for possessions.

A friend of mine has an elderly mother who prided herself on living alone. But she was followed home, twice, on pension day, and was mugged as she went to put her key in the lock. She is afraid to live in her house now. The loss of her own place is the second worst thing that has ever happened to her — after being widowed — but nobody would tolerate her talking about it and crying about it for more than a few days. She just had to bear it in silence.

Everybody I know has been robbed, whether it was a car vandalised, or a burgled house come home to, or a purse snatched in a shop. Everybody. I also know a few people who do these things. The ones I know are very stupid and limited. I remember a friend being absolutely devastated by the theft of her bag because her address book was in it, twenty years of addresses, the central tool of her trade.

You can take it for granted that whoever stole her bag doesn't have an address book. Doesn't keep a diary. Doesn't have a cheque book. Owning these things, like owning a house, makes us seem to the young criminals a quite different species. To them, they and their peers, who own nothing but clothes and videos, are the real people. We are the aliens.

They can be sorry for themselves, and for their own kind, but not for us. Some girls took my neighbour's bag, and she is so small and old that they looked through it in front of her. She had no money at all — there was nothing there except her medical card and her free-travel pass and that sort of thing. They took the bag anyway. She had to spend weeks queuing up to replace all that, anxiously explaining herself to the ESB, to the Social Welfare, to CIE, to the Eastern Health Board.

This would be classified as a petty crime. What's petty about it? In her way, this lady is a representative twentieth-century figure. She did nothing to deserve what happened to her. The crime against her was arbitrary, motiveless. And the girls humiliated her for their own amusement. The best that can be said about what happened to her is that she's much more willing to die than she was before.

But we fail the humanity of the thieves, just as they fail ours, when we write them off as animals. It is open to anyone to spend a day in the courts. If you do, and you look and listen to the people up on robbery charges, you have to recognise that they have been stunted by unvalued lives. You have to recognise that they were made, not born. This has nothing to do with bleeding-heart liberalism: I don't feel one bit liberal about the strutting boys in their trainers who terrorise their fellow-poor and anyone less strong than they are. I feel the rush of hatred too, and the lust for revenge. But the courts strip the inequities of our society bare. These callous kids were babies once, and babies are pure potential. You know that you could have stood in the maternity ward all those years ago and, on the basis of home address alone, said: "This one will be the judge. This one will be the man in the anorak standing in front of the judge."

What can we expect, in a society so dreadfully divided between the haves and the have-nots, but that some of the latter will prey on the former? We accept that a third of the population live on the poverty line. We accept that only a handful of the most exceptional of the children of the poor will make it through to third-level education. We accept massive examples of greed and dishonesty in public life. We accept the values of materialism. What do we expect then — to be left unharassed, we who have all the privileges?

People do grow out of crime. It comes about when the girlfriend gets pregnant, or they start making good money at the job, or they get a house, or they win a cup at weight-lifting. As soon as they have something — as the rest of us have — to protect. Jail doesn't decriminalise people; a stake in society may. But we've got thousands and thousands of young people who cannot expect a stake in society. Is it reasonable to expect them to oblige us and to respect us? To be nice? To accept their lot?

There is a low-level war on the streets of Dublin. But it is an ugly little war. It is not against the rich: the rich don't allow themselves to be vulnerable. It is essentially a war between the poor and the not-much-better-off. The little old ladies, for example, are front-line troops. More and more of them are finding that their declining years have been poisoned by the spread of street crime. And, for all we know what to do about it, so will ours be.

Power and Obedience

In Galway the other night the company I was in started talking about a local controversy. Some Leaving Cert girls, it seems, as an end-of-school prank, had invited a male stripper to lay on a surprise performance for the teachers, religious and lay, and for the girls. This was very much unappreciated by their elders. The head nun cancelled revision classes, cancelled the debs' ball, and in general, demonstrated to the girls where, as a matter of fact, power lies.

The people I was with never got round to discussing the rights and wrongs of this event. We were all so astonished at the girls having even thought of such a thing that we got no further. Even the youngest among us, not long out of school, could hardly believe the change there has been since her day. It would never have crossed our minds — any of the men and women there — to try even the mildest joke on the authorities in our schools. And as for a male stripper! The world would have come to an end. God knows what would have happened. We'd have been murdered, for sure.

"But then it's all different now," someone said. "Kids *like* going to school these days. They don't dread it the way we used to." And then, the horrible, unforgotten stories began to be told. One woman, when she was five or six — before her First Communion anyway — had been slapped by a nun. When she told her mother, her mother took her back to the school to demand an explanation. The nun looked the mother right in the eye and denied ever touching the child. Next day, the nun assembled the school, and made the child kneel in front of it and repeat after her, "I am a liar. I am a liar." In this woman's voice, you could hear the bewilderment of the child she once was, as well as an enduring bitterness.

A man said that it hadn't been too bad for him. There were only two masters in his school who beat pupils and one of them only punished you "when it was reasonable. If you were messing, or that." But the other was a sadist, who used to lift the boys up by the short hairs beside their ears. He taught maths. Once a boy explained a maths problem he'd written out on the board to others, when the master was out of the room. For that, he was beaten so savagely that he was left unconscious. "What was his crime?" the man who was telling us this is still asking, thirty years later. "What was his crime?"

All of us could remember the special pain when the cane missed your palm, and caught your fingertips instead. We all, the men and women there, know what it's like to have your ears twisted. Chair-legs, pointers, fists — anything and everything was used against children in those days.

And it was no use appealing to home. Most parents thought that if you were chastised you deserved it, and probably deserved more of the same. Or that it was the school's business, and that parents couldn't interfere with a school. Or, that they'd been beaten themselves and that it hadn't done them a pick of harm.

That's the question, isn't it? Was it harmful? Because if it was, then most people over the age of about twenty-five years are likely to have been harmed. Not that they'd admit it. Men, especially, sturdily insist that if anything, being hit did them good. Made men of them. Should be brought back for joyriders, vandals, hooligans — other people's children, in short.

I think it is true, myself, that just being hit, as such, doesn't harm you, or at least that it didn't in that culture, where it was altogether accepted. But the context did matter. Where it was unfair, or out of control, or part of personal vendetta, then it terribly disturbed the child's task of making sense of the world. And I think that it was, generally, harmful. That it inculcated a sense of powerlessness on the one hand, while teaching authoritarianism on the other. The individual was a nobody, in a world of more powerful beings. Power was always out there, in the hands of the wielder of punishment. The notion of personal authority, of rightly having your own place in power-relations, simply couldn't develop in the climate of fear.

I think of a quiet man I knew, who once told me about his school. Everyone bullied him, because he was so meek. But one Brother hated him. One icy winter's day, for example, the Brother soaked his scarf in water, and sent him out to stand in the yard until the scarf should freeze. It took five hours. This man never asserted himself in life. He married a forceful woman, who walked all over him. He did his little job, quiet as a mouse. It is hard for me to see no connection between what he suffered as a child and his subsequent timidity. It is hard not to believe that if he'd gone to a child-loving school, his natural sweetness might have led to his being valued, and thus to valuing himself.

In fact, I find it difficult to believe that there is no relationship between our society at large and what we witnessed as children. And it was as small children we witnessed it, at least for me. Secondary girls' schools didn't use corporal punishment, the ones I went to anyway. Yet we might have been better able to take it when we were older, instead of at seven or eight or nine.

What threat, I ask myself, did people so small appear to pose, that they could be treated like that? What was going on? However bold we were, how could they have done it to people so much smaller than themselves? Make them flinch and howl and be humiliated? "Ah, sure, we got over it," people say. But if they did, how is it that those episodes are always remembered, when so much else of childhood is forgotten?

How did all this affect the relationship of ordinary people to the other people, the ones who have power over them? You notice that we have no Tiananmen Squares here, that we don't assemble to demand accountability, no matter how bad things are. We don't go after the people in power, we don't follow them around saying, "What happened to the promises you made?" Or "you lied to us." Or "you let us down." Grievances we have in plenty, but what about outrage? What about confronting them — making them pay? No, that's not something we do, and I don't think it is altogether fanciful to see a link between that passivity and the prudent passivity we learnt at school.

The kind of country we have is commonly called "conservative". Well, if conservatism includes an unwillingness to rock the boat, a fear of change, a dull acceptance of the status quo, those are all attitudes that were inculcated in us, from our earliest years. It isn't as if we chose them, from a wide menu of things we might have been. To be like that was the wisest course. And not just in the schools, of course. From de Valera down to the parish priest, from the home to the guards' barracks to the doctor's surgery, the two poles of that world were authority and obedience.

Now, we have a more diverse kind of world struggling to come about, and young people to cope with it who never knew what it was like to be afraid to go to school. Here's hoping that that will make a difference, and that enough of them will stay here long enough for us to see the difference. The male stripper, it seems to me, was an awfully bad idea, on several grounds. But the road that led to him has been climbing all the way.

Spirit of the Nation(1989)?

When Charles J. Haughey made his first entry into Irish public life, his was literally a worm's-eye view. At fifteen or so he joined the Local Defence Force and spent a lot of time crawling around in wet fields, prepared to repel the invader. Now, he travels the country mainly by helicopter. From up there in the air he reads the landscape through the preferred perspectives of his later years — archaeology, history, literature. "It's so *crowded*, Ireland," he said to me this week. "It's so full." Someone else might see emptiness and sameness, but his is the best-informed eye in Ireland. There's not much going on down there that he doesn't either know about or is interested in finding out.

One of the things he has known better than most is that there are many Irelands. If he has read them all correctly this time, he will be returned with the majority he seeks, and if so, we will see for the first time what he is like when he has nothing to do but govern. If he has guessed wrong, there will be considerable personal pathos in his position. He is already — along with Neil Blaney — the most senior figure in the Dail. No one else survives from the 1950s. He is by far the most widely experienced politician in Ireland — anyone who cares to leaf through the 1,600 pages of his collected speeches, *The Spirit of the Nation*, will be struck by the enormous range of the detail he has mastered in his day. "He has followed his course," Des O'Malley says. "He has pursued his objectives with a single-mindedness unique in Irish politics." If he fails this time, then the people will have decided that Mr Haughey's course, Mr Haughey's objectives, are not to be endorsed. And if not now, then, probably, never.

The first of the Irelands Mr Haughey commands is the Northside, which is not just Dublin's northside but everywhere people live in streets and kids go to big, tough schools. He knows all that from the inside — playing football, robbing orchards, taking the bike out to Portmarnock for a swim. He was something of an exception in being very clever — first in Dublin for a scholarship — and very bookish. He haunted Marino library. But not all that much of an exception. His personal friends — still Northsiders — a motor-trade businessman, a judge of the Supreme Court, an auctioneer — would all have been the same kind of boy, reared in very modest circumstances but with the brains to transform them.

Mr Haughey would have been the first in the history of his family to go to college, to make money, to continue educating himself and to have the means to express personal taste. This experience differentiates him from the older, professional stream in Irish life, where families have produced solicitors or doctors from way back, from British times even. It is one of the things that makes Haughey seem always an outsider, an anti-establishment figure, permanently challenging, even when he is in power.

His supporters in his own constituency feel this in him. They defend him, even when he isn't being attacked. Last Sunday, he was there to be talked to on the steps of Artane church, and he was far more serious with his questioners, far less patronising than he is with, say, the press. In fact, he wasn't patronising them at all, and they weren't deferential to him. Between him and them there is a huge shared network of relations, schoolfellows, friends of the family, local characters; and, like most Irish TDs, he has a phenomenal memory of every detail of this.

Like almost all Irish TDs, too, he is asked for, and promises, help and favour. The difference between him and the TDs who complain about this clientelism (in private) is that he believes in it. "Why should they hear from some faceless bureaucracy that they've got a pension? Why shouldn't they ask someone they know to get it for them? Why shouldn't someone they know personally tell them they've got it?" He was fervent about this. He doesn't see political patronage as keeping the people in subjection. He sees the politician as protecting the individual against indifference. What's more, he sees this as the way the Irish people like to do things. And his commitment is to preserving the Irish way.

He wandered away from the church, unhurriedly. More avuncular these days than he used to be. More genuinely calm. He left behind the usual lively seminar on his character. "Sure I know he has a few skellingtons in his cupboard," a lady said. "But sure which of us haven't?"

What is a skeleton in one of the Irelands isn't necessarily a skeleton in another. His lifestyle, for example, and how he came by it, are discussed in Ireland's Southsides but not in its Northsides. Not that anyone begrudges it in itself. He lives like an exceptionally cultivated squire, spending his money on his island and trees and deer and paintings, rather than on gold-plated jacuzzis. His affluence doesn't cut him off from the people. I knew two little boys who were sent home early from the Gaeltacht for being bold. They thought if they hid for a few days, and then reappeared at the train station, their parents would never know. So they went out to Kinsealy and hid out the back of Mr Haughey's house for three days. Someone gave them out food.

But he did acquire wealth in a mere seven or eight years, in very poor times, and before entering a profession — politics — that usually impoverishes its practitioners. He made enough to buy the house and lands in Raheny which he sold in 1969 for a profit of £154,000 — equivalent, in today's terms, to about £1.2 million. It was worth so much more because houses were built on it.

"How was I to know that Dublin would expand northwards?" he said to me. "It had always expanded southward up to then. When I was young, Dublin ended at Donnycarney village."

Otherwise, he refused, as he always does, to discuss these matters.

But he surely knows that it is impossible to make money in Ireland without other people believing that you've made it by pull, contacts, insider knowledge. When it is made by politicians, a further range of fears is evoked. It is because of Mr Haughey's reticence about these early years that there has always been attention paid to his relationships with rich and furtive individuals. Or, at least, it has always been paid in certain quarters. Not by the people at Artane church. They don't care who Charlie knocks around with. The "climate of confidence" hasn't reached them yet, and they couldn't care less what corners might be cut in getting prosperity to them. As usual, they trust Mr Haughey — and no one else — to send it their way if he possibly can.

Where the "climate" has had an effect, people are going to have to choose between the habit of deploring Mr Haughey's ways and the imperatives of self-interest. Out there, in all the Southsides, there has been an indubitable change. People have savings, and they know what the inflation rate is and what it has been. They have loans, and they know about interest rates. Their houses are suddenly worth much more. A son or daughter studying, say, architecture, now has a lively chance of a job in Ireland.

Are those people likely to go back over the past, to remember the one moment when — as was widely experienced — Mr Haughey preferred a passionate, personal impulse to the interests of the bourgeoisie? Twenty years ago the British army came into the North and in the lurid and confused scenario that ensued, Mr Haughey was to find himself in the dock. History will one day uncover the facts. But from the point of view of domestic politics what happened next is what matters.

He left that court almost entirely alienated from the Fianna Fáil establishment and the Fianna Fáil business connections. He turned to that other Ireland, which is neither northside nor southside. He went down the country, and there he served his time.

Liam Lawlor, TD, was barely into his twenties then, but he had ambitions of his own. He drove. Thursday nights, Friday, Saturday, even Sunday, they met at the Green Isle Hotel and set off for anywhere — Ballybofey, Cahirciveen — anywhere a sizeable number of people had invited Mr Haughey to speak. They never mentioned the recent past, Mr Lawlor says, and neither did the people they would meet. It was unspoken. Murmurs of "He's a Jack man", "He's a Charlie man" were as near as anyone got to being explicit. It was a quintessentially Irish situation. It wasn't about what it appeared to be about — the Lemassian message of modernisation which Mr Haughey was preaching. No one knew what Mr Haughey had done or not done. And no one declared themselves either.

Mr Haughey used to turn on the car light as he got near the destination and go over his handwritten speech. It always had a local content. This mattered quite as much as the "republicanism". A celebrity had taken the trouble to come to people who habitually feel isolated. "They never forgot it to him, " Tom McEllistrim said to me in Kerry. "I told them that he was a great man — that many the grant I got from him when he was in Finance, and those were the days when grants were a new thing. But it wasn't that. It was that he'd come to their function and shaken their hands." In the later leadership challenges, Mr Haughey always could have appealed to the party faithful, over the head of the parliamentary party.

Three years Mr Haughey spent like this. No other modern Irish politician has put in such work. Three years of chicken dinners. Castlemahon was the leading brand of chicken then. When he was elected leader, Mr Haughey told me, one of his children wrote on a mirror at home, 'It was the Castlemahon that did it.'

The arms affair, the split in the party and Mr Haughey's departure and return were the grounds for much that has happened since. Not just in practical, but in mythical terms. From then on he had that attribute of the romantic hero, that he had been away, and that he had come back. But there were squalid consequences as well. There were those among his colleagues who would not trust him to appoint Ministers for Justice or Defence. When that veto became inoperative he appointed Sean Doherty to Justice. From that appointment stemmed many of the famous grotesque events of 1982-83. These are always lumped together, even though some of them, like the MacArthur business, were merely grotesque. The enduring thing, post-Doherty, is that Mr Haughey's appointments in the field of security are scrutinised as no other Taoiseach's have been.

Mr Haughey's enemies could make a much larger collection of skeletons: his friends could hardly make a smaller one. But either way, there was much much more to him than that. His provisions for the elderly, for example, were not just generous but imaginative. Thousands and thousands of people who never had the means to travel have discovered their own country and their own vitality through the free-travel scheme. He changed the quality of life for the old. He was an expansionary Minister for Health. "I can assure you," he said to me with emphasis, "I can assure you, that it gives me not the slightest bit of pleasure to have to cut back the very programmes I put in myself."

He generated the first pieces of pro-woman legislation in the history of the State. And advised by the poet and critic Anthony Cronin—a typically original and challenging choice of non-political associate — he reaffirmed, in contemporary Irish society, the position the artist held in Gaelic Ireland.

Where he could be, in ways that did not disturb the status quo, he has been innovative. Wholesome reform, or radical changes of structure have never even appealed to him. "Why should I shove the people on faster than they want to go?" he says. "Nice and steady, nice and steady, that's the way."

This is exactly what the left and liberals, in general, have against him. That he doesn't lead, but follows. They see his position on divorce as symptomatic. But they often go on to assume that his pacing of himself alongside the most conservative element in the country is an exercise in cynicism. They do not consider that he might actually like, even love, Ireland the way it is and might see no great need to reform it — or to take the superior stance implicit in telling it that it needs reform. A lot of Irish people know that our society is unjust and dishonest and double-faced. But, deep down, they think it's wonderful all the same, and that this is the most charming country in the world. Michael D. Higgins throws out the suggestion that in this, Ireland's view of itself and its view of Mr Haughey are the same: he may seem shabby to other people, but under the shabbiness there is a king in disguise.

People of Mr Haughey's age were the first heirs of independence. Many of them, like him, had parents who had taken part in that struggle. When he entered the Dail, it still had members like Dan Breen, and, of course, Eamonn de Valera. To those of Mr Haughey's generation who were in any way romantic-minded, Ireland seemed like a marvellous new gift, a place to be endlessly explored, to be cherished as it had come to them. It was only recently freed: it would be impertinence to seek to change it.

That pride can be heard in Mr Haughey's voice when he talks about Ireland in Europe. The phrases "sovereign state", "equal among the community of nations" roll off his tongue in a special way. One is reminded that he represents Ireland abroad with great diligence and dignity. But when he remarked that he had once said to President Mitterand that "everyone else in the Community had to give up something to join, but that for Ireland it was pure gain", the real Ireland sprang unbidden to mind. Mr Haughey must know the growing reputation of Ireland as the "fiddler" of the Community. He must know that dishonesties accepted in sections of Irish life are perfectly unacceptable to our European partners. He will have to face that element of Irishness if he is to deal fairly; not just represent the interests of Ireland to the Community, but the interests of the Community to Ireland.

But is he able to look at Ireland with the same clarity as he looks at other places? Is he not too implicated in it? Led into endless pragmatism by his very feel for its complexity? The two go hand in hand, he and his country. That is why criticism that is directed at his personality — as if it were an autonomous force — is inadequate. Over and over he is attacked for the country not being other than it is. But it is as it is. It is unnaturally passive, through its partition of its natural dissenters in the North and the drain of its young people. It is capitalist, not socialist. It is Catholic, not Protestant. It is tribal, not civic. Those were the parameters of the Ireland of his youth, and he has not thought to change them.

And that, perhaps, is where history's estimate of him will start from: that he was a caretaker, in a situation that cried out for more than that. It wasn't that any aspect of Irishness needed to be destroyed; it was that the relation of one sector to the other, one power to another, one person's rights to another's, needed, and needs, to be the business of the leaders. It must be said, however, that plausible contenders for the role, leaving Mr Haughey aside, fail to spring to mind.

Next week, he submits himself again to the judgement of the people. Like all politicians, he is in their power, not they in his. If he returns to government, his critics would do well to remind themselves that his position is a democratic one — that he will be the elected leader of the elected representatives of the largest political party in the country. If they don't like that, there is little point in going on about the special and demonic nature of the man. They'd be better off carrying around the placard I saw at student demonstrations this week. It said, 'If Fianna Fáil's the Answer, It Was a Stupid Question.'

50,000 New Babies

This woman was telling me the other day that where she lives nearly everybody is on the labour. But this didn't stop them, of course, from going berserk at Christmas and getting taxis home from the shopping centre with the toys and all kinds of extravagances. The result is that nobody has a penny in January. "Especially the ones with big families," she said. "They're completely cleaned out." And I said, automatically, "Well, what are they doing having big families, if they're on the labour?"

As if I wasn't from a big family myself. My elder sister had her own children going to school when my youngest sister was still going to school. It all seemed perfectly normal to us. The only thing is, as I got older, I was sorry for my mother. That's one of the things that is rarely said on the subject of big families — that they have implications for what the father, and more especially the mother, might have made of their lives. Child-rearing can't develop all the potential of all humans. It doesn't develop, for example, all those things which are necessarily solitary.

But arguments against large families usually start from the children, they not having asked to be born. Almost everyone can point to some house they know where in spite of the manifest inadequacies of the parents, in spite of the obvious stunting of the children, in spite of a complete absence of material or emotional resources, baby after baby keeps arriving.

The worst example I ever saw was down the country. The house was full of pale brothers and sisters who sometimes burst into vicious, *silent* fighting. They were not the children of the household. They were being fostered. Their own mother was mentally slow and their father molested all his children, as a matter of course, until they were taken away. Everyone knew: the social workers, the priest, the guards. But who could stop this pair having children? No one could. So the foster-parents had four of these children already, and expected another one, every eighteen months or so, as long as the mother's womb held out.

Something should be done, you'd think. Something should be done about families where they'll obviously all have to emigrate. Something should be done about families where the children get themselves out to school and then fall asleep on their desks because they've been up all night watching videos.

There are families where the children live on the streets from as soon as they can stagger — little bullet-headed, dirty-mouthed children, tense with fighting a social war for their parents. Something should be done. And about the little girls bowed with minding their mammy's babies, who'll have their own babies before even they bloom.

But what is the something that should be done? I well remember the derision here when a documentary was shown about China's drive to reduce population. A woman in every village has the right to call on all the other women to check whether they'd taken their pills. The village has the right to demand that such-and-such a woman have an abortion. All of this seemed ludicrous as well as vile to free-born Irish people.

We don't have any of the reasons for having large families that the poorest people on the planet have. We have old-age pensions and we have machines to do our labour and we are not likely to die young. Yet in the matter of having as many children as happen, the Irish behave as if they were an endangered species.

State coercion, as in China, is out. Though there, at least, coercion was a universal policy. The trouble with state intervention here, or state persuasion, is that it would inevitably be directed at some rather than others. It would be that poor people shouldn't have big families. Or stupid people shouldn't. The rest of us, however, would be free to do as we like. As it is, we discriminate in every possible way against the identifiably under-privileged. But if we were to direct a policy of birth control against them, discrimination would be taking a quantum leap. Being able to have human children is the one thing that all human beings share.

If we are a community at all, the one rough thing we have in common is that we're humans — equally human, if not equally anything else. If we were to say that X or Y isn't allowed have children, would we not be creating a sub-human category? I know that in fact a great many respectable people do refer to rapists and murderers and even mere vandals as sub-human, but it is a long way from that to institutionalising a category of second-class humans. How would you like to be the only child of parents who were forbidden by the state to have any more children? Any move to control family size would have to apply to all of us.

If you tell someone that they may not have a child, you are not only judging them but you're pre-judging the child. Who can say what a human being might not be? Of course you can go by probabilities. You can say that the abused child of a single mother crack-addict in a rat-ridden room is likely to be such-and-such. But you can't know. You just can't look at a baby and say that there is no hope of happiness or goodness for this person. Anything could happen: anything has already happened — often, in history.

The dreadfully neglected children we see are the children of the poor because the poor can't hide. But the rich can hide. They can hide what they do to their children in a welter of nannies and expensive schools and air tickets and holiday homes. And maybe you can damage children all the more effectively the more resources you have. Maybe you can wreck two children just as comprehensively as you can wreck ten. Maybe neither riches nor poverty has anything to do with it.

Because the middle-classes aren't necessarily good parents either. I think that the middle-class code of stability and moderation and conformity is probably very helpful in giving children a shelter within which to grow. But the shelter becomes a prison when anything goes wrong inside. The neighbours can't go in and the social workers don't call. A man I know went to a house near his to complain about a dog, and was accidentally let in. He discovered that there was not one stick of furniture in there, except for the expensive curtains, and not one bit of food. The father had lost his job, it seemed, long before, and the whole family was pretending they were still prosperous while they all but starved. Was that a better or worse thing to do to the children than feed them on chips and let them burn cars?

The size of a family, or even the resources of a family as related to size don't seem any kind of reliable indicator of well-being. I know a large family of bright, confident children who live with their parents in one room. Anyone who knows the parents thinks them useless. They are useless, from the point of view of the community. But not from the point of view of the children, because mysteriously enough they are good at being parents. You would have predicted, back when these two no-hopers married — because she was pregnant — that their partnership would be a disaster. But things are more obscure than that. However they work things out between themselves, and between themselves and the children, they have made a successful home.

I'm as shocked as the next person when the Pope lands in some country creaking under the weight of children and anathematizes birth control. But I'm shocked too, at how much is given away when a vasectomy is exchanged for a transistor radio. The ability to find a mate, and with that mate make humans in your own image — if it didn't happen so often we'd be struck speechless by the grandeur of it.

No wonder the state falters in approaching the family. About 50,000 children will be born in the Republic this year. We operate under the myth that they'll all be all right — that like the sweet little wizened babies we see in the New Year newspapers, they're being born into happiness and love. But some of them won't be happy and won't be loved and won't have access even to the crumbs that fall from the rich man's table.

And as to what any of the rest of us can do about it ... You can't even say to your own brother that he's ruining those kids of his. You can't say to a woman in the bus queue to please stop hitting her baby. The state should be able to do what the individual cannot do, but children, as much as land, are property — private property — and except in the most gross of circumstances, no trespassers are allowed.

Huge areas of life, including what people do in the line of having children and bringing them up, escape from society altogether. They're private. You can consciously try not to live too greedily yourself. You can consciously work for equity in educational opportunity and health care and the like. But after that, all you can do for the 50,000 new babies is to wish them good luck.

Dartish-Speak

It may seem odd, when our larger European future is the question, to be talking about something as trivial as an accent: the accent that children of the Dublin middle classes are using now that is arguably the first new native accent of an independent Ireland. But our idea of ourselves is formed in all kinds of ways. Just as we are affected by the European currency crisis, so we're affected by the internal realignment of allegiances signalled by this new way of speaking. It is the badge of a new élite. More explicitly than anything else, it expresses that élite's sense of its economically advantaged position in this society. It redraws one of our maps.

I think a lot of people have noticed it. It came up, for example, at an Irish class I went to for a week during the holidays, when there was a general discussion about accent and pronunciation. The teacher mentioned the voice of the young woman who does 'AA Roadwatch' on 'Today at Five'. I am struck by her accent myself. I find myself waiting through the news items until it comes to her, and then hurriedly trying to analyse what it is she is doing to the words she uses: in particular, to the word "southbound", which is somehow a key to this new accent. I repeat it over to myself — "southbound, southbound" — but I can't say it the way she says it.

The teacher said that the pupils of Dublin's southside all-Irish schools speak Irish in this "Roadwatch" accent, too. Or call it a DART accent. Connoisseurs say that it is found along the line of the DART, becoming ever more pronounced the nearer it gets to Glenageary. It is the accent of DART-served schools. I'm told that they don't have it in Belvedere, for instance, and sure enough,

Belvedere isn't on the DART. On the other hand, you hear it all the time in Grafton Street, which isn't on the DART either.

We used to know where we were with accents. Almost precisely. There used to be — just counting the South — about four main ones. There were country accents: they're all different from each other, of course, and they're not even all rural, because they include the cities of Cork, Galway and Waterford, and hundreds of towns. But from the vantage point of Dublin — and accent is all about vantage point— they're all from "the country" anyway.

Then there were Dublin accents. There were rare oul' Dublin accents, as in the gruesome ads for "Old Mr Brennan's bread". There were Trinity accents. And there were anonymous accents. Mr Haughey, for example, is anonymous; Gay Byrne is anonymous Dublin; the President, Mrs Robinson, is anonymous Dublin, even though she's from Mayo. Perhaps there's a fifth accent called anonymous rural. MEPs develop anonymous rural. Broadcasters, except for sports broadcasters, are inclined to the anonymous rural. Even James Joyce, astonishingly, on the recording of his voice that survives, has a kind of all-purpose rural accent — Irish, but not from any given place in Ireland.

The anonymity is not about place but about class. Or not exactly class, in the English sense, but education. Education isn't an indicator of economic privilege, but it is an indicator of privilege, if only the privilege of having parents who care. The less you sound native to wherever it may be, the longer you've spent at school. The exceptions are so obvious that they more or less prove the rule.

Joe Duffy, for example, is highly educated, but he was obviously impervious to any tips about elocution that came his way. Jim McArdle, of *The Irish Times*, who sometimes reports on cycling for RTÉ, bends even the most exotic

Italian and Belgian names to a robustly Dublin pronunciation. They, and a few others, stand out.

Standard received pronunciation in this country is placeless. It can have a hint of this or that local influence (though Cavan and Monaghan are problematic), but not more than a hint. But no one accent, until this DART one, was expressive of social background. I don't count Anglo-Irish accents because they are not new. As far as I know, they've been the way they are for ever. They are natural, in the sense that they've come down the generations, like all the other accents of the Republic.

But there is one homemade, unmistakeable accent which might be proposed as the grandfather of the DART accent. This is the one you hear around the Law Library. It is vaguely English, as if its speakers, if they didn't quite go to an English public school themselves, knew a lot of people who did. As far as the pronunciation of words goes, it is not a progenitor: no other group in Ireland talks like that. (At my most charitable, I believe that it is a necessity forced on advocates by the awful acoustics of the courts, and that the pompous slowness with which they speak is really just an effort to be heard).

But what the Law Library and the new accent have in common is an absence of timbre — a lightness, a thinness, a kind of sexlessness, an ostentatious lack of vigour in taking on a sentence. The lawyers may be trying to copy a particular accent but the young people are not. What they appear to aspire to is accentlessness. They don't sound English or American or Australian, or at least not consistently. They manage not to sound anything — not anything recognisably Irish, and not anything else either. They are, in fact, minimalists — speakers of an English that has about as little personal identity as a spoken language can have. Why this — an accent perfectly suited, say, to the dealing room of an international finance house — should be the preferred accent of our best-placed young people, is wide open to speculation.

But that they would develop a speaking style of their own was predictable enough. Young people used to be just old people who weren't old yet. They wore the same clothes, read the same books, listened to the same music, were involved in the same politics, as their seniors. Drank in the same pubs. Believed older people could be learnt from, for heaven's sake.

All that is over now, and the young now furnish their own ghetto. But there are ghettos within the larger one. You can tell the castes apart even by the gloss of their hair, never mind the cost of their clothes. Now, as soon as they open their mouths, you can also tell which one is going to college, and which one isn't it and never dreamt of it. Even which college: the new accent is much more associated with UCD than anywhere else.

I don't know whether DART is spoken only by Dubliners. It would logically be the preferred style also of monied students from rural Ireland — the kind whose parents buy flats and houses in Dublin for their children to use while they're at college. It is, and is meant to be, a "yuppie" accent. And yuppies, it seems, must eliminate native or traditional elements in their self-presentation. This is ideologically expressive. I see in a report from Zimbabwe in the *Times Literary Supplement* that it happens there, too. The war of independence, the writer says, is just a memory to young urban Zimbabweans. Evidence for this is a curious new fashion among the teenage children of privileged families, whose imitation of English intonation has earned them the sobriquet of "nose brigades". In the malls and discos of Harare, they can be seen wearing gaudily decorated pith helmets — solar topees — a fashion roundly condemned by Hove (a Zimbabwean novelist), who told a reporter he would "soundly beat any child of mine wearing such a thing; it's a sign of disrespect to those who suffered under the colonial régime."

Well, I don't know that I agree. The one sure way to evade neo-colonialism is to neither know nor care whether you're being neo-colonial or not; to treat the whole thing playfully. Back at that Irish class I mentioned, a man told me that his children — from a comfortable part of Dublin's Northside — have taken to speaking in *Commitments* accents, and that, what's more, when they went to a Gaeltacht island this year, the young islanders, too, had taken to speaking Irish with a *Commitments* accent. That sort of thing comes and goes, I imagine, and adds to the gaiety of nations.

But even if the impulse behind Dartish is liberating, I can't get to like it in itself. I feel a kind of insolence behind all it rejects. I don't like its sectionalism. Especially I don't like how weak it is, how pallid and infantile compared to other full-blooded accents around. It is as featureless as the suburbs from which it comes. It has none of the originality of underclass speech. In fact, it is determinedly unoriginal, as if the people who speak it have nothing to prove. It expresses nothing except a generalised tedium, which means that words like "yes", "Terenure" or "Heineken" are (a) too boring to pronounce in full, and (b) the property of the caste who pronounce them thus. It is not that I want everybody to sound like Miceál O Muircheartaigh, but I don't see why the healthiest, best-fed young people in the entire community have to talk as if they're permanently exhausted.

Not that what I might say could make any difference. Isn't the whole point of the new accent that it has nothing to do with the oldies — especially, nothing to do with the pathetic provincials who actually reared the children who speak it? Doesn't it say that they refuse to be the children of any particular home? That if they're at home anywhere, so to speak, it is with each other, in such affluent enclaves as Ireland has to offer?

This isn't the first time or the first way, of course, that one generation has marked itself off from its predecessors. But what is different about this development is that it is, presumably, irreversible. Imagine. This accent is with us for ever. The nose brigades are here to stay.

Housework

It was on a package holiday, cycling in Austria, and the group included two very pleasant English couples. We came to Mauthausen. The Nazi concentration camp there, and its terrible adjoining quarry, where thousands and thousands of people died horribly, can be visited, if you can bear it. There was a quick discussion between the two husbands and two wives. The wives made little *moues* of distress and became all helplessly feminine at the thought of going near such a place. The husbands began to puff up, manly and protective. The decision was reached that the big, strong men would brave the visit to the camp, and the little wifeys would go shopping. And so they both did, each sex well content with the other.

Those couples were thriving, as far as I could see, on the traditional distinction between the public and private spheres. He'll mind the world out there: she'll mind the home. I can see that it is in the interest of the human race as a species that this should sometimes be the case. Sometimes. When women are very pregnant, or when there are small children to be reared, the woman needs protection and support — not that many women don't manage without it. But that fleeting time in the individual woman's life has been extended to define womanhood altogether. Minding children for five or ten or fifteen years incorporates, in our system, the task of minding their fathers for fifty.

Which — if it suits both parties — is one way of spending your life. But there's no particular reason why the idea of women in the home should be favoured over other ideas about women. There is nothing more normal about being a housewife than not being. If you ask yourself in whose

263

interest it is to promote the notion that women are homebodies and men are out in the world, you may reply that it is in men's interests. They are made relatively free by this arrangement. And so it is a notion most powerfully propagated, and represented as "natural". The English women at Mauthausen were formed and shaped by century upon century of propaganda about how they should behave so as to be what the world calls womanly. The conditioning is so strong that I felt for a moment "unnatural" myself, for feeling that I had to go to the quarry.

Inherited stereotypes make it hard to discuss the perceived conflict between women who do paid work outside the home and women who work unpaid within the home. I say perceived conflict, because, mostly, more has been made of it by people hostile to women than by women themselves. The overwhelming majority of women are in perfect agreement on the matter. They would like both. All things being equal, they would like, at different times in their lives, and in different proportions at different times, to bear and raise children *and* to do interesting and useful work outside the home and earn money.

Almost anyone who impedes women from one or another of these fulfilments is an ideologue. There are mothers, and promoters of motherhood, who make a huge fetish of that particular role, and denigrate the many other marvellous things a woman might do with her life. And there are some women — usually sickened by the world they see around them — who want nothing to do with it. If they could, they'd destroy the present world, motherhood and all. A detail of the Kilkenny incest case — that neighbouring men, when they got out of the pub, rang the poor abused daughter and her mother with obscene proposals — is the kind of thing, repeated, that can make you a separatist.

Ireland has more mothers working full-time in the home than any other EC country. This is simply because there are fewer opportunities to work outside the home here than anywhere else. There are very many women who would work outside the home if they possibly could. They are full-time mothers, certainly, but how often is that their choice? And if one of the young women in Ireland who has no hope of a job, much less a career, chooses to have a baby, the choice is not the same as it would be if she'd thrown up a highly paid job as a hairdresser on a cruise ship, say, going around the world. Numbers, in other words, mean nothing. That a lot of women are full-time mothers but no woman has ever been, say, chief executive of a major bank, doesn't make motherhood more "natural" to women than running a bank. But, of course, motherhood may be more desirable than anything else around.

Lots of women in societies like ours do decide, usually along with their partners, to get pregnant such-and-such a number of times, and have such-and-such a number of children, and to work full-time in the home for such-and-such an amount of time. They make a general plan about reproduction, based on their resources and values. Having children is by far the most interesting thing they can do.

They choose. They make a choice. A choice that has the whole dignity of the human being behind it. The dignity of the choice should be kept separate from the issue of how undervalued the work of mothering is. For the world as it has been run so far does indeed undervalue work in the home. But the woman who freely chooses to do it has given it her value — has honoured the work with her self. She should fight for improvements in pay and conditions, the same as in any job. But let it be clear that this is not the same as resenting the job in itself.

The note of resentment that often characterises housewives' descriptions of themselves come from interiorising the values of the world. They sense that work with children in the home is looked on with contempt. They feel that women who work outside the home are treated with more respect. They try to win respect for what they do, partly by stressing the alleged element of sacrifice in their work and partly by denigrating non-mothering women.

But it wasn't women who designed a world where paid work is admired but unpaid work is not. It wasn't women who designed a world in which child-care is unpaid. It isn't women who ask the mothers of toddlers, "But what do you do all day?" The value system we have inherited is challenged by feminism. It is that value system that says that women and housework are relatively unimportant. Not feminism.

When it is firmly established that to choose to work full-time in the home *is* an important choice, and is a *choice*, then rearing your own children in your own home can be looked at for what it is. It is an extremely demanding job, but it is also an exceptionally varied, interesting, contenting and comprehensive job. I have never seen a woman, no matter how successful, move around the workplace with the same fluent ownership of the space as women display in their homes.

I have never seen a woman in the workplace who is not sometimes or always alienated by the work she does. Minding the children of your own body is not alienating. When the situation is not distorted by something else — by poverty, by having no loving support, by having had no choice, by having nothing else to look forward to — then surely there is no better job.

All my sisters have had children. I haven't. But as far as I know, there is no fight between us because we've had different lives. So easy is it, in fact, not just for us but for women in general to appreciate that circumstances and choices have led one to this destiny, another to that, that I mistrust most discussions about women's roles. The problem is not between real women. It is between external views of what women are or should be.

And it is not being born female that is problematical. The problem is absence of opportunity and absence of financial independence. And absence of intellectual confidence. That last one is the one that can be tackled now, today. Fight: don't whine.

Don't fall into a role. When a woman says that she's "only a housewife", or when she complains that she hasn't had a holiday for ten years because she has so many children — as if her fecundity had nothing to do with her — or when she decides that remembering the Holocaust in a concentration camp would injure her delicacy, she's propping up the old roles.

But they're not worth it. Men are not the strong ones, women are not the weak ones, and motherhood is not what makes women valuable. We need truthful, particular ways to describe human diversity.

Inventing Café Society

The *Irish Press* group of newspapers is to me much more than a business in trouble. We were more or less reared on a *Press* wage. My father went off to earn this money, usually in evening dress, like a band-leader, every afternoon. He could be found again, around midnight, at the desk he used in Burgh Quay. He'd be banging away at the typewriter, doing the 'Dubliner's Diary' he wrote under the pseudonym "Terry O'Sullivan" for the next day's *Evening Press*. Out the back, the presses would be rolling thunderously with the latest *Irish Press*. I couldn't bring myself to walk down Poolbeg Street last week, when all that action, once so purposeful, was stilled.

There's no other word for what my father was than "a gossip columnist". But that's a word that has shifted meaning so totally over the last three decades that he would hardly recognise what it signifies now. "Gossip" is now about "personalities"; who those personalities are, and what is proposed as newsworthy about them, are key aspects of contemporary Ireland. The decline of the *Press* newspapers might be said to be due to getting contemporary Ireland wrong. Or, to staying too long with an out-of-date Ireland.

My father had an enthusiasm, which nowadays would seem painfully naïve, for his job. If he went to a function room in the Gresham for the launch of a new type of Irish door-handle, and then to Jurys to a press conference about some mussel festival, and then to a reunion of Army comrades, and then looked in on a Rose of Tralee heat, and then opened a new pub in Dun Laoghaire, he would enjoy every minute. Because everything about Ireland seemed full of vitality to him, and interesting, and a credit to the country and the people. Those were the early days of what are now public relations machines, publicity machines, advertising machines. The whole idea of celebrity was just getting started. There was a certain innocent *joie de vivre* around, as if Dublin was just being discovered as a metropolis.

He died before he retired. But he was ready to retire. He had seen the nature of those evening paper social diaries change decisively when John Feeney (who himself died, appallingly young) started being amusingly acerbic about people and events in the *Evening Herald*. My father and his generation were more like local, provincial journalists, in that they didn't say anything at all if they couldn't praise. That was already old hat, and he knew it. Gossip had become personalised. The people writing it invented personalities for themselves — to the point where the teams of people who work on something like a Nigel Dempster page all know exactly how to sound like Nigel Dempster. Nobody expresses uncritical enthusiasm any more, except for various rich men and socialite women.

What readers want from gossip columnists is the illusion of access to a raunchy café society, or to the parties celebrities attend, or to that way of life depicted in the tiny black-and-white photos at the back of glossy magazines, all women falling out of their ball-gowns and men mouths open in mid-neigh. The glossies are fair enough: they're the house magazines of people who are almost exclusively interested in the doings of themselves and their peers. There's hardly any text — at most a sort of 'Jennifer's Diary' narrative about who attended the polo match or how the marquee was decorated or who dined with the bridegroom's mother. Society photographs are also a system of reward. There are circles of — above all — wives, who live very strenuous social lives for charity, and whose suits and hats and jewellery at lunches and so on are indicators of their husband's status.

In my father's time, columns were invariably illustrated by photos of the prettiest young women to hand. The sexism was blandly seamless. The dynamic wives raising money for hospitals are in a more complex position. Their activities are as legitimate a part of Irish life as any other — much more useful than most— even if they only happen so as to be photographed.

But there are real difficulties in Ireland in pushing the notion of a sparkling café society. These difficulties are made clear by even the most cursory look at the paper which has most relied on this notion, and which — arguably — has been successful because of that, in ways where the Press papers have failed. The *Sunday Independent* would be our *Hello!* if it could.

Like many Sundays, this is a newspaper not very interested in news. It doesn't rely on expert, authoritative, news analysts. Nobody would turn to it for "the definitive account", except, perhaps in the field of crime. There was a skirmish lately about its politics, and about whether its editors give it a certain ideological tone to please its owner. But I don't think many people buy the *Sunday Independent* for its politics, or take it as more than another bunch of opinions among the many each Sunday touting for an audience.

They buy it for gossip. Who Dunphy is ranting on about, or whether the Terry Keane page is going to shed its seventh veil, or to be told whether Turks are better lovers than Connemara men, or to see the thousandth photo of Michelle Rocca and hear Hugh Leonard's thousandth attack on nuns. And they buy it because in a rickety, uncertain, eccentric and badly expressed way, it is trying to invent an Ireland purged of any of its traditional meanings. An Ireland composed of celebrities and personalities, "gossip" about whom is enough to satisfy readers, as in *New York* magazine, or *Vanity Fair* or the *Daily Express*. And people like this lightness. Gossip reigns.

The problem with this enterprise however is that there are no Lady Thises and Honourable Thats to thrill to here. The occasional vague interview with some Anglo-Irish ancient is no substitute. We're not England. And we're not America either. The effective absence of libel in America means thrillingly offensive gossip is possible. Here, the best that can be done is to out long-dead models as alcoholics. This is a small, and on the level of socialite gossip, achingly repetitive country.

The answer the *Sunday Independent* has found to the absence of a celebrity class is to propose that its staff — the people it pays to work for it — are themselves café society, that they're the most glittering people around, and that photos of them behind a candelabra, or accounts of them getting drunk with some poet, is itself celebrity gossip.

With this, the wheel my father started comes full circle. His mild hero-worship for the likes of P. V. Doyle has been turned upside down. In the contemporary world, not the celebrity but the celebrity-maker is king. Some day a cultural historian will look back at what became of the *Press* papers and the complex of reasons that led to their present decline. No doubt the diaries and columns will be scrutinised, they being a rare expression of a paper's sense of itself.

"They were too modest," the historian will murmur. "And at the end of the 20th-century, modesty got you nowhere."

Being Free

A few weeks ago, I went around the travel agencies in Dublin looking for a cheap ticket to anywhere where the skies would be blue. I arrived at one agency at the start of the lunch hour. Most of the staff seemed to have gone to lunch, even though the place was packed with customers, themselves free for just that hour. Service was so slow that person after person gave up after waiting about thirty minutes or so, and went away. Those in the queue stood, because there were only a few seats. It was almost unbelievable that paying customers were being treated in this way.

But nobody complained. Far from it: when they did at last get to one of the assistants, each person put on an ingratiating little smile, and began by apologising, as if being there at all was their own fault. When they were shown, say, a brochure — a brochure soliciting, after all, their money — they'd say humbly: "Is it all right if I keep this?" It couldn't have been more clear that a holiday is a thing so special and so desired, and everything to do with planning a holiday casts such a radiance, that even propping up the wall of a Dublin travel agency is all right. Magic phrases rose above the confessional murmurs ... "Two adults, two children, Orlando"; "Alcudia, half-board"; "on the beach, about a mile from Rhodes town ... "

As far as I know, in some hundreds of years of social theorising, it never occurred to any prophet to mention holidays. Not even the most prescient political scientist guessed what leisure was going to mean to the masses by the end of the twentieth-century. The thought quite gives one pause. How likely are contemporary Marxes and Proudhons and Pol Pots and Socialist Workers to be right in their forecasts, if the forecasters of the nineteenth century got it so wrong? Or got part of it so wrong? Only futurists of a Jules Verne-like brilliance could have foreseen cheap air travel and all that flows from it. But an exceptionally gifted student of the human soul might have intuited that workers — white collar as much as blue — would themselves take in hand their sense of their own condition, and manage to infuse it with elements of anticipation and reward.

Not that sunshine holidays bought off the revolution, exactly, but that they make people happy, and are an area in which people feel autonomous. Having something wonderful to look forward to in the future alleviates even a near-tolerable present, and holidays are easier of access than heaven. You can see that sunshine holidays have become the heart of the heartless world by the way people carry themselves on holiday.

People of different backgrounds may find different forms of play to pass the day in, and may pass it in different company; the working class mostly with their families; the middle class, it seems, more often with friends than relations; the wealthy always with their peer group. But there is one central sensation which is the quintessence of the sunshine holiday, and it is the same whether you spent the day with a puzzle-book on your beach-lounger, or studying Piero della Francesca's narrative technique, or water-skiing behind one of your yacht's motor-boats. That is the evening sensation. The sensation of being showered and fresh after a hot day. Of having a drink and a meal ahead of you. Of looking as nice as you're ever going to look, in your tan and your light clothes. "This is the life," they say as they step out arm-in-arm into the warm foreign dusk. And it is, oh it is, the life.

This is the sensation which best sums up, at least in these times and in the so-called First World, the feeling of being free. (And who would have thought, 100 years ago, that freedom would be a sensation, not a condition!) And the privileged can't buy a keener sense of it than the underprivileged: it is the same for everybody. Everybody who can get to it, that is.

For the great Mediterranean tourism industry is underpinned by people who have never felt this ease. Through windows, down the back alleys of fashionable Greek islands you glimpse sweat-stained kitchen-hands. Kurds. Egyptians. Grim men far from their homes in Africa stalk beach restaurants with their trays of wood carvings. Tired Moroccans slowly pull sweeping-brushes across the floors of airports.

But their day may come. Nobody ever thought, after all, that in Europe unemployed youths and obscure clerks and laundry women and widows with nothing but their pensions would pause at the top of aeroplane steps to put on their sun-glasses before going down on to the sizzling tarmac.

And at the same time, millions of peasants are being freed from terrible lives by the spread of tourism. Yet "blight" is what the privileged feel free to call the tourist urbanisations that now command the east coast of Italy and the east and south of Spain and parts of Turkey and the Algarve and Majorca and so on. The place where I went on my cheap ticket last week, halfway between Almeria and Malaga, was exactly what is meant by "blighted". The bare, beautiful mountains once swept down in folds to the sea, and in the valleys between ridges there were orchards and olive groves, and there were little white-walled villages above shingle beaches where the men brought up their fishing boats.

Now, the headlands have been sliced away and gouged by earth-moving machines and skyscraper blocks of cement apartments stand side by side for miles on end, so close to each other that they cut out the other's light, above the grey rubble beaches. Anywhere a few almond trees are left, the bulldozers are moving in. The villages have been swallowed by hypermarkets and concrete esplanades and highways. There is no nature for miles.

But who would choose the peasant life, now? Those orchards weeded by hand, irrigated by hand? Those white-walled villages with one communal pump for water? Those baking hillsides, and the labour of harvesting olives for pence, for half-pence? Those who would prefer their landscapes unspoiled — as I do — should consider whether they want other people's human potential to be trapped forever within the simple life, for the sake of the tourist's patronage.

The huge hotels and shopping malls and bingo halls and fish restaurants that cover what once were dry clay fields around the Mediterranean are industries, exactly as if factories belching smoke and clanging with the noise of fork-lift trucks had been built on those fields. The innocence of swimming and the brilliant blue of each day and the physical release of shorts and flip-flops transform these places in the tourist's perception. But they are industries, heavy industries, even, in the environmental destruction they wreak, and their profligate use of water.

Some day these places will be archaeology. In the meantime, they offer what most people both want and can have. They are hallowed, however ugly they may be, by the happy ease they offer to burdened humans. They are huge sites of transformation.

Sexuality and Punishment

Garret and Angela. They even sound like nice kids from a tennis club, don't they? Garret and Angela. Garret FitzGerald was writing recently about how sexual intercourse between teenagers was exceptional in Ireland prior to the 1960s, and of how this caused him and his friends no unhappiness.

"On the contrary, we enormously enjoyed the consequent lack of constraint in our social relations with — many! — members of the opposite sex that flowed from the fact that premarital sexual activity was simply not an issue."

Angela MacNamara then wrote in to join Garret in regret for those wholesome times when, to quote her, "One could enjoy many friendships, much social fun ... "

I don't begrudge anyone a happy sheltered youth. I only wish it had been like that for all of us. But I'd like to put in a word for the truth of how things were for the majority in the bitter, unloving 1950s. The fact is that the sexual security of privileged boys and girls was bought at the expense of the underprivileged. There was sex in Ireland, urgent, mute, ignorant sex. The class who frequented dance-halls, rather than tennis clubs, could tell you. If there wasn't full sexual intercourse, that's because the penalties for it were so terrible.

The casualties of that system of social control are with us, in the form of ageing men who have never held a woman in their arms, and women with memories that burn. To praise the sexual restraint of the 1950s to them is like praising a diet in front of Famine victims.

Girls were punished so terribly for getting pregnant that in courting they tried very hard to get the boys to stop. Stopping was the only widespread form of contraception. If they couldn't control his drive, or their own, or if they didn't know how babies were made, and they became pregnant, they had to leave home. They had to hide. They had to be walled up in remote mother-and-baby homes, or they had to get the train to Belfast or the boat to England. Children themselves, in the utmost loneliness and fear, they had to face pregnancy and birth. Then, they had to say goodbye to their babies, the flesh of their flesh.

Garret FitzGerald said in his article that "it has become politically incorrect to suggest that any of the former constraints on sexual behaviour might have been socially useful." They weren't very socially useful to Irish girls with swollen bellies walking the streets of London.

They were useful higher up, perhaps. I presume they served the purpose of ensuring the virginity at marriage of nice boys and girls. But then, nice boys and girls weren't dependent on sex for what the world might offer of sweetness and excitement and affirmation. Nice boys and girls had parents who took them to Connemara and they had school debating competitions and they had "hops" they were collected from and they had careers to plan and they had each other. But down at the grass-roots, where the dances began at 10.00 and ended at 4.00 in the morning, life was not so warm.

Children were treated roughly, at home and at school. The destiny of those who left school at eleven or fourteen was to go into serfdom in England. Few valued the poor. Few mourned the capacities that died within them as they grew up. No wonder the dark lanes around Parnell Square used to be lined with burrowing couples after the ballrooms closed.

I remember a girl I got talking to once on the boat to Holyhead going out on to the deck with a complete stranger who gestured to her across the bar. They weren't the only ones, I'm sure. What they did was a mixture of pure despair and pure liberation. Who wants that madness back?

These days, evidently, boys and girls can have sex if they want it, so a person of the opposite sex can be a person, to be talked to, and not just an embodiment of sex. Nowadays, what only the sons and daughters of the bourgeoisie had in the 1950s is available to everyone: boys and girls can be friends. This is such a huge advance, in terms of humanity, on the near-savage fear and attraction that there used to be, that I would want to hear better arguments than any Garret FitzGerald has advanced to favour a return to "former constraints".

He says the constraints were "socially useful". What does this mean? They saved the State money, sure enough. No money was paid out for the rearing of non-marital children. Orphanages cost a bit, though on the evidence of the heart-breaking accounts of what life was like for Irish orphans, not very much. But apart from money, what has this society lost by its young people becoming at ease about sexual intercourse?

What is un-useful, socially speaking, about that freedom? Control of their sexual behaviour has passed from state and church and parents to the young people themselves. It can be hard on them, I know. It just is a hard thing, finding out how to handle sex. But no matter how the new responsibility works out, it is unthinkable that there could ever be a return to the double standards of the recent past, and its cruelty.

The new era is only beginning. Eileen Flynn still wouldn't keep her job. Dead babies are still found in ditches. Young men still run out on the pregnant girls they promised to cherish. But the old punitiveness is breaking down, all the same.

It is not allowable to express hatred for women and their wombs, even if it is felt. We can at least hope that the number of Irish people damaged by social attitudes to sexuality will decrease. Maybe, to take an example, there will be less incest, now that young people have a vocabulary with which to describe sex. That would certainly be useful. One of the major constraints of the past that Garret FitzGerald was praising was silence.

It was indeed socially useful to cover up terrible things like incest. It did make for a more stable community. But the thought of what we allowed happen to the helpless so as to preserve that silence should make us bow our heads. The death-dealing place that Ireland was in the 1950s hardly bears remembering. For girls beginning to sense the world it was like being locked in a compound, with old, male bullies up in the watchtowers. The place is a hundred, a thousand times better now. Even those who have been kept out of the general improvement — those who get the least education, the worst housing, who belong to maybe a third generation of the unemployed — even they are profoundly better off.

At least they can run their own sex lives. They can make love left, right and centre if they want to, and they can have babies outside marriage if they choose to, or inside marriage, or they can decide not to have babies, as they so wish. They are autonomous in this area of their lives at least.

This greatly increases the chance of their being as happy during their teen years as Garret FitzGerald was. And surely to God happiness, or the hope of it, is as useful an agent of social cohesion as fear ever was.

Schools and Sadism

There are straightforward historical reasons for the scandal of Goldenbridge. First, there were bound to be bad nuns. "Entering religion", as it was called, was an extremely difficult road to take, and many young women must have taken it for the wrong reasons. There were social pressures on girls to enter.

To the world, it was the height of respectability to have a daughter a nun. To a girl educated by nuns, as most of us were until the 1970s, to continue in that milieu often seemed a more plausible option than trying to get into the civil service or going to dances till you found a husband. Becoming a nun meant you didn't have to deal with sexuality at all; your parents would be pleased with you; you would be secure, and you would have much more status than most women. In the fervent atmosphere of the old convent schools, this might easily present itself to a girl as being madly in love with God. But if she wasn't, really, madly in love with God, she was stuck in a relationship calculated to drive her mad.

What's more, even if she was a fulfilled Bride of Christ, she might have to teach children or run an orphanage or nurse sick people to prove it. Even though having a "vocation" in no way qualified her to do these things, and she may have been grossly unsuited to her lifetime's task.

There was a concept, very popular when I was a girl, of "breaking the will" to make one worthy of God's love. It was a fascist's charter, of course, which is why it was so popular with administrators. Lots of schools were keen on breaking the wills of bold, sinful, children. But the teachers themselves were controlled by this idea.

So if you longed as a nun to go on the missions, they made you teach maths in a suburb. If you were gifted academically, they put you in charge of a kitchen. Generations of young women went along with this, and humbled and disciplined themselves and confessed sins of pride when their perfect docility gave way. They flogged themselves and fasted and poured out prayers so as to fit the square peg of themselves into the round hole provided for them. No wonder some of them went mad.

There was a silliness surrounding vocations. A big, spotty, adolescent girl would come into class alight with excitement. She'd whisper to her friend; the friend would whisper to her friend, and finally the news would be out: "So-and-so felt a hand laid on her head and heard an unearthly voice saying 'Come, Follow Me!'" And soon after, so-and-so would be taken away for an intimate talk with a popular nun. How many of those girls eventually found themselves full of anger, and turned that anger to rage? How many of them used the strength of a thwarted personality to infect their communities?

Entering religion, then, could be done in bad faith. That's the first thing. But society as a whole was in bad faith towards nuns. By the 1950s, the great nineteenth-century orders of nuns had been reduced to serving the Irish patriarchy, the same as everybody else. The care of children, especially, was fobbed off on them. And nobody valued children, unless they were well-heeled children — a system then and now promoted by the priests who insisted on running expensive private schools so that there would always be an "us" and a "them". It was no wonder that a nun here and there internalised the cruel values of the power structure. You could do what you liked to ordinary children, and you could take any amount of frustration out on poor children. I don't know why the Sisters of Mercy are standing in the pillory alone. A great many of other "religious" should be standing beside them.

You cannot talk to a group of Irish men about their schooldays for two minutes before someone starts telling tales of brutality. An ear deaf from a blow; a stammer from constant humiliations; a terrible episode of incontinence in public from fear, and — over and over again — a brain never used because all the boy wanted from school was to get away from it. The kind of mad sadism many men remember didn't happen in respectable girls' schools. But physical punishment was common.

I went to schools run by four orders. One was the Irish Sisters of Charity. I was cast as St Gabriel in a tableau when I was seven or so, posed at the end of the school concert, standing above the Holy Family with my wings spread protectively. But I saw my friend in the audience and waved my wings at her. The nun beat me around the room afterwards with the leg of a chair. Later, I was a pupil at a Sisters of the Holy Faith school. The nuns had a long leather strap as part of their habit — it was attached to their belts. But the head nun had a special, double-thickness strap which was kept in a cupboard. I was strapped with it many times, and it reduced me to a snivelling supplicant, squeezing my red-hot hands between my knees and begging for forgiveness.

This was trivial stuff, but it suggests a context for Goldenbridge. And the lid hasn't been lifted yet on the industrial schools, or on the runaways the farmers hunted — at £5 a head — and returned to those schools, or on the gardaí who put women who had children outside marriage into mental homes for life at a nod from their respectable families, or on the awful things done to "boarded-outs" — the slave labour of modern Irish agriculture. Almost everyone supported the régime. A man I met yesterday, for instance, told me that a Brother beat him so badly he was in bed for a week, after emergency treatment in hospital. As soon as he could walk, his mother marched him back to school, to the same brother. She asked the brother to continue to put manners on the boy, and said how grateful she and her husband were.

People are reluctant to face the truth. But I believe the truth is that what lay behind the cruelty perpetrated on children was Catholicism itself. It developed the concepts of sexual wickedness and maternal sin which were used to facilitate the expression of sadism. And the more general ordinary abuse of children was in part a consequence of more Catholic teaching, this time on contraception. It was known that almost all the children of large families — almost all children — would never have a stake in Irish society, never have children here themselves, never count for anything. Their eventual unimportance in London or Springfield, Massachusetts was visited upon them early. Why would their minders or teachers value them? Their country didn't value them.

Why would you cherish the orphans in your care? What was their destiny? Well, one destiny was to become a skivvy in a convent. Every convent had a pecking order, and the skivvies, scrubbing the mud off tons of potatoes, in their poor broken boots, were at the bottom. Why would you lavish love on a child who is only going to be a skivvy when she grows up? The burghers of the town came down to the nun and got a skivvy ....

Contemporary Ireland floats on a sea of grief. Many, many people are guilty of causing it. This isn't about one nun or group of nuns, though they have much to answer for. But they are scapegoats, too, for others still hiding.

ISSUES

The Mystery of the General Good

On my way in to work I pass beggars with their babies, and women in furs going into boutiques to collect dresses that have been flown in from England. I could buy a mackerel on the way for 25p, or I could buy handmade chocolates. I pass chip shops and dining clubs, brasseries and hermetic pubs, vegetable stalls and gourmet delicatessens.

In the bank this morning, the man in front of me in the queue was the cart-pusher, who comes along the gutter in the morning vaguely trailing his sweeping-brush. The woman behind is famous for her dinner parties. Each thing is part of the whole: privilege and poverty all in an intimate, intricate mix together.

Even the people most trapped in ghettos — the very rich, the too-famous-to-go-out, the very poor — know what the others do, and a little bit about what it's like. There's bound to be a relative somewhere whose condition is quite different from the rest of the family's. Even politicians, who never travel on a bus, meet an awful lot of people who never travel in a car. You can't really seal yourself into just one way of life here. Other people keep breaking in.

RTÉ television shows ads for expensive toys, and at the same time shows scenes of deprivation from home and from abroad. *The Irish Times* talks about champagne and golden baubles, and also talks about the homeless and malnourished and hopeless. The mix reflects the way things are. It wouldn't make sense, to most people, to censor affluence because of guilt about misery. Not only are a lot of people in actual fact comfortable enough: in actual fact, that is what everybody aspires to be. Having money is cheerful and exciting. Who ever wanted as badly to be poor?

But it jars, the mix. It jars, the silk lingerie alongside the itinerants. It is just not okay to come out of a shop with your parcels and stumble across a glue-sniffing child. Whatever there is left in us of a desire for social justice, even if it is no more than a persistent unease, comes alive at Christmas time. You make yourself conscious of your own good fortune by conjuring up what the opposite would be — what it would be like if you had no home or if you lost the children or if nobody wanted you.

Ordinary people don't know why things are as they are. They don't know how it comes about that some are fortunate and some are not. They feel themselves to be individually compassionate — they would make things better for other people if they could. But they see no route from themselves to the general good. They don't know what to do, except be charitable.

In theory, that is what politics are for. We are an electoral democracy and we can use the ballot to express, through legislation, the will of the people. In practice, this is not how politics in this country is perceived. People grasp that they can elect politicians, and choose between the persons offered to them. They can even elect parties. But the connection between party and policy has long since been lost, at least in the centre and on the right. Nobody even listens to what politicians say before an election. And after an election, what power have the people then? If we were asked, for instance, by referendum, whether we want the recommendations of the Commission on Social Welfare implemented, I have no doubt that we would say that we most certainly do. But no government implements them. Something stops them: the size of the task, or the Department of Finance or, for all I know, the International Monetary Fund. We really have no way of making the Government's priorities the same as our own.

And leaving politics aside, most people don't know anything about economics. They see no connection between their own good fortune and the bad fortune of others. Nobody ever points out any connection, except in the line of making them feel guilty. But they don't want to feel guilty, and they don't believe they are guilty. They're glad that they're safe and warm and have money to spend, and they really, really don't understand why someone mightn't have worked for five years, or why a single mother would trap herself with more than one baby, or why a poor man would spend his whole dole money on drink.

If it were clear to people that mortgage tax relief, for instance, or private schools, are in fact connected with the despair of the underprivileged, they might allow their moral sensibility to open up to those things. But they're trapped in little pieces of information, and anecdotal knowledge, and a view of the poor based on the cleaning woman.

Yet, if asked, of course everybody would say that they want things to be better, that they don't want anybody to suffer; that of course they don't want itinerant children to burn to death in a field of mud; of course they don't want teenagers exploited in low-paid jobs; of course they don't want there to be women who can only get through Christmas on valium.

And it's not just because it's more comfortable for yourself if everybody around you is comfortable. It is because — in my opinion, anyway — people would much rather be good than bad. And they have an idea of the good, which derives from Christianity, and it has to do with other people. The thing that baffles them is, how do you get from here to there? How can one person, in one life, move a whole society towards social justice?

Can there be any kind of plan? But then do people at heart believe in planning? At Christmas you notice more than any other time how great the role the accidental and the random play in the individual life. There are going to be people who are dreadfully unhappy this week and all by accident, through no fault of their own or ours, nothing to do with money, even. That your lover left, or the daughter moved to Australia, or all the old neighbours are gone. It is known by everybody that even leaving aside the big things, like whether we have good health, or when we die, the way our lives work out is essentially ungovernable. This is never mentioned as a factor in political culture. Some politics depend on the notion of steady progress towards an achievable goal. But, deep down, people don't believe that events can be made as orderly as that. So those politics appear unreal, and that in turn affects their chance of success.

It goes against the grain of experience to believe that general reform is possible all at once, or that it can be brought about increment by increment, with everybody knowing where they're going. But piecemeal, minor reforms are within our grasp. One family can look after one other, less fortunate, family. One pressure group can establish a need, and struggle to meet it: think back ten years ago, there was no one to help the victims of rape. Twenty years ago there was no single parent's allowance. A hundred years ago there was no alternative to the workhouse. Obviously things do get better, even if it is obscure to most of us how it is that they get better, or when the exact moment of change is, or what are the ideas that eventually move in from the edges and become the centre.

It seems reasonable, if not to believe, then to hope that things will continue, bit by bit, to improve. That there might be a Christmas when there will be less to hurt the conscience.

We're hardly going to go on, are we, letting the number of our homeless grow and grow? Or are we? Is it endemic to our economic system that an underclass must develop, and that we must harden our hearts?

Sexual Harassment

I was waiting for someone in a pub the other day. It was just before the lunchtime rush, and the boss was having a cup of coffee. He had positioned himself on a low stool, beside the entrance to the counter. The lunchtime waitress was hurrying in and out of there, and every time she passed he grabbed at her legs and tripped her. He was laughing, but his eyes were intent. He was absorbed in his little piece of sadism. She wasn't laughing. But she has to put up with it, doesn't she? He's the boss. He has power over her.

On the radio I heard Professor Denis Donoghue explaining that in America, when teachers are alone with students, the doors of the rooms are left open for fear of allegations of molestation. Tom Rafferty, MEP and former professor, seemed amused. They never had to do that in Cork, he said. It's just these crazy litigious Americans, isn't it? But Professor Donoghue put him right. Sexual harassment is commonplace in universities, he said. Teachers have power over students. Of course they sometimes use that power to exact sexual favours from the young.

Power is the key. That is why harassment is properly dealt with under employment legislation. The Labour Court stated, in 1984, in the case of a woman who had been driven to resign from a job in which she had been continuously subjected to unwanted advances, that "freedom from sexual harassment is a condition of work which an employee of either sex is entitled to expect." Fine words, and I'm grateful that they exist. But in real life there is a huge gap between what women feel harassed by and what men will accept is harassment. It was only a *joke*, they say. Can you not take a joke?

The Labour Court recently had a look at a joke and decided it wasn't all that funny. It happened in a hotel, on a company training weekend. Two women were sharing a room. They left it in the evening, tidy, presents packed for their children etc. When they came back, the room had been wrecked. Beds stripped, furniture in piles, bedclothes in the bath and every single thing belonging to the women interfered with in some way. Their underclothes, including soiled underclothes which had been put away, were arranged on the bed in a 'sexy' way. An overnight bag had been stuffed with clothes and then it had been zipped up, around a roll of cotton wool, so that the roll protruded. An armchair had been overturned on the bed so that its webbing underside faced the room. A curling brush had been thrust through the webbing, so as to protrude.

The women thought a sexual pervert had done this to their room. Back at work on Monday, one of them went to the personnel manager to ask why the Garda hadn't been notified. That evening the managing director, the engineering manager and the same personnel manager called to her house. They had done it, they said. It had been meant as a practical joke.

A practical joke. Innocent of aggression. Innocent, of course, of phallic overtones. Totally innocent. A prank. The Labour Court made the pertinent point that since there were many more male than female employees on the weekend, why not play a prank on a male?

But you know and I know, don't we, that it wouldn't be so much *fun* if it was just done to a bloke. It wouldn't have that *frisson*, would it? And what has that *frisson* to do with? Why, it has to do with threat, with aggression, with the delicious thought of the women coming into the room and having to deal with the mock-penises sticking out at them. It has to do with savouring the thought of the women's helpless fear.

What makes these men think that sexual aggression is funny? Have they ever seen a woman amused by it? Are they happy to see it directed at their own wives and daughters? Would they let the same daughters take risks with it? No, they wouldn't. But they're evidently so thick that they don't realise that there is a spectrum which goes all the way from having your breast pinched to being raped, a spectrum that goes from intrusion to violence. A spectrum of aggressive acts. All of them remind women of all the others. Getting into your room, playing with your underwear and leaving triumphant symbols behind are most certainly actions that belong in this spectrum. And if the three men couldn't see this, surely their peers in the management of the company could see it? What were they doing, defending these actions?

I pity the woman who took the case. I can imagine how hard it must have been and how everybody, at work and in her community, will sneer at her for causing a fuss and will blame her. Women are always blamed in these circumstances. Yet she didn't do anything. She didn't get the key to their bedroom and play a prank. She caused nothing. But she'll be stigmatised as your woman who caused all the trouble. I admire her. I am swept with shame every time I think that when I saw the waitress being harassed in the pub I didn't even speak. I should have had the courage to speak.

All some men can say, when you raise the subject of harassment, is, "Sure you should have seen the skirt she had on her. Asking for it, she was." But the fact is that women have the right to make themselves attractive. They often are trying to attract someone. So are men. Why shouldn't people try to get off with each other, the end result being so delicious? Why can't a woman wear what she likes and retain the right to make her own decisions? Why shouldn't she assert her sexuality? It doesn't harm anyone. It doesn't threaten. Not to mention that if she hides it, and does not dress in the way men find attractive, then she's written off as boring, weird, gay, frigid etc.

Sexual harassment has nothing to do with real sex. It has nothing to do with the pleasures and the perils of an honest pass — and everyone has made a pass at at least one other person sometime, otherwise the race would have died out. It has nothing to do with the hints and glints and voltages between attracted people.

What it is is an abuse of power. Behind it there is always some way that you are going to be punished for resistance. Maybe he's going to hit you. Maybe he's going to gossip about you. Maybe you'll be out of favour. Maybe you'll lose your job. To avert punishment, you have to pretend to see the joke. But I don't think women are going to acquire the sense of humour in question until they are as strong as men, as violent, and as immune from pregnancy.

And until they have the same power. One of the men, for example, who degraded the women's bedroom, was the personnel manager. Since the incident, the same personnel manager has given an unfavourable assessment of her work performance.

Knowing Travellers

Someone I know bought a derelict cottage recently. He was working on it at weekends, and one weekend the copper-piping for the plumbing was delivered to the site. A local came up to see him and said that travellers had been noticed looking at the copper. So he slept in the shell of the building for a few nights until all the copper had been installed and the place was secure.

When he told me this little story he said to me: "I'm only telling you this in private. I'd never say it in public." In other words, he's a decent man who wouldn't dream of contributing to the anti-traveller feeling around. On the other hand, he unhesitatingly believed that the travellers were going to steal the copper.

There are not many subjects on which such double-think is commonplace. Abortion is similar, in the passions it arouses and the absence of a middle ground. But liberals here are actually more free to express their views on abortion than on the travelling people. They may have worries about the whole travelling way of life, and fear an element within the travelling people. But they will not give voice to any of this, for fear of being seen to line up with the vociferous minority which would be glad to see the travellers in punishment camps, and their women sterilised.

Thus, the argument about travellers polarises people into those who hate them, and those who are driven by that hate into a blanket defence of the travelling people which ordinary people cannot quite accept. Claims are made for the travelling way of life which settled people, by definition, cannot understand. And the travellers are charged with so many and such horrible crimes by their detractors that their defenders have to deny any criminality at all.

Dublin County Council recently had a special meeting about their plan for halting-sites. During the meeting, one councillor said that there was a fear among settled communities that the presence of travellers would lead to an increase of rape and in attacks on old people. He was shouted down, and withdrew the remark.

I'm glad that he did so. But it is more of the double-speak. He was only reporting, accurately, what some people do fear. If those fears didn't exist there would be no problem. But the fact is that there is a problem. I don't see what is gained by acknowledging the problem, but refusing to acknowledge the reasons for it.

I have never had the opportunity of knowing a traveller on equal terms. The closest I've come was a settled traveller I met in Cork. She always kept her hand over her mouth, because her lips were split and her teeth missing, thanks to her late husband. But she was the gentlest, most good-humoured of women. When I met her, her children were teaching her to read and write and she was learning at a great rate, because she wanted to be able to help them at their homework.

Just one meeting like that can dissolve the stereotypes. But anyone with eyes in their head can see the healthy children and the spotless caravans that some travellers can manage to present in seas of mud and in rain and frost. And anyone can listen. More and more, travellers' own voices are being heard. There was a young woman on the Gay Byrne Show not long ago, talking to him about the way travellers handle courtship and marriage. She was wonderful. If anything, she was patronising the rest of us.

If this smacks of a naïve plea to recognise the humanity of the travellers, that is because their enemies deny their humanity, so you have to start the discussion at zero. "Animals," people say. "Savages." "They've all got AIDS."

Journalists get long, usually anonymous, letters about the filth of the travellers, their neglect of their children, their thieving ways, the viciousness of their assaults, the way they terrorise old people all over the country. Usually, one thing has been done to the writer by a traveller, or someone thought to be a traveller. And in their distress and fear they see travellers everywhere and crime everywhere and the whole of living ruined for everyone by all travellers.

You can assert to such people that travellers *are* humans, that they are our fellow Irish people, and are, on the whole, as law-abiding as the settled people, on the whole, are. But this cuts no ice. The one thing that stops the tirade is to point out that which is self-evidently true: the babies of travellers come into the world as innocent as you or I, and whatever it is that goes wrong happens in and through society.

Almost the whole of travellers' lives is on view. A man beats his wife in the street and a hundred people see. Settled wife-beating happens behind closed doors. The travellers line up outside the employment exchange with bottles of wine in their hands, or sit in their vans swigging from the bottles. Meanwhile thousands and thousands of settled people are drinking in pubs or in front of the telly or handing around the sherries. Many people neglect their children, but hardly anyone knows. Yet everyone sees the travelling children sniffing glue. Everyone sees the women with sunburnt babies sitting all day in front of a cardboard box.

Everyone can identify a traveller at once, the weather-beaten faces and the motley clothes. Their beautiful women and children, such as Nan Joyce and her children, have a special sort of beauty. So the travellers have no privacy from us. They are "other". Their otherness is more than disquieting: between us and them there is an abyss of understanding, and in that abyss the nightmares about their nature swirl. What you have no understanding of you can endow with any feature.

It is this mythic element that makes reasonable planning for the travellers so difficult. Because, on the face of it, the problem they present is soluble, and it should be possible to bring about an Ireland where everyone has access to water and sanitation, and where we, the comfortable ones, don't have to put the others out of our minds on cold winter nights. There are about 12,000 persons — persons, not families — on the road or staying at halting sites. Even if that (1996) figure is a great underestimate, that's still a very small number of people. There are millions of us — surely it is possible to set up a network of sites and schemes where travellers can escape from the degraded living conditions which we impose on them, and then calmly blame them for?

Or, do we want to go on like this for ever? The argument from compassion has never worked: we've accepted for decades that travelling children suffer and die in far greater numbers than our children, and not many people care.

But what about the argument from self-interest? The very people who most loathe and fear the travellers must see that the cycle has to be broken sometime. They must see that while attitudes to the travellers remain so hostile, traveller children are born to alienation, born to be increasingly hardened by their experience of life, born to grow up unable to like or pity or make common cause with their oppressors. "Why don't *they* do something? Why don't *they* understand us?" some settled people cry. But truly, what society has done to them is so much worse than what they do back, and all of us are so multiply advantaged compared to them, that it will take a long process of reparation before we can talk of mutuality.

Animal Rights

This morning, Clery's department store in Dublin opens, for the first time, without a fur department. Furs are gone. No more buying the wife a musquash for the anniversary. No more of those stiff little squirrel jackets that mothers used to lend daughters going to dress dances. "There's just no demand for them anymore," says Clery's management, and theirs is not to reason why. But apparel is always immensely socially significant, and for furs to disappear from the shops of Western Europe and North America tells us something about the nature of our times.

Mainly it tells us about the power of unreason. The anti-fur lobby do not want women to wear furs, and towards this end they have left incendiary devices in shops, smashed windows, harassed fur-wearers and financed a very clever advertising campaign. They've been amazingly successful, given how many other pressure groups, similarly trying to improve us, have failed. It is more or less unacceptable — in certain quarters, at any rate — to wear furs now.

Which is a pity, just when furs were getting cheaper and cheaper, and beginning to lose their Western association with idle luxury. They were getting cheaper because animals were being farmed for their skins, just as animals are farmed for food. But the anti-fur people, like all fundamentalists, are not interested in discrimination. It suits them to pretend that every fur coat is a threat to the last few members of some beautiful and declining species. It suits them to find offence in all furs, even your grandmother's fur collar, where the animals in question have been dead for 100 years. Further, they have placed the question of wearing furs somewhere in a vaguely moral or emotional landscape. They have evoked guilt, without defining the sin. But if you try to think, as opposed to feel, about the issue, several things will strike you at once.

First, this is a local, not a universal matter: you don't find an anti-fur lobby on the streets of Murmansk, or trying to convert the Inuit. Secondly, it is directed against women, always a softer target than men, or men or women together. Thirdly, it does not make sense. If the aim is to stop the exploitation of animals by humans, then they should be leaving their incendiary devices at meat counters and in shoe shops, and putting up posters showing cruel people doing grotesque things like eating rashers.

But, is that the aim? Or is the anti-fur lobby more about expressing something than achieving something? Isn't a lot of animal rights emotion at bottom an expression of disgust at humankind? Animals are nicer than people, animal activists believe. Animals, they point out, do not inflict war on each other, or abuse their children, or pollute the planet, or tell lies. No more they do. But they do not write books either, or devise political systems, or tell jokes, or nurse you when you are dying. They are different from us. One of the ways in which they differ is that we have the capacity to use them for food and clothing, and they do not have the capacity to use us.

Thus, for example, the Koreans farm rabbits and make cheap rabbit-fur coats. I have such a coat. It cost £230 and it should last for twenty years. But will I be allowed to wear it for twenty years? A girl pushed me into a doorway in London, so overcome with emotion that she could not speak, and handed me a leaflet about our cruelty to dumb animals. This confrontation raised in an acute form my rights as opposed to a Korean rabbit's rights. Is it wrong that an animal should lose its life just so I can be warm? Should we leave all animals strictly alone, and if we do, what will become of humankind, since the declaration of peaceful co-existence would be strictly unilateral?

I find it very difficult to formulate the rights of a rabbit or a chicken or a rat or a sparrow or a mosquito. We all agree on killing mosquitoes, do we not? Except for followers of the Jain sect, of course, who brush the pathway ahead of them as they walk, so as not to crunch any living thing. Their position has the merit of logic. Mosquitoes are as alive as elephants or white leopards or Fido or Puss. They are less rewarding, but they are just as alive. For all we know, they have emotions, too. We do not really know anything about the non-human species, not sharing a language with them. The absence of language is plainly a comfort to some people: they can lavish love on a pet or on animals in general and never be challenged. But such relationships are not of the same order as relationships between humans. You can get a dog or a cat to be loyal to you in return for your protection: human love is a lot harder to win.

Sentimental feelings towards all animals as such is quite a new twist to humankind's dealings with the other species. So far, we have worshipped them, made them sacred, attributed magic to them. Tortured them. Trained pit-bull terriers to fight each other, trained bears, trained cocks, trained greyhounds to kill hares, falcons, shrews, borzois, wolves, hounds, foxes. We use animals for transport, we race them against each other, we send them into space. We inseminate them, farm them, battery-farm them. We eat them: fish, birds, eggs, flesh, milk. Dogs and cats are singled out to be individually loved, but on the whole the fate of the animal kingdom has been, and is, to serve us.

This would seem self-evidently right if we lived in the Amazonian jungle or in Outer Mongolia or anywhere human existence is at issue. Survival there is in direct proportion to the ability to master animals. But in the urbanised West, all that is distanced. Animals are represented by domestic pets, and Bambi, and the harmless things in zoos, and wildlife films viewed in the comfort of your own home. Respect and admiration for the natural world has grown where first-hand knowledge of it has been lost. So we are left without any sturdy sense of where we are in relation to animals. We want to save dolphins, but not rats; wear shoes from the hides of farmed animals, but not furs from the skins of farmed animals; eat fishes, but not meat; love our own cat but not next door's dog; respond to the helplessness of animals, but not the helplessness of our own species.

It is not one of bit surprising that there should be so much inconsistency about a subject so complex. I cannot imagine that all human beings everywhere will ever share a common attitude to all animals everywhere. It seems to me eminently an area where you make up your own mind. For myself, I draw the line at making animals suffer or die for my sport, not so much because it's bad for them as that it is bad for me. But I accept that animals die for my food. And since they have skins and furs, I accept that they die for my clothing, too.

I would far sooner abandon the Korean rabbit fur because it was probably sewn together by underpaid, exploited Korean human beings, than because rabbits die to make it. And, by the way, the rabbit meat is used to make pet-food for the dogs and cats of the West. What did you think pet-food was made of?

Innocence Ruined

One morning last week I was walking down the Rathmines Road at about eight o'clock. I was going for a swim. Going past McDonald's I saw a woman, surrounded by children. She was calling in to someone inside the restaurant, asking what time it would be open. She was a small woman, and the children were very small. I counted them — six little girls, and the baby she was carrying looked like a boy. The older children were laden down with bags and bundles. McDonald's wouldn't be open for another hour, so they walked on. A duck and her ducklings.

I said to the woman that there was another café around the corner, and because she was so burdened I ran round to it to see when it would be open. It would be open at half-past-eight. I could guess what this little troupe were doing on the street, but the woman told me anyway. They'd run away from the caravan they live in at first light. Her husband had been beating her. You could see the bruises.

There's a refuge for battered woman in Rathmines. She'd been there already, but she'd been told to come back at half-past-ten when the health people would be there. So she and the seven children were looking for somewhere to shelter for the next few hours. They stood there, all with the same blue eyes. Matter-of-fact, they were, as if it's just another thing you do in life, to pack up all your worldly goods and set out. The mother had organised the evacuation with such precision: the baby's food had been prepared, the bundles were distributed according to what each child could carry. And they were all spotlessly clean, hair and clothes. How she had managed this, in a caravan, I just don't know. I thought maybe I should go with them to the café in case they were refused service. The woman had a traveller's voice. But they were such an orderly little group that I expected they would be all right.

So I went for the swim. There was me, paying money to get exercise. There was she, getting miles of exercise, whether she liked it or not. I went home via the café. They were sitting at some tables outside its door. They had no cups or anything in front of them, so I don't know whether they'd eaten. The baby was chuckling away, but the little girls were bored. "What time is it?" one of them asked me. She had her schoolbag with her. Maybe she would have preferred being at school to trailing around with her mother, though you could see the confidence they had in her. I said to the woman: "There are eight of you, and there's only one of him. Could you not have thrown him out?" "That's easier said than done," she said.

I rang the refuge later. They have twelve families there at the moment instead of ten which is their maximum, and the place is so crowded that they're sleeping on floors. But they had made room for her. She's there now.

I could go and see her. She's used to people with accents like mine asking her intimate questions. I could give her advice about housing and contraception and barring orders. But who am I to exploit her powerlessness further? The rich and powerful never tell you anything — you wouldn't dream of asking. People like her tell you everything, because you might be able to help them. But I can't help her.

Except by asking the broad question — what put her on the street? And you may say that whatever it was, it has nothing to do with us. We can't help it if he beats her. It's between themselves. We have nothing to do with it. As a community, we designate people to protect the weak. We designate the Garda. Of course, it's hard to get to the phone when you're being beaten up, and of course this woman had no phone. Still, in theory, you can always send for the guards. And we do provide refuges for battered women. Not nearly enough of them, but some. Not many women have to walk the streets with their children all night. Only a few. You could say that there is no more the community can do about what is essentially a private matter.

But there is more the community could do. It could begin to become conscious of the extent to which some men think they own their women and children, and the extent to which they feel entitled to wreak their power over them. Everyone assents to this. Beating your own wife is far more acceptable than beating someone else's wife. Why?

Why is it that no one interferes? Why is it that wife-beating is considered distasteful and upsetting, but isn't considered a grave offence? It is accepted as a part of life, something that always happened and always will happen, as if it were part of "nature". But there is no one nature. We construct nature. What we think is natural, and therefore outside human manipulation, changes all the time. For example, it once seemed natural to be amused by the mad, and people went to Bedlam to laugh at the inmates. For example, it once seemed natural to do anything you liked to animals. You could prod a poor bear to dance in the street. That's over now. What is "natural" has been reconstructed. To the point where I can say that if a man cruelly beat a harmless and devoted pet animal there would be public outrage. Whereas there is no outrage at a man beating the woman who "belongs" to him.

"Why doesn't she leave him?" is what people say. Why is it assumed that she is free to change things, but he isn't? Why is he assumed to be changeless? Why are there refuges for women, instead of refuges for men, where they could go or be sent to sort themselves out, and try to find some insight into their behaviour? There is one self-help group, in north Dublin, where men who habitually assault their partners have come together to confront what they do. Why is there only one such group in the country? Look at what women have done, for themselves and for other women, over the past twenty years. First they started all the services that men's abuse of women make necessary —

services for single mothers, rape counselling, refuges. Then they moved on and today, literally all over Ireland, women are involved in self-development through schemes and groups and personal initiatives, and through the arts. Thousands of them are hoping to change themselves and to understand things better, with the hope of living more fully.

Where is the corresponding vitality in the world of men? You'd think that they were perfect the way they are. You'd think patriarchy was perfect, even though patriarchy underpins beatings and abuse and rape and walking away from the responsibility of your own child. "Feminist" men claim to be such because they are personally blameless and because they support women. But why don't they support men? Why aren't they out there working with rapists, the same as women work with rape victims? Why does no man take responsibility for his brothers? Even about themselves too many men are lazy, and get by on the minimum of insight. In practice, the only men you meet who know anything much about themselves are men who have struggled to give up drink, because they have had to reflect.

Of course, someone is going to say that I'm generalising about men. Yes, that's exactly what I'm doing. Individual men are as likely as anyone else to give their time to the Vincent de Paul, or to be dedicated probation workers, or to lend their energies to social change, including all the changes that have come for women. But it is on the general level, it is as a mass, as a gender, that men are to date so much less conscious than women.

Yet it is on the level of consciousness that change must come. Just as it did about Bedlam. Barring orders and more refuge places aren't the answer to wife-beating. The answer is self-education, especially the self-education of men. The ideal people to get a process of self-education going are not officials, not social workers, not doctors, but other men. Ordinary men. But that kind of thing is not the kind of thing men do for each other.

I don't know why that man beat up the woman I met. I don't suppose he knows either. I don't suppose she knows. And above all, I don't suppose that the children know. But they were there when it happened. They were learning. So that's seven more small human beings who have seen with their own eyes that brute violence makes things happen. The implications of such a lesson are social as well as personal. We will be dealing with them. But even if it meant nothing in social terms — even if the only victims of that night's violence were the women and the seven children — look at the extent of what those children have lost. Theirs is innocence ruined, even though their mother is so brave.

The New Order of Divorce

It looks as if we will have faced — within a single decade — the questions raised by abortion, twice, and by divorce, twice. The subjects won't go away. At both ends of the spectrum of opinion about these things they are lumped together, like bacon and eggs. Extreme conservatives are opposed to both in any circumstances; radicals see both as a simple matter of human rights. In the middle of the spectrum, however, the two issues diverge. They feel different, and they're talked about differently. They have different consequences for the society we're all trying to live together in. Abortion is by far the most psychologically powerful of the two subjects. But I think that — leaving aside for the moment intrinsic right and wrong — if you judge the availability of abortion or divorce in this country simply as social change, then divorce is by far the more momentous.

For one thing, abortion is a private matter. The provision of abortion isn't, of course, and neither is the legislation which might govern such provision. They are by definition in the public sphere. But actually having an abortion is private. Even in cultures where it is not necessarily furtive, it is not a matter for exhibition. It belongs to a whole category of things about women and their bodies that women only talk about in exceptional and intimate circumstances.

Even where there is no guilt there is regret. An abortion brings about an absence. There is nothing, really, to say. You don't hear news of an abortion passed around the family, or discussed in the workplace. So the actual social impact of abortion is negligible. After all, we have it now. We live alongside the 5,000 or so women a year who've been to England. We don't know who they are — or want to know — and they don't want to be known. I imagine that it would be the same even if the procedure were carried out in this country. It will no doubt be said that to have abortion available here would change society — would bring about a perceptible public decline. But in that case, why haven't we felt the decline already, emanating from these thousands of women in our midst?

Whereas divorce is going to change the way we think and feel about some central things — for everybody. For one thing, if it is accepted here, it will diminish the perceived power of the Roman Catholic Church. Or, at least, of the Catholic Church locally: I don't think the Catholic Church in California, say, makes much of an issue of divorce. It isn't just a matter of authority and obedience — of our choosing to do something they don't want us to do. Their teaching on contraception is very widely ignored, without any particular consequences. But contraception is not felt to involve the sacred and the sacramental. Very few people approach their sex lives in that frame of mind. Getting married, however, is different. If ever ordinary people really, really try to consign an action of their lives to God — if ever they consciously appeal for grace — it is when they get married. The undertaking is so serious and so perilous that prayer seems entirely appropriate. What will become of that intersection of the natural and the supernatural when everybody is perfectly aware that the same vows might be made twice or three times? That not everything is staked on the one venture?

Divorce, after all, is about remarrying. It is not about marriage breakdown, which happened, happens and will happen, whether or not there is divorce. I heard the Taoiseach, Albert Reynolds, talking about his fear that divorce would impoverish women. Someone should make it clear to him, once and for all, that it is marriage breakdown which impoverishes women, not divorce. We already have all the circumstances of marriage breakdown. We already have second and subsequent relationships and families with several parents and women left high and dry to bring up children and men striving to make one wage stretch to two households. All that we already have. What we don't have is multiples of people legitimately called husband and wife.

You can imagine the scene in graveyards. Which widow will be the important one? At christenings, weddings, and re-weddings, it is not just the grannies who are going to be stunned. All of us — except the international jet-setters — are going to have real difficulties expanding on the concepts we inherit. The most fundamental of those concepts is the family. Even a brother-in-law who has been married in for thirty or forty years can continue to seem not one of the real family. When the chips are down, in crucial family discussion like whether to put an aged parent into a home, or how to divide a legacy, the persons who have merely married in will find themselves ignored, often. The family is the one unit that survives even an otherwise general social disintegration; it is the one group to which the anti-social are loyal. Until now there has been no question as to who belongs to what family. But a succession of marriages of equal status will change all that.

It will also, one might suppose, deal something of a blow to the romantic ideal we all carry around. This is the notion that there is just one other person in the world who is exactly the right person, and that you find that person and — each loving the other perfectly — marry him or her, and go on loving till the end. This ideal coincides with the Christian ideal. It is also the most practical, the most hygienic and the most child-protecting arrangement to hand. But the problem with basing a life-arrangement on love is that love's claims are just as imperative second time around.

"Love" is the value to which divorce defers. But the love industry is so powerful — think, for example, about popular music — that it is a value which is hardly ever examined. Part of the confusion I feel about the culture of the United States, for example, has to do with the meaning of the word "love" there: it seems to be of transcendent importance and at the same time of no importance at all. Here, love is accepted as sufficient reason for getting married, but the absence of love is not accepted as sufficient reason for ending the marriage. With divorce, romantic love moves even more centre stage than it is already. It receives further endorsement.

And, of course, that — the endorsement of romantic love — has all kinds of implications. It affects who we think of as valuable, and at what stages in their lives. It massively supports individualism: it imports a kind of optimism into popular thinking. The point of love, after all, is that it makes one happy. The provision of divorce would make being happy an acceptable social goal. The thousands of little personal systems of pessimism which in fact keep life going here will lose a bit of their status.

None of these philosophical shifts are entailed by the provision of abortion. So it seems to me. That's not an argument either for or against abortion. It is just an attempt to separate two issues, and to ask the question why one is so hard-fought by conservatives when the other is in so many ways so much more anti-conservative. I know a girl who is pregnant and she and her boyfriend are thinking of getting married. Up to now, I'd have begged them not to do it until they are more certain. But I found myself thinking the other night, "Sure, what does it matter. They'll be able to get divorced, if it doesn't work out." And it occurred to me that I'm the first of all the long line of O'Faolains who ever lived to have that thought.

The Gay B&B

There's a small guest-house in central Dublin, in a pleasant, prettily decorated, nineteenth-century house. They're all the rage now, these town-house places. Just inside the door, in an illuminated frame, there's a large photograph of the President. That's common enough. Only — not so common — beside Mrs Robinson there's a portrait of Danny La Rue. He performed the opening ceremony of the place a couple of months ago.

The guest-house is attached to a gay sauna club. You get free admittance to the club (worth £7.50) when you stay a night in the guest-house (B&B, £25 single). It's Ireland's first gay-run accommodation, and it's mainly meant for gay men, although anyone, of course, can stay there. And it's as stunning a sign of social change in Ireland as you're likely to come across.

It asks more of the rest of us, in the line of abandoning old attitudes, than gays have hitherto done. Last week, for example, we had World AIDS day. Everyone knows what gay men have suffered through AIDS, and more or less everyone on such a day, if they think about it at all, feels sympathetic. It's easy to be sympathetic towards somewhat distant people, especially when they are comfortably defined as victims. The guest-house, however, is a detail in the life of a perfectly self-confident, if sexually specialist, part of the community, which has its own entrepreneurs and its own business life. Sympathy is quite irrelevant. Then again, next Friday 170 gay men and lesbian women will attend a gala dinner in a hotel in Dun Laoghaire, where they will present the Minister for Justice, Mrs Geoghegan-Quinn, with the Hirschfeld Award.

This award is to mark the forthright way in which the Minister presented the arguments for Ireland's progressive sexual equality legislation. It is fully expected that a wonderful night will be had by all. And the conferring of the award will be another moment in social change. A great many people in Ireland still have the knee-jerk reaction that the only thing the Department of Justice could possibly want with homosexuals would be to keep an eye on them. But there are no threatening laws now, no in-built criminality, nothing which a homosexual person can get into trouble for that anyone else wouldn't get into trouble for, too. Obviously, all the implications of this have yet to work their way into every corner of the social fabric. For example, the Army appears to have an unresolved problem. But the Gay and Lesbian Federation is now as likely as the Irish Farmers' Association or the Pre-School Playgroup Association or the Soroptomists or any other body to invite a Minister to dine with them and receive an award. They're not just normal — they bid fair to be boringly normal.

Yet it is not possible to recover in just a few months from the millennium or two during which homosexuals were formally reviled and ostracised. Gay people themselves probably adjust more quickly than outsiders can — they always knew that in everything except sexual orientation they were much like everyone else.

But I can imagine real shock, on Christmas Day, when people watching British television find that, simultaneously with the Queen's speech, Channel Four will be showing Quentin Crisp delivering a 'Heartfelt Message from New York'. I'm sure there will be people who think they are quite unbiased who, nevertheless, will say that this is going too far, that it's sheer impudence, that Christmas is a family occasion, that camp old queens like Quentin Crisp shouldn't be on earlier than nine o'clock at night, and that the programme is offensive to the elderly and to children. Forgetting that if you really mean it that gays are equal, and Channel Four feels like scheduling some gay entertainment at the exact moment which a British audience would consider the most solemn and sacred of the year, then you can't protest because it's *gay*. You might protest because it's boring, though nobody ever does that about Her Majesty's address. But you can't protest that Quentin Crisp is *inappropriate* without getting your liberal credentials into a twist.

The partners who run the guest hotel in Dublin are living witnesses to the speed with which change has happened in Ireland. Surely no other European country has changed so fundamentally, and with so little anger?

Twenty years ago, Liam and Tony opened Studio One, the country's first gay club, and they got a certain amount of harassment from members of the Legion of Mary, who reported them to the Garda. Just for existing, really. But that was the very least you would expect, given the times. De Valera was only dead a few months when Studio One opened. On the whole, everyone had a great time. And the club did well: visitors to Ireland — the late Johnny "Crybaby" Ray, for example — would dance there, and Irish gays took their place among the nations of the earth, so to speak.

But abroad, they say, and especially in England, Irish gays were despised. Even more than the rest of us, they had to put up with jokes about the bog and potatoes. Now all that has been turned right around, as the new guest-house signifies. Now, gay Ireland is an élite place. Visitors are coming here because of our legislation. Some are looking out for business opportunities. Until this year nobody was prepared to put much money into the Irish gay scene, and it is relatively undeveloped. Some are coming just for holidays. There are even kitchenette suites in the guest-house for long-term guests.

At the moment, there's a man from France staying, and a Scotsman, and some English men. But women book in, too, and they've even had a nun stay — a real one — to their great bewilderment. I said it might have been Helen Lucy Burke in disguise, come to sniff the mattresses.

The "anything goes" days, however, are over. In the club next door there's a glass box where money is collected for AIDS research and AIDS charities. The community buried a close friend with funds from that box not long ago. But gay men have learnt to live with AIDS — the same, Liam says, as people in the North have learnt to live with the forms of danger which surround them. It has only been five years since David Norris said, to the packed congregation at a cremation in Glasnevin, that "this death will be the first of many." Before that, apparently most people thought HIV infection was just an American thing, and you wouldn't get it if you stayed away from Americans.

But the five years have changed sexual behaviour. Changed it, not stopped it, which is what homophobes hoped the plague would do. Yet it is surely people who are pretending to themselves or others that they're not really interested in sex who accidentally have risky sex. If you know where you are, and with condoms practically coming out of the woodwork, you're about as safe as you can be these days. The point of a gay sauna is to get off with other gays. Sauna clubs, indeed, are such a practical idea that it's a mystery they don't exist in the heterosexual world, instead of deafening dance floors and sour wine.

The club was there for years, behind the house that has now been made into a hotel. It used to be a grocery shop. But the old man died, and the upper storeys were empty, and Dunnes Stores took away the custom. Most of the street was derelict. Now three blocks of new apartments are going up. The private education colleges which are taking over inner Dublin have moved into the vicinity, bringing in hundreds of young people. Some of the pubs have become international-type bars. Life is pouring back into an area which has done nothing but decay for years.

A few years hence the plain, grey street will be altogether modernised, and the way it was for so long will be forgotten. It will seem quite unremarkable that the local hotel is a gay one. Our citizens will be like Amsterdamers are now, or Berliners — not amazed by anything. Nobody then will see anything unusual in little things such as that the hotel's brochure says "Good morning. We do hope you had a good night's sleep and indeed an enjoyable night on the town." Or that you get a complimentary glass of champagne with your full Irish breakfast on a Sunday.

Evidently, many Irish men suffer greatly because they are gay. Every day you see the viciousness with which straight men punish them for what their existence says — that the peace and quiet of the heterosexual marriage bed isn't everything. There must be many, many men in Ireland who will never in their lives be held in a passionate embrace, because heterosexual bigotry has forced them into darkness. But that is only part of the story, and the story so far. Liam and Tony represent another possibility. They've never been victimised. They've been happy and amused, most of the time. They apologise to nobody. Moreover, a few weeks ago, the elegant façade of the guest-house won a prize in the Business Face of Dublin Awards, sponsored by Jurys Hotel Group. They accepted their certificate from the Lord Mayor. That's where they're at. They're businessmen.

When maternity leave for mothers first came in — only twelve years ago — some employers looked on fondly as their women employees went off to have a baby. Once. Then when women took time off to have second babies, or even third ones, they got furious. "They're *taking advantage* of the legislation," I remember one boss saying to me.

They thought there could be progressive legislation, but that things would stay the same — that nothing would really threaten the status quo. But legislation changes everything. The decriminalisation of homosexuality will have effects more far-reaching than most people have bothered to imagine. The guest-house is just a little thing: but it is a portent of the Ireland to come.

Crime & Punishment? —
The X-Case Sentence

The easier tasks of women's liberation are begun. But what, now, about liberation from fear of men? What about liberation from powerful men's indifferent contempt for the perspectives and experiences on which that fear is founded? We live in a society streaked with rottenness, where children and young people and vulnerable women are not safe within the family circle. Nor are they safe outside the family circle. Take a commonplace fact — more than nine out of ten women in Ireland are afraid to walk alone at night. If they hear heavy footsteps behind them they go icy with fear. They are at heart afraid of all but a few men.

It is time to say that the most obdurate, intractable problem that they have is male violence, and the men who are not violent themselves, but who forgive male violence, and belittle its effects.

Half the population, at night, are prisoners! And if they defy imprisonment, and walk home at their ease the way a man would, and are raped, we live in a society where it is perfectly imaginable that a judge will say that the convicted man is a good footballer, or a good employer, and give him a light sentence. If he rapes a child he's almost certain to get a light sentence. The most appalling thing about the reduction of sentence in the X case was that it was perfectly reasonable. The judges informed themselves about the usual sentences in cases of unlawful carnal knowledge. The X-case man's four years was actually pretty stiff compared to the usual. Forty-seven out of fifty cases of carnal knowledge in recent times got less, including just fines, or suspended sentences.

It is time to force a change in the judicial culture. The length of a sentence makes no difference to the harm already done. But sentences are all *we* have. They are the sanctions which express our estimate of this or that crime. And four years for ruining every single thing in a child's life *is not acceptable*. And I mean "every single thing". The psychiatric report on the X-case child said "that she needed psychiatric help and that her therapy would involve the working over of her experiences with the accused ... she also needs a course of medication to facilitate the necessary psychotherapy." The psychiatrist believes that this would "enable her to regain a normal, healthy, *joie de vivre* and to have the confidence to enjoy games and dancing and progress academically ... " That's the account of the damage to the child which the court had before it. But it is not generally known that her parents' marriage did not survive all this, no more than she did. The courts don't take such things into account. But a life can be murdered as certainly as a person can be.

No one up there seems to recognise the burning, choking anger that women especially, but women-understanding men, too, feel at the way sentencing seems sensitive to everything about the man, but insensitive — dead — to the value *women* place on being able to live in our bodies (and our children in their bodies) with health and joy and confidence in our sexuality. It came out again last week — Ireland's most shaming statistic. Only five per cent of confirmed — confirmed — cases of child sexual abuse are prosecuted.

And I know why. I know what happened in the case of a child I loved. Three years old she was, when she was first corruptly used. And what happened when she began to tell, years later? Why — the garda had a word with the priest, who had a word with the abuser. (Of course, the working assumption is that gardaí and priests are never paedophiles themselves, ha, ha). The patriarchy, so to speak, offers to fix matters up above our heads. As if it weren't patriarchal arrogance in the first place that prepares gluttonous men to use, as if they were things, the little girls they pervert. Only his own engorgement is real. Not her self, in all its delicacy. Does it not strike anyone else that the most wicked thing the X-case man did was to impregnate the child? He didn't have to impregnate her. He could have spared her that.

Come into the parlour, the smiling Oirish invited, last week. I wouldn't recommend any female to accept the invitation. Recently, in the west of this country, a father was found guilty of the most terrible crimes against his children. He raped and sodomised and brutalised them almost incessantly. No neighbour intervened, as far as I know. A son who ran away from "home" over and over again was returned to the man who owned him every time. A journalist I know went to the area and talked to locals. "There wasn't a thing wrong with those girls that I could see," a man who lives near the scene of horrors said. "They were as well-fed as any girl around here." Why, then, had the son finally exposed his father? "He's doing it for money. All he's in it for is the compensation."

In the Kilkenny incest case, some of the father's drinking pals used to phone the poor, beaten wife and daughter with obscene suggestions and requests. Don't come into the parlour.

Last week, after the X-case sentence reduction, and the arguments given for it, I was physically stooped. I felt as beaten down as when, after the Birmingham Six appeal, we went back to the Old Bailey to hear the Lord Chief Justice read out the verdict. He didn't just throw out the appeal. He did it with contempt. He all but jeered at the men.

Listening to him, as an Irish person, I bowed my head. I felt as if his words were lashing my back. The Court of Criminal Appeal here last week didn't, of course, make offensive remarks. But what the court offered as mitigating factors in the X case left me with the same feeling of absolute helplessness in the face of the power of the judiciary. And exactly the same feeling that the way people who are really powerful in the society I live in think and see things and estimate things is so utterly different from the way I do that I despair. I despair of being understood. I despair of understanding. I have no hope of understanding that a four-year sentence is right for what that man did. I do not know what the judges mean, when they say of the X case man that he was a "good family man". To what family was he good? His own?

I thought that there'd be a rest after the latest round of abortion-shriek. That we could come out and play. But there's no end to the insults that rain down on women. I beg the judiciary to take notice that they *must* teach themselves to imaginatively grasp that women's bodies when they are penetrated *may make a child*, and that that makes penetration and the threat of penetration more horrifying than men can know. The courts *must* reflect women's as well as men's perspectives on sex crimes.

If the next fifty cases of unlawful carnal knowledge turn out as tolerable for the perpetrators as the last fifty, we will have to bypass appeals to the judiciary, and demand of the politicians that they introduce mandatory minimum sentences. Why not? What is the independence of the judiciary to women, if that independence extends to independence of women's heartfelt beliefs and feelings? Four years! There is not a woman in Ireland thinks that just.

The Abortion
Debate Recollected

I had the feeling, listening to the Supreme Court judgement on abortion information, that with the settling of that part of that issue, Ireland was free at last to move.

Onward, it seemed to me. For the first time in twelve years no one concerned had already announced their next step. Not that there'll ever be any real end to the fight about abortion. The anti-abortion people must continue to call for another referendum, and are no doubt tirelessly canvassing county councillors and so on. Activists on the other side must continue to demand abortion on Irish soil. When the whole thing started off, and the "pro-life" amendment turned up out of the blue, that was the counter-demand. It was articulated at a meeting in Liberty Hall by Dr Noel Browne: free, safe, legal abortions in their own country for Irish women.

Looking back on the whole thing, it seems to me very telling that it was Dr Browne who spoke. The abortion argument here hasn't been rights-based. It ended up with the lawyers, but it didn't begin with them. It was the overall innocence and vulnerability of the unborn child that was offered for our contemplation, not its rights. And similarly, the argument for abortion stemmed not from any notion of the rights of the individual but from compassion, from knowledge of mothers and grandmothers and friends trapped and ostracised and destroyed and forced into exile by Ireland's treatment of women.

Noel Browne's mother's life was exceptional in the amount of suffering it contained, and in the tragic heroism of her fight for her children. But many women had it very hard. Many women gave themselves for their children.

And so there was a picture of what it has been to be a mother in Ireland in people's heads. No matter, then, how the structure of the abortion argument proposed women as the enemies of children; all the way from the former bishop of Tuam saying that the womb was the most dangerous place on earth for babies, to the mother and the unborn being separately represented before the Supreme Court. Nobody really believed it. In the experience of all of us, Irish women have not, to put it mildly, been casual about pregnancy.

Because we were going on experience and imagination, the X case changed everything. Logically, it should not have done. If you're against abortion you're against abortion. If a wealthy, thirty-year-old career woman who's afraid of losing her figure has no right to an abortion, because abortion is wrong, then neither has a raped twelve-year-old girl. But our abortion debate, as I said, was never rights-based, and therefore it was inconsistent and — essentially — unprincipled. People just referred the child's crisis to their own situations. "If she was my daughter ... ", they said, and voted for the arm's-length abortion we have now.

In retrospect, it was always going to be extremely difficult to stop an amendment that conceded anything at all to the mother from being interpreted to the disadvantage of the unborn. And looking back on the whole thing now, that's the mystery I'm left with. What was supposed to happen if the anti-abortion people had got everything they wanted? What was their ideal Ireland going to be like? I have the most sincere regard for the commitment of, say Brendan Shortall. Just a few weeks ago, listening to him on the radio, his heartfelt eloquence on the subject of the unborn rooted me to the spot. I have great regard for William Binchy's intelligence, among others, and for Des Hanafin's knowledge of Ireland. But what did they and their colleagues want in the end? They never said. Did they intend that every fertilised egg be brought to term? Because if they did, they would have had to subjugate our democracy to that one purpose.

I don't know whether the balance we've arrived at — allowing abortion, while signalling abhorrence of it — will last for long. But for the moment, it is an answer of an oblique kind to an appallingly difficult question. No authority had much influence over the answer arrived at. Like rights and principles, authority has had to bow to the people's pragmatism. The answer is neither black nor white. Going to England for our abortions is self-contradictory, and it pleases no one. But it works. Its one virtue is that it is functional.

We could be a lot worse off. We could have abortion clinics here, and violent pickets on them. Who can deny that there is violence and anger just under the surface of Irish life? Or we could have — and as far as I know, this is no exaggeration — pregnancy testing at airports. The letter-writers are out in force in protest at the Supreme Court's ruling. But what do they want? If they get another referendum, what do they want to put in it this time?

I have learnt a great deal from the whole abortion controversy. I have come to respect the depth and importance of the debate. I'm not sorry that the fundamental mystery of life itself was examined at length by this society, even if it was so often done at the expense of the loving empathy that grown women deserve quite as much as the unborn do. But sometimes I wonder whether the anti-abortion campaign was as centrally about abortion as I am supposing here.

For one thing, it sometimes seemed to have a much wider agenda than abortion. Some of the same people and the same feelings seem to be mobilised also against homosexual rights, against contraception, against sex education, against feminism, against single mothers, against divorce, and even against the child in the X case, in attempting to minimise the outrage done to her.

More or less everyone in the country would agree that the gift of life is beyond our command, and that our dealings with it must be of a different order and quality from anything else we do. It has demeaned the anti-abortion cause, in my opinion, to use it as a stalking horse for a commonplace conservatism. There is nothing conservative about being pro-life. There would be no abortion in any of our utopias.

Again I think that anti-abortion fervour was often about other things besides abortion. I think there are an awful lot of people in this country who feel excluded and unheard and held in contempt. Often, at meetings, I would see that a certain kind of educated middle-aged man, in particular, was enraged at being forced to listen to a plurality of voices, when no one was listening to him. I'm not saying that their anti-abortion feelings weren't absolutely sincere. But the rage was even larger than the issue. They would still have been angry, even if travel and information and the whole lot had gone as they had wanted.

It is Ireland they are disappointed in, and their own place in it. It is the erosion of certainty that is threatening them. A lot of people in this country want to go back to the simplicities of an authoritarian era.

Of course, there's more to say. The silence of the women who've been to England, for example, was deafening. But now that the first phase of the abortion debate is over, one can wish for a period of peace, and a turn towards the ordinary in the psychic life of our nation. Before 1983 nobody ever talked about abortion. Then it swamped us for a decade. Now, maybe, we can find rest somewhere between those extremes. We can learn how to colonise a middle ground.

BELIEF

Irish Atheism

I was talking to a woman the other day, a single parent, who supports herself and her daughter by long, night hours of cleaning. She had just got a note from her daughter's school, telling her that she'll be making her First Holy Communion in June. This woman dreads the expense; it is not just the outfit for the little girl, but something presentable for herself that she has to get. Why, she wanted to know, can they not wear their school uniforms? Why indeed. As it is, I've met mothers who shoplift to clothe their children for these occasions.

However, the grumble about the clothes turned into a larger complaint. Had I seen, she wanted to know, the amount of money that children collect on their Communion visits these days? Fivers and tenners, single pounds are too small to offer. "Surely it's meant to be religious," she said, "not all about what you're wearing and how much money did you get?"

Well, yes. It is. But what interested me about her disgust at the secularisation of this sacrament was that, as far as I know, she doesn't believe in God herself. She certainly doesn't practice the Catholicism she grew up in. So what's it to her, if the material is wiping out the spiritual?

She belongs to what I think might be quite a sizeable number of people, former Catholics, who go along with the externals of belief, so that their children won't feel like outsiders. The implications of this position don't really worry her at all, and she wouldn't call herself a hypocrite. Neither would I use the word hypocrisy in this context. Whatever it is these people are doing, it is much more vague and instinctive and pragmatic than hypocrisy is.

It starts with marriage. Imagine a man and a woman, neither of whom would dream of accepting Catholic teaching on celibacy before marriage, or the procreative purpose of marriage, or anything else the Church might preach. They haven't been to Mass in years or to Confession for decades. But they want to get married in a Catholic ceremony in a church, and they'll readily lie about their beliefs, even all the way through a pre-marriage course, to get that kind of wedding. They say that they don't want to upset the mammies and the grandas and so on, and, of course, that's true. But it is also true that their non-belief doesn't seem to them an important thing, worth arguing about in the open. It is not a positive unbelief; it is not convinced atheism. It really just boils down to not liking and not practising the religion they were brought up in.

And anyway, people usually get married so as to celebrate each other, and to say to the world, in the most solemn terms they know, that they commit themselves to each other. In this culture the vast majority of people don't know any terms more solemn than those arrived at during the history of Christianity. It takes real independence to turn one's back on this huge reservoir of meaningfulness, and to settle for the literalness of the registry office.

Next, there's the question of Baptism. Again, the emotions cry out for the big gesture, and endorsement by tradition. A christening is a welcoming of the baby to this earth, and an induction of the new human being into the community, leaving aside its denominational aspect. And, in any case, I suppose that atheist parents think that it doesn't matter very much, because the baby doesn't know what's happening. Their own example of unbelief, they assume, will set the child right.

And so it all begins. But is it a good way to live — to see to it that the children appear to be Catholics, while steering clear of the whole thing yourself? To exploit their powerlessness? To send them out to Mass, while you stay in bed? To give them money for Missions in which you don't believe? To accompany them proudly to First Communions and Confirmations, even though they have never seen you pray?

I see why people do this, of course. They want to give their children protective colour. It is extremely hard on a child to bear the burden of dissenting from the majority. Only a few children in the country can get through the educational system without encountering teachers and schoolmates and schoolmates' parents who would make no bones about their hostility to unbelief. How could any loving parent ask a child to pay for his or her parent's views? Outside Dublin it is very difficult even for an adult to retain standing while eschewing communal practices.

The children know. They know that some of the people around them really believe, and they know that no one at home does. But they have to live as best they can by the double standard. It is only about religion that this arises. Whatever other convictions the parents may have, even minority convictions, like vegetarianism, or using Irish as the language of the home, the children will be reared by them, quite straightforwardly. After all, what else can you rear children by, except your own convictions? But few people will take the risk of not hedging their bets on this, profound, subject.

But if this leads to anything it must be to the creation of adults who take neither belief nor unbelief seriously. Perhaps that is why there are so many socialists in this country, and even communists, who are perfectly at ease with religion. It used to be part of the work of the left to attempt to disenchant people with heaven, so that they would cry for justice here on earth. But Irish socialists are as keen on heaven as anyone else: they have to be. To stand on atheist principle, to refuse to join in prayers, say, at funerals, to say that religious funerals are so much mumbo-jumbo, would be to proclaim yourself utterly marginal. A nutter. Offensive. Nobody would dream of doing it.

Nobody is supposed to take any ideology seriously enough to make a display of it. Any non-religious ideology, that is. So people stay quiet, and somehow believe that by not going to Mass they are taking a stand against religion or the Church or clerical power or something — that like Stephen Dedalus they are flying by the net of religion. But are they?

All religions must have members who fall away. It must always be a personal difficulty for anyone, of any religion. But Catholicism is so vast here, so saturates all aspects of life and death, that to leave it means leaving the protection of the pack, being alone.

It is a process or a decision with myriad social consequences. Perhaps in this sense it is right for parents to keep their children enrolled in Catholicism as a way of life, even though they do not accept it as a revelation of the truth. Perhaps, too, Irish atheism is rarely more than tentative, as if God might come along at any minute and prove it wrong. The woman who faces her daughter's Communion wouldn't be complaining about the cost of it if she had money. But she would still disapprove of commercialising the sacraments she doesn't believe in. Nostalgia and wistful hope are far, far more powerful over the human heart than the dry pleasure of having a perfectly logical position.

Sin

I had a small, personal, breakthrough in my relationship
with the present Pope recently. My eye was caught by some
new pronouncement of his — something to do with women
not being allowed to wash a priest's feet, in the ceremonies
associated with Christ's Passion. I found that I couldn't be
bothered to read on. I've finally lost even interest, never
mind anger, at this kind of thing. I wish the Pope well. I'm
sure he would wish me well, if he knew I existed. But we
haven't been on equal terms for a long time now: I've cared
what he said, but he hasn't cared what I said. Now, we have
at least indifference in common.

This doesn't make any difference to the kind of
home-made arrangement with the Catholic Church that I
have evolved for myself. Authority is no problem if you are
in a position to ignore it. But there is something, something
far more fundamental, that makes an invisible barrier
around me, and makes me feel lonely, even when I am
doing and saying exactly the same things as the rest of the
congregation.

One of the ways people of my age and educational
background remain impressed by religion is in always
being conscious of the shape of the Christian year. I feel its
hollows and its plateaus and its great climbs to its peaks.
I take Good Friday, for example, with some seriousness,
even though lots of people I know are just glad of a day off
work, and watch videos and swig away at the vodka, and
the best of luck to them. This year I went down to the
Pro-Cathedral, to the ceremony that begins at 3 p.m. Radio
Two bopping away on the car radio, along the sunny, empty
streets. And then, another culture, inside the cathedral
doors.

331

Bus conductors, girls in skin-tight jeans and high heels, neat couples with neat children in matching coats, ancient men, women who carried carrier-bags full of shopping with them when they went up to the altar to kiss the cross, and again when they went up to receive Communion. All there, because a man was crucified in Palestine two thousand years ago. You don't have to be a Christian at all to be deeply impressed by all this. That it should mean so much, and that people, who look so ordinary, should have such grandeur in their private selves.

The ceremony was based on the Gospel of St John, which begins with the arrest of Jesus, and ends "and the tomb was at hand, and they laid Jesus there." The gospel was read by one woman, with another as Peter, and a priest as Christ, and us, the congregation, as the crowd. We had to bring Christ to Pilate, we had to choose Barrabas, we had to say "Crucify him! Crucify him!" We were murdering Christ. And I presume that it is from this that all the rest of it springs, the Confiteor at Mass, the calls to repentance, the idea of being saved, the penitential practices, the life-long attempt to be free of guilt which is the lot of the ordinary Irish Catholic.

I couldn't say the words, myself. I couldn't help it. I just stood there thinking: in what sense did I murder Christ? Of what am I guilty? Even poor Pontius Pilate — how was he guilty? He behaved exactly like any colonial governor; he could have been a particularly obtuse Northern Ireland Secretary. Obviously, he thought the whole lot of them were crazy, and he did his best, for a while, to grasp the situation. Then — no doubt in the interest of civil order — he gave in. He was a man caught in his own circumstances. He *couldn't* see more than he saw. He acted as best he could in the time and place, which is all that most of us can do.

And if I'd been there — though, being a woman, I wouldn't have been — who is to say that I would have murdered Christ? Couldn't I have been Mary Magdalene? In other words, why are we assumed to all be guilty, all the time, even though common-or-garden experience teaches us that guilt is only appropriate when we know what it is that we are doing, and that it is rarely collective? We certainly object to South Africa sentencing six people to hang for being part of a crowd which brought about a murder. We know that that isn't just.

Bishop O'Mahony made it clear in his sermon in the Pro-Cathedral that the Via Dolorosa is here — it is West Belfast, and the Gaza Strip. Christ's sufferings are the sufferings around us. This makes the actual Passion of Christ an exemplary story, and I think it is increasingly felt among the young that this is what it is. But what I don't understand is, where does this leave the history of the Catholic Church? Since when did it interpret the Gospel as being about injustice and inequality and the grasping of privilege by the few? And anyway, what about redressing suffering, instead of feeling for it? Christ's Passion was inevitable: it fulfilled the prophecies. Is human suffering, equally, inevitable?

On the 'Late Late Show' that night a woman made a plea for the sense of sin to be restored, before Irish life goes to the dogs altogether. Why *sin*, I thought to myself? Why not self-respect and a sense of civic duty? Between those two, we would have little to worry about. But the bishop on the panel — Bishop Comiskey — reads the world in essentially the same way as the woman does. Penitence. Repentance. A return to confession. We cannot truly be renewed until we relearn the practice of frequent confession, the bishop said.

Repent for what? What have we done, other than live along as best we can, admittedly often failing in goodness, but also trying, really trying to be good? When I was in Medjugorje, it was one of the things I found hard, that the pilgrims there were being called to repentance, although they were already as decent and pious as people are likely to be. How does it happen that Mary never appears in the Pentagon, or to Hitler's Supreme Command, or at the

Cannes Film Festival — which I assume to be an orgy of materialism? Some people I know came back from Medjugorje and now fast on Wednesdays as well as Fridays, to atone for the sins of the world. These are poor people, loving people. Why them, to atone?

There seem to be two levels of discussion about religion in this culture. On the one hand, there are theologians, and the sermons and writings of the clergy. These take certain points of departure for granted, such as that we are all in a state of sin. So they naturally never explain *why* we are, except perhaps by reference to the sufferings of Christ, which only starts the circle again. On the other hand, the faithful don't look at it as their business to worry about the "why". They just believe, full stop. But there must be some hidden kind of middle discourse, something that I might be able to follow myself. Or does not feeling guilty actually disbar you from being a Catholic?

I look at my little god-daughters. They're only six: they never feel guilty about anything. One of them nearly burned the house down, and was half-murdered, but still, I could see, she didn't *know* how to feel guilty. But she will be inducted. She goes to Mass, and beats herself enthusiastically on the breast and says "through my fault, through my fault". Eventually, this will have meaning for her. But what meaning? Will it not simply be a guilt she learns on the authority of the priestly caste, which they, in turn, are the only ones to relieve? And could there not be some relationship with the endless beauty of the New Testament that involved the mind more, and the psyche less?

It may well be that you must have a *sense* of sin to be a Catholic, or at least to join in the liturgy of the Catholic Church. It may be that having a concept of sin is not enough. I imagine that there are more people than myself who don't know where they stand about these things, but aren't quite content, all the same, to just not think about them at all.

In a way, of course, they don't matter. They're luxury worries, and they don't affect how we live our lives in actuality. But sometimes I wonder whether there are not real strains implicit in a Catholic culture for everyone except simple, believing Catholics, and whether those strains are not the more important for being personal, not social.

The Beauty of the Bell

Every few years, someone gives out about RTÉ transmitting the Angelus bell. This attracts some comment, and then the subject is dropped, till the next time. But it is perhaps worth pointing out that you can hardly walk a hundred yards in Ireland without coming across something — a cross scratched on a rock, maybe — which reminds you that the culture of the Irish people is a Christian one.

Most of our historical experience has developed in and is made manifest by the Irish language. And it is impossible to be a social being in Irish without constant reference to Christianity. "God bless you," is the English for the common Irish greeting. "God and Mary be with you" is the common reply.

The announcer on Radió na Gaeltachta sometimes signs off with "*Go gcumhdaí Dia sibh*". I would not call myself a believer, but I like to hear this said. Who would object to the invocation of a sheltering God? And a phrase like this is hallowed by age and use. As are the curses, lullabies, proverbs and so on which are the domain of God and the Devil and Mary. If a person were to embark on the (weird) project of speaking an Irish purged of religious imagery they would soon be in trouble. What's more, they could not fall back on English. What after all, does "Good Day" come from? Or "Goodbye"?

We do not go on holidays to Turkey and object to the call of the muezzin, or complain about Buddhist bells in Thailand, or protest about the great peals from the carillons of English cathedrals. We take it for granted that this country or that values this or that religion. In Ireland, the religion of the majority happens to be a Christianity more Mary-centred than the Christianity of the biggest minority. But there is no theological difference between us, as there is between, say, Muslim and Hindu in India. The general story of the Angelus — the Incarnation of Christ — is one every Christian honours. And it is difficult to know who is entitled to be offended by the Angelus' three 'Hail Marys'.

The national broadcasting station is Irish. It comes from and is supposed to address the culture of this country, which was not and is not a secular culture. RTÉ broadcasts the Catholic Mass and Protestant services and no one, so far as I know, objects. So why object to the Angelus? Anti-Catholics, if anything, should be down on their knees in gratitude to Radió Éireann for not giving in, back in 1950, to considerable pressure to broadcast the Rosary. The Angelus bell was chosen precisely because it is a call to prayer but not a prayer itself.

The expert on these and many other things, Dr Sean Mac Réamoinn, used to write about matters religious under the pen-name "Oisín", because Oisín was the first Irishman on record to stand up to the Catholic Church. Not least on the matter of bells. Oisín came back from Tír na nÓg to find St Patrick in possession. God be with the old days, he more or less said, when we in the *Fianna* listened to the sweet birds, now there's nothing but you and your oul' bells.

But bells themselves are not, of course, the issue. I take it that they are objected to as signifying twice a day that the national broadcasting station kowtows abjectly to the jack-booted oppression of the Church of Rome, so to speak.

I've suffered from Rome myself. Girls and women do. But I can't for the life of me see that the answer to that is to attempt to expunge signs of my fellow citizens' faith from public life.

I don't doubt that the Republic of Ireland must move towards a conscious pluralism, and that there must be an end to the imposition of Catholic teaching on non-Catholics. There have been what to the non-Catholic eye are sectarian outrages perpetrated here, especially in the areas of health and education. But the way to combat those, surely, is to publicise them, to protest against them, to take legal action against them where possible, to elect the kind of politicians who will get into power the political parties which will attend to them, and in the meantime, to evade them.

This however is of a quite different order of seriousness to objecting, say, to crucifixes being hung on hospital walls. Some may find the imagery of the cross offensive, but it doesn't harm them. Some may dislike seeing a missionary collection box on a chemist shop's counter, but the denominational gesture doesn't endanger, whereas a refusal, on grounds of conscience, to sell contraceptives might. I don't like seeing lawyers and judges going off to the Pro-Cathedral to get a blessing on their year's work. But as long as their judgements are not sectarian, their display of religious allegiance is their own business.

There seems to be a great deal of point in anti-clericalism, but none in casual anti-Catholicism. The strain of popular anti-Romanism you come across in Northern Ireland — all cloven-hooved priests and randy nuns and betrayals of the secrets of the confessional and Papal gluttony — is surprisingly hurtful, even to someone like me. How much more painful, then, it must be to believers to hear it proposed that public recognition be withdrawn from the Angelus prayer, which has been in use for at least 700 years, and which must, therefore, be meaningful. There would need to be serious reason to support taking it off the airwaves.

Is the serious reason our treatment of Protestants? We never speak about Protestantism in the abusive way Dr Paisley and his like feel free to talk about Catholicism. But neither were we just or fair to the Protestants in this State. If it is the case that the Marian aspects of the Angelus do indeed reawaken in our Protestant fellow-citizens the insult of the special place the Catholic Church once held in the Constitution, or the *Ne Temere* decree, then RTÉ should certainly not broadcast it. But I don't remember ever seeing such a point made by Protestant leaders. Nor do the forms of popular devotion — May processions or neighbourhood grottoes or visiting visionaries from Medjugorje or pilgrimages to wells blessed by association with the Virgin Mary — constitute, I imagine, the problem for Irish Protestants.

RTÉ television shows a painting or other art work when it broadcasts the Angelus bell. This is the single and only moment in a day and night's television that refers to history, to art, to religious inspiration, and to what to most people who have ever been born is the mysterious nature of existence. The accompanying sound of a bell is part of worship all over the planet and always has been. There's a beautiful bell from Cashel in the Hunt Collection, and it is from the ninth century. The human voice is not adequate to everything humans have to say. That's why there are bells. Reason is not always the appropriate discourse. That's why there are prayers.

These are deep things. Denominational arrogance has of course caused great harm on this island. But beware lest the attack on sectarianism becomes a cheap, trivialising, iconoclasm.

The Silence of
Reasonable
Catholics

I stood respectfully in a village street last Thursday, as the Corpus Christi procession went by. Little boys scuffled along. Little girls in their First Communion satin scattered rose petals with a certain housewifely frugality. The ladies of the ICA intoned the prayer about saving us from the fires of hell and leading all souls to mercy after each decade of the Rosary. The master led the schoolchildren with a strong voice: *"sé do bheatha a Mhuire, atá lán de ghrásta ... "* Old men tramped by in heavy boots. Fashionable people with continental tans ambled along saying the Hail Mary. They sang 'Sweet Sacrament Divine' and 'O Sacrament Most Holy' as the monstrance was taken around the village. Every pub and shop and house had been tidied and cleaned and had found some flowers to flank the statue or holy picture propped on best tablecloths. There was Benediction outside the church, and then the sergeant waved the pent-up traffic through, and the whole thing ended in a welter of tractors and tourists' campers and bread-vans, and the pubs opened, and the shrines were taken in.

It is a rare thing to see Irish Catholicism out in the street like that. For all that almost everyone in the country goes to Mass, and can be heard making the responses there, Irish Catholicism is all but mute. There is no general forum in which Irish Catholics speak as such. There seems to be no desire to speak about the faith, or if there is a desire, no language to use. Religious allegiance marks whole lives:

340

a person might be educated entirely by religious, go on trips to Lourdes or San Giovanni as holidays, enrol in the Third Order of Saint Francis, have relatives who are nuns and priests, pray night and day. Yet no one would think it strange for such a person never in their lives to say anything at all about any aspect of their religion.

This would be understandable if Ireland were like the US, and it was a settled fact that people's religious beliefs were their own business and that there was a distinction between matters of state and church matters. But Irish Catholicism is being challenged as never before. The institution and its role in society are under interrogation. It would seem next to impossible, by now, to be an unself-conscious Irish Catholic.

Yet you hardly ever meet a Catholic who has the words to tell you why they are a Catholic. Soon there aren't going to be enough religious to control the Republic's educational and health services, and the church is going to have to ask lay people to carry on its work. The religious have trained the people they will hand over to. But how well have they trained them? Will there turn out to be a cadre of lay Catholic administrators able and willing to hold out against the pervasive secularisation of the contemporary world? In thirty or forty years, when men and women with specific religious vocations have lost their institutional power, how Catholic will our institutions be?

We are heading into a post-clerical Ireland. Not a post-Catholic one, of course: even in the deprived and ravaged communities where the church is least strong there has been the usual great crop of First Communions. The people will be Catholic. But when it comes to arguing the case for a Catholic as opposed to any other kind of Ireland, how well will the people make the argument? The clerics may have trained the laity in obedience. But if I came to live here from, say, the Netherlands, and discovered that I couldn't get my tubes tied in the local hospital because Catholic teaching forbade it, who of all the Catholics around could explain the teaching to me? Who could argue the case for enforcing the teaching in Irish hospitals? There must be a case, other than that the Vatican so decrees. But what is it? Have the people any training in Catholic philosophy?

What is the case for having clerics as the managers of the State's primary schools? I can see why the Catholic Church would want this. But why should Irish people as a whole want it? If I were a Northern Protestant, who reluctantly decided to throw my lot in with an all-island Ireland, who could explain to me what this society believes it gains by having Catholic priests in this position? If I called to my new Catholic neighbours and asked — not as a criticism but to gain understanding — why the priest was also the school manager, would any neighbour be able to tell me? "Well — it's traditional," they might say. But why is it — if it is — a valued tradition?

"Why" is a word not much uttered by Irish Catholics. "How" is preferred. We knew how to proceed through life, I remember, all the way from how to make an Act of Contrition to how to renew the pledge if there turned out to have been sherry in the Christmas trifle. But "how" will not be adequate when Catholics have to stand up in a mixed society and say "I want special treatment for the Catholic position because ... " We will have to learn how to discuss the complex interactions of the spiritual and the social. Catholicism can be strong by force in Ireland, but it won't be a strong intellectual force until Catholics — not just trained theologians — know how to talk about what it means.

Catholics are spoken for more often than they speak themselves, so the nuances of their voices are frequently missed. Most Irish Catholics I know are happy to be Catholics, and privately it is a serious matter with them to try to be good Catholics. But they know they can't make other people be good Catholics. I suppose that it was that kind of *realpolitik* about their faith that lay behind the decision Catholics made in the travel and information referendum to assert abhorrence of abortion while facilitating those determined on getting abortions. No hint of the possibility of that principle-splitting came from any spokesman for Irish Catholicism.

Still less from the vociferous right-wing orators who put themselves forward as the true representatives of Irish Catholic thinking and feeling. I was listening to one of these recently. The person started off from an anti-abortion position most people would share, but within seconds was raving on about mentally handicapped people being deliberately starved to death in Irish hospitals and children being turned on to sex by the "Stay Safe" programme and divorce being deliberately introduced by conspirators to take from the Irish the religion they had fought for, and the Pope being the true ruler of the whole world — all other religions besides Catholicism being quite simply wrong. This fundamentalism is very unfair on the majority of Catholics who worry about threats to their religion, who hanker after simpler days, and who are not at all mad.

But it is the extremists who get on radio and television and bombard newspapers with letters. The country is full of decent, reasonable people who are committed Catholics. But the hardest thing to find in the country is a decent, reasonable Catholic who can argue and debate the big questions facing Irish Catholicism. I blame the institutional church which kept its people dumb. It never taught them language for fear that their profit from it would be that people would know how to curse — that the faithful would want seminars as well as processions.

Death

The funeral rituals of priests differ in some details from those of the rest of us. Not many people know that. Ordinary people, when their coffins are brought into the church, are placed in front of the altar feet first. Priests are placed with their heads closest to the altar.

We will be buried with our heads to the headstone. Priests are buried with their feet to the headstone. And this applies to priests of the Church of Ireland, too, though I think only Roman Catholic parish priests are buried in graves lined with brick. Practices like these that set priests apart have grown up over the years because, whatever about priests themselves, ordinary people want priests to be people apart. If they were not, they would not seem to us to be suitable mediators of the different levels of significance we're aware of in our lives.

It is almost impossible to imagine an Irish funeral without a priest. Yet outside commentators seem to think the Roman Catholic Church here is falling apart and in rapid decline, in the wake of recent scandals. They forget this one fact. People here believe that they need priests. Not that they need them to be good or wise or hard-working, but that they need them in themselves.

Down the centuries, we have been perfectly well-used to priests fathering children, cheating on deals, bullying, drinking, exploiting the poor and so on. This has probably contributed to a certain two-facedness in our culture. But it hasn't made any difference to the faith itself. I doubt whether the present, very much more shocking, revelations will make much difference, either, though reasonable people think that they must.

But a religious culture, like ours, is about everything. Churches and priests are only a part. And reason is only one element in all that goes on between birth and death. We don't want to die, for one thing, but we're given no choice. That isn't reasonable. The people we love die, and we have no power even over the manner of their going. And vast as the individual ego is, it seems to become extinct.

To deny this, we posit a God who knows the meaning of the brief trajectory of human life. And when we go, we need that passage to be set apart. The Humanist Association in Ireland creates, and performs, when asked, an increasing number of secular ceremonies for bereaved people who can't stand religion. The booklet *Funerals Without God* is their best-selling publication. But mostly, the deaths of even the most thoroughgoing Irish agnostics are marked by religious ritual. And a proper, decent, Irish funeral is still religious. Who would want to go into the dark alone — without a community?

I don't know that I can get very close to belonging, myself. But I was in the presence of the real thing recently, at the funeral of an elderly lady related to us by marriage. Her whole send-off was so perfectly done that I asked a nephew, afterwards, to see could he arrange for me something like it — a modest, heartfelt, traditional, Dublin funeral. The only difference being that I would be ashes at the end, whereas Mrs Devitt was interred with her late parents and husband in Mount Jerome. I even assigned my Credit Union shares to my nephew to pay for it.

But now I realise that you can only have a funeral as authentic as hers if it arises from the truths of your whole life. The very church we were in had always been a sacred spot in her landscape. As a young woman she had walked up to Mount Argus with her mother, particularly when someone in the family needed the "cure" from Father Charles. She went to the Easter ceremonies there, because the Passionists could provide the priests for "a full altar".

345

Her grandson was an altar boy there. She would have been gratified by her own funeral there, connoisseur of funerals as she — typical of her generation — was. "She could describe coffins in detail," her daughter says with affection.

The celebrant of the funeral Mass had not known her personally, yet he was the central, the one indispensable, figure in the occasion. He had familiarised himself with her life before the service. So he was able to make everything he had to say pertinent to this particular woman, who had led a life of unsung bravery after she was left a widow in straitened circumstances. Above all he was able to look at the congregation, and especially her grieving children, and assure them that, as Christians, they did not hope for eternal life — they were sure of it. If a foreign journalist had tapped me on the shoulder after the Mass and said: "Scandals. I've come about the scandals and the decline of the church in Ireland," I'd have looked up blankly and said: "What scandals? What decline?"

The scandals are only a part of a whole. What has the undoubted decline in the credibility of the clergy, for instance, to do with the hymns a young woman with a pure voice sang at Mrs Devitt's funeral? "Oh Mary we crown Thee with blossoms today, Queen of the Angels and Queen of the May." 'Ag Críost an Síol'. 'Ave, Ave'. 'Sweet Heart of Jesus, Fount of Love and Mercy'. These are cornerstones of popular culture. And belief resides in them, irrespective of hierarchy.

Outside it was freezing, of course. The little crowd pulled their coats tight around themselves as they waited on the steps to pay their respects to the family. Work colleagues of her children and the like had been at the Removal of Remains the night before. Somehow there is a protocol everybody knows.

Then there was the slow gathering at a wind-swept corner of the cemetery. The grave-diggers who could have come straight out of Shakespeare. The profoundly

346

beautiful last prayers at the graveside, and the fact of earth. Outside the gates the Men With Caps, purple-faced with cold, supervised car parking with many an audible reference to pub opening hours. And then the warm pub, where her neighbours had been thoughtfully brought in a limousine, and where tea and drinks and a big, hot, meal was laid on for everybody. And there the talk turned often to Mrs Devitt and her place and her times.

Everything was properly done. Everything is mixed in together, in the native way of doing something important. All the other pieties are intertwined with the religious one. There isn't a separate thing called "religion" in ordinary life. "Religion" cannot decline and leave everything else untouched.

Conversely, a strong edifice which is not religion props religion up. If half the priests in the country were scandalous and the other half were covering up for them, this funeral would still have been a product of Irish Catholicism. And that still feels right and natural. Foreign papers please copy.

The Other World

There are some apparitions happening again in Co Cork, and I see the Bishop of Cork and Ross quoted as saying about them that "it's a silly season for silly people". Oddly enough, the last time I heard the word "silly" used like this was in Mostar, a town near Medjugorje. The local doctor, a committed socialist, was talking with contempt about the pilgrims who flock to Medjugorje. "They're children," he said. "When you think of all that the world needs — they're so *silly*."

I said that I didn't think they were silly: I thought they were needy. What's more, I thought that on a human level, Medjugorje was a wonderful place. People seemed to expand there — to be more whole. Even I felt it. Irrespective of visions and visionaries and dancing suns and rosary beads changing colour. The doctor, however, continued to be as scathing as the Bishop of Cork and Ross.

The doctor wanted to build a just and reasonable society. He found mystery distasteful. But the mysterious exists, and some people have an appetite for it. A few years ago, thousands were travelling to Ballinspittle. Why that year, and not the years in between? Some commentators said it was the abortion referendum, and the psychic upheavals it led to. I don't know that the *zeitgeist* is so easily explained. Why Cork? A Mayoman said to me that it's because Cork isn't in an all-Ireland final this year. Not that Mayo is an entirely rational place. I was there on Midsummer Eve and there were bonfires all over the place.

Do committed socialists — like the doctor — see fairies (as I did) when they were children? I'm not suggesting that fairies and religious apparitions have anything in common. Fairies have no doctrinal or ethical implications. Mine didn't have, anyway. It is just that in both cases, other people don't believe you. Most people probably do not believe that there are manifestations of the Virgin Mary in Co Cork at the moment. Yet they must know that the people concerned are not telling lies. There are, of course, impostors and hysterics and the like in the apparition business. But that is as nothing compared to the thousands, if not millions, of people whose lives have been transformed by the inexplicable.

People who were quite indifferent — who couldn't care less — did see the sun dance at Fatima, and did leave their crutches at Lourdes and did see the statue move at Ballinspittle and do fast and pray with a special intensity because of the message promulgated at Medjugorje. And those are just examples from within one Church in one place — Europe. If you were to contemplate all the magical and miraculous elements in all the religions of all the world — the chicken-bones on altar-steps, the white rags tied to desert tombs — then you'd begin to wonder whether "silliness" is the right word for what is going on.

In Ireland, things are always turning out to be multi-dimensional. At the well of Saint Gobnait in Ballyvourney recently, some woman had left her rings. There were bright toggles — that teenagers tie their hair up with — twisted around the little rail of offerings, under ancient trees. At a remote well in the Burren — a toothache-cure well — someone had left a coat-hanger. What were they doing with a coat-hanger, miles from the road? In Leitrim, the lady went to get me a piece of string. If I rubbed this piece of string on a certain tomb, and then wore it, I'd never have back trouble. All perfectly normal. Perfectly normal to go seven times around a bed of stones on your knees. To find a rock in a field with a cross scratched into it. For Ann Lovett to have gone to a grotto to have company in her terror.

There are invisible presences everywhere. My five-year-old friend, Jack, has an invisible friend called Billy. We — the adults — have to hang around, waiting for Billy to find his coat. A teacher — a practical woman — called to see her mother. She met a tiny little old lady coming out of her mother's house. This was, of course, the banshee, and sure enough, she found her mother dying. A colleague at *The Irish Times* was shown his way home one night on the Aran Islands by people who had drowned seventy years before. In these circumstances, why wouldn't statues move? Given that religion is the great repository of images, given that it engages the deepest emotions, given the daring acts of the imagination that it exacts on a daily basis.

The stir of cities hides the numinous. But think what space there is for visions in other lives. How desolate Knock must have been, thirty years after the Famine. How remote Garabandal and Medjugorje are. How lonely the life of a little girl like Bernadette, gathering firewood, or the children at Fatima, minding the sheep. I can't pronounce on the authenticity of Marian apparitions, but I can say that it is evident that we need to believe that we have a mother, who loves us.

Parish priests get caught in the middle. So one was saying to me, recently. On the one hand, he has his congregation, proud and excited if there are manifestations in their midst. On the other, he has the higher authorities, who very understandably want this kind of thing kept in check. Quite apart from the problem of meaning — and some visions seem, like my fairies, to be meaningless — there is a materialisation of faith implicit in the miraculous. "Give us a sign!" people shout at the Creator. As if there were nothing there without a sign.

I can quite see why a teaching Church cannot allow the folk to run hither and thither. But for myself, I like it that people persist in mingling the everyday and the otherworldly. It is an ancient and a universal practice. And although, on a public level, one would like Ireland to be run in a reasonable, pluralist, modern way, there is more to living here than being a citizen. There is a capaciousness not so much of belief as of endlessly suspended judgement, which to my mind is precious.

This is not to say that everything is the same as everything else. I met a woman once who was bottling plums in brandy, at enormous expense, as part of some obscure act of worship picked up by her from a visionary in northern Italy called Mamma Rosa. I wouldn't put that kind of thing even on the same spectrum, however far away, as belief in, say, the Resurrection. But people will do anything to try to make sense of the uncertainties of life and the certainty of death. They use the senseless to make sense. They make a construct out of what they have to hand, often with enormous ingenuity. I never saw a statue move, and don't expect to, and don't want to, but I've met people who have seen such things. It's the people who leave you awestruck — not the statues.